Rotter/Bendl

# YOUR COMPANION TO ENGLISH TEXTS

## Comprehension
## Analysis
## Appreciation
## Production

Kollegstufe/Abitur/Universität

MANZ VERLAG MÜNCHEN

Herausgegeben von Ute Kretschmann

Unveränderter Nachdruck der zugelassenen Auflage

Manzbuch 299

15 14 13 1987 86 85
Die jeweils letzte Zahl bezeichnet die Auflage bzw. das Erscheinungsjahr

 · Umschlagentwurf: Ingeburg Rothemund, München · Gesamtherstellung: Verlag und Druckerei G. J. Manz AG, München/Dillingen · Printed in Germany

ISBN 3-7863-0299-5

# TABLE OF CONTENTS

## PREFACE

Teachers of advanced courses in high schools and universities continue to deplore the inability of students with seven, eight, and even nine and ten, years of secondary study of English behind them to express themselves in a clear, correct, and comprehensible manner in writing.
As we see it, what is at the bottom of this distressing inability of advanced students to write good English is the fact that until quite recently English was taught mainly for **receptive** use in secondary education in Germany, and students were not really expected to reach a high level of proficiency in its **productive** command as well. The inevitable outcome of all this was, of course, that by the time the students reached the newly-introduced 'Kollegstufe' or went to university, they were to a large extent unprepared for the new demands. They found themselves suddenly confronted with the necessity of expressing themselves in the foreign language on difficult controversial subjects without having first been given enough practice on fairly simple and straightforward matters. In other words, they were asked to start writing at an advanced level, and about complex problems, with a number of the necessary steps leading up to that level having been left out or not taught extensively enough.
So what is needed urgently – and this little volume hopes to fill this gap to some extent – are books setting out to teach systematically all the various test skills, such as writing summaries, letters, compositions, etc.
In this situation, we have done our best to provide appropriate material for advanced English studies and to give students and teachers as much practical help as possible. The result is a new type of course book: its purpose is not mainly to provide practice material, although this has also been included to some extent, but to teach, progressively and systematically, the skills which students have to master if they want to be successful in their examinations. Since it concentrates on teaching basic techniques, the book can be used in the 'Grundkurs', the 'Leistungskurs', and for private study; many of the points it covers will also be found extremely useful for university students.
Our main intention has been to increase the students' competence in written communication, with these as the important points to concentrate on:

1) Students must know precisely how to approach texts – how to read them, how to guess unknown words, how to use their dictionaries, etc.
2) They must acquire definite criteria by which texts can be analysed – and thus better understood and appreciated. In particular, they should

come to grasp the implications of a text, which are sometimes at least as important as its explicit statements. In short, they must gain more feeling for English style.

3) The approach must be as comprehensive and systematic as possible so that students – after studying the material – may feel prepared for any non-literary text.
4) Students must be put in a position to express their findings and their own ideas in a correct, concise and convincing form, and also to produce longer texts of their own.

In a word, we have tried to promote the competence of students in the fields of

**text comprehension,** **text appreciation,**
**text analysis,** **text production.**

A second aim has been to familiarize students with certain routines and techniques so as to enable them to work more economically and effectively. All the suggested methods, such as methods of word guessing, making full use of the dictionary, using the file card system in vocabulary learning, collecting useful expressions, and so forth, have been tried out in practice – and they work, as our students at the Gymnasium Erding have found out to their profit.

To round the picture off, we have included important information about letter-writing (ch. 7), because it is a special form of text production which often comes up in exams; about translating from English into German (ch. 8), because translation ('Version') as a test skill in its own right is still found in some examinations; and about writing a research paper (ch. 9), because it is something nearly every student will have to come to terms with sooner or later.

We would like to express our gratitude to all those whose writings have proved useful to us (for books and articles we are particularly indebted to cf. 'Acknowledgements'). We are thankful to Professor Dr Alfred Wollmann (Universität Köln) and Akademischer Oberrat Dr Werner Sedlak (Universität München) for scholarly advice and much-needed encouragement; and to the 'Staatsinstitut für Schulpädagogik' in Munich, and especially to StD K. Hartmann, for many valuable suggestions. Our thanks also go to Mrs Joan Dobell, B.A., who read and checked the manuscript from the native speaker's point of view. Our very special thanks, however, are reserved for our students at the Gymnasium Erding with whom all the material offered in this book was tried out and who made many helpful practical suggestions.

**W. Rotter**
Altenerding, December 1977 **H. Bendl**

## HOW TO USE THIS BOOK

**This introduction is meant to be read! Without it the structure and purpose of the book may not become clear.**

### To the Student

This book can be used in various ways and for a number of purposes because

1) it provides some basic information on important aspects of working with texts;
2) it teaches basic working techniques;
3) it can be used as a reference book;
4) it provides language material in tables on problems of text analysis, text appreciation ('Stilkritik'), and text production.

This means that the book can be read through as a whole or in part, or can be consulted for certain items to be studied separately or simply for reference.
The best course to take is probably to read the book all the way through and then to pick out certain chapters or individual points for detailed study in class or in private; the 'Table of Contents' and the 'Index' can be consulted for guidance.

### 1. How to obtain basic information on important aspects of working with texts

This covers everything from word formation, etymological and semantic connections (1.3.3) to information about problems of vocabulary (2.2) and of finding suitable reading material (2.3); it also covers most of the contents of chs. 3–7, which deal with the question of text classification (3.1–3.4), types of questions found in exam papers (4.1–4.9), the most important stylistic and rhetorical figures (5.1–5.3) and provide information on the process of communication (6.1), on how to make ideas clear (6.2), how to develop ideas and support arguments (6.3), how to organize ideas and structure texts (6.4), and on letter-writing (7.1–7.3).
Some of this material can simply be read through and then looked up

again as the need arises; most of it, however, has to be studied in detail, e.g. etymological and semantic connections (1.3.3).
You will find that this section contains lists of Latin and Greek roots, with a number of English words derived from them, and French and German parallels, like this:

| Latin Root | Basic Meaning | English | French | German |
|---|---|---|---|---|
| haereo | I stick | adherent: sb sticking to a cause = supporter | adhérent | = Anhänger |

This is just an example; you will see that the lists take up quite a number of pages – and all this information is meant to be carefully studied! To show you the practical value of it a number of exercises have been provided for this section. Here is one easy example; you have to guess the meaning of the word in bold type:

To make sure that the envelope couldn't be steamed open he put some **adhesive** tape round the edges.
Correct answer: **adhesive** = sticky (from haereo = I stick)

The lists are by no means complete, of course (only the most frequently found roots have been given), but the idea behind it is to make you aware of etymological and semantic connections you might otherwise have overlooked. This in turn may lead you to be on the look-out for similar connections, even if they haven't been included in our lists. Though you may find this somewhat boring and theoretical at the beginning, you will soon discover that you can save time in learning words because with these links you can retain them in your memory more easily. Moreover, you will also find that understanding 'difficult' texts and guessing unknown words becomes a lot easier once you consciously start looking for parallel words in other languages.

## 2. How to acquire basic working techniques

This includes the techniques of reading a text (1.1), practising one's reading comprehension (1.2), and guessing unknown words (1.3) as well as working with the dictionary (2.1) or practical vocabulary work (2.4); it also covers the techniques of paraphrasing (4.10), summary-writing

(4.11), giving an overall interpretation of a text (4.12), and of writing a research paper (9.1–9.7). Inasfar as translating a text into German is a question of following a certain technique in the sense of avoiding a number of pitfalls, ch. 8 comes under this head, too.
Again, some of this material can simply be read, e.g. 2.4.1: practical language work in the field of grammar, but other material will have to be studied closely, the section on summary-writing, for instance (4.11). The main point, however, in all these cases is not how often or how closely the relevant sections in this book are read, but that you do make use of the suggestions offered here in your own work.
It goes without saying that such a thing as writing a research paper can never be successful, in the sense of somebody spending only a minimum of time on it **and** obtaining a good result, without the proper technique. All the relevant chapters should, therefore, be carefully worked through.

## 3. How to consult 'Your Companion' as a reference book

Practically the whole book can be used for reference purposes, but there are a number of chapters which consist primarily of reference material – material which ought to be looked up again and again. These include the chapters on etymologies (1.3.3), on text types, text groups and text forms (3.1–3.4), on questions on the text (4.1–4.12), on stylistic and rhetorical figures (5.1–5.3), on definitions (6.2), on planning written work (6.4), on the various types of letter (7.1–7.3), on preparing a working bibliography (9.2), and on the final version of a research paper (9.7). Of particular importance are obviously the TA and TP tables in chs. 3–7; they should be studied again and again. The TA tables comprise language material suitable for text analysis and text appreciation, the TP tables material useful for your own text production.
What you should do whenever you feel unsure about a particular aspect of working with texts, especially about how you can express yourself on a certain problem, is to consult the index and perhaps the table of contents for the exact page numbers where this particular aspect is dealt with in this book, and then read this section again.
For instance, if you want to make sure what the precise difference is between 'humour', 'irony', 'satire' and 'sarcasm', you should go to chapter 5.1 and read up the respective sections; there you will find a definition of each term, together with one or two examples or illustrations, and you will also be provided with language material in tables to help you to formulate your ideas in correct English.

You will immediately realize the importance of being able to distinguish rhetorical figures and stylistic devices if you study the model text 'A Woman's Tears' at the beginning of ch. 5 and the corresponding worksheet with model questions and suggested answers. You will also find that a student will very likely be lost if he is confronted with a text of this type (its content is of no real consequence; what counts is the way the author has presented his topic, in other words his style) and a number of questions on the author's style, such as:

- 'Decrying the Crying Game' (l. 68) – Determine the stylistic figure contained in this expression. What are its implications?
- What is the tone of the whole passage and what effects is the author aiming at?
- Exaggeration recurs throughout the text. Find instances of it and show how they contribute to the general tone.

Questions such as these are meant to test the student's powers of text analysis and appreciation, but it is easy to see that he will be in trouble if he does not know the technical terms (e.g. 'pun', 'alliteration', etc.) and what they mean, or does not know how to say in English what he has found out, or both.
This type of question (i.e. questions aiming at text analysis and appreciation) is becoming more and more common in exam papers. Consequently, whenever you come across rhetorical and stylistic figures in any text you may be studying, you ought to try to determine what they are (perhaps with the help of your teacher at first) and then go and look up the relevant sections in this book and inform yourself thoroughly. It is only with a lot of practice that you can penetrate into this most interesting aspect of language studies.

## 4. How to increase your linguistic competence in text analysis, text appreciation and text production

It has already been said that this book offers some language material in tables and that the TA tables are for text analysis and appreciation and the TP tables for text production.
You will find these tables most helpful for your practical work because they will help you to increase your linguistic competence in precisely those fields where you need to be most competent.
Irrespective of whether you want to determine the exact text type or text form (3.1–3.4), to answer questions on a text (4.1–4.10), or to appreciate

an author's style (5.1–5.2) – do make ample use of the relevant TA tables. Here is a demonstration of how this could be done.
You will sometimes be asked to analyse the composition or structure of a text, e.g.

- Try to determine the structure of the text.
- Examine how the author has arranged his ideas.
- Divide the text into parts. Try to find headlines for them, etc.

If you go to ch. 4.8 you will see that a TA table has been included there to help you to formulate your findings in correct English. Here it is:

**TA Structure, composition**

| | | | |
|---|---|---|---|
| The text | divides into<br>falls into | (×) paragraphs<br>(×) parts<br>(×) sections | |
| The author passes from A to B by | a subtle<br>an abrupt | transition | |
| In the . . . paragraph, the author | passes from A to B<br>takes up B<br>returns to A | | |
| | evades the subject<br>digresses from the main topic<br>varies the theme<br>changes the topic | (cf. → diversion)<br>(cf. → digression)<br>by alluding to . . . | |
| He | goes into<br>does not go into | details<br>particulars | |
| He then supports his argument by | a quotation<br>an example<br>a comparison<br>a contrast | (cf. → argumentation) | |
| He draws the conclusion that . . . | | | |
| He | distinguishes | | between A and B |
| | makes<br>draws | a distinction<br>a comparison | |

p. t. o.

**TA Structure, composition** (continued)

| | | | | |
|---|---|---|---|---|
| He | → contrasts | A with B<br>A and B | | |
| | compares | A with B<br>A to B (in the case of a simile) | | |
| The second paragraph | forms a<br>offers a | slight<br>strong<br>striking | contrast | to the first para.<br>with the first para. |
| The author | plays off | ideas | against each other | |
| | → balances | sentences<br>paragraphs | | |

You can now take the expressions you need for what you are going to say from here, like this:

- The text divides into three parts; or:
- In the second paragraph, the author digresses from the main topic by alluding to . . .; or:
- He then supports his argument by a quotation, etc.

It is obvious that you cannot possibly memorize everything these tables say; if you tried to do this you would have misunderstood their purpose completely. What you should in fact do is to consult this book again and again and read up the relevant sections whenever you have to write anything that has to do with a particular aspect of text analysis and appreciation.
The same thing is true when you have to produce a text of your own, whether a relatively short comment, or a longer essay or a letter. Here the TP tables can be used. They will give you a choice of connectives necessary to link ideas within sentences, within paragraphs, or from one paragraph to the next (chs. 6.2–6.4 and 7.1–7.3).
So, in the case of an argumentative essay, the following table (cf. 6.4.6) gives you a choice between a number of useful expressions and connectives:

**TP The main body: opposing other views**

| | | | | |
|---|---|---|---|---|
| Those who advocate A attack B for various reasons:<br>Those out to support A often argue that such a procedure will . . .<br>They are among the first to point out that . . . | | | | |
| Firstly<br>Secondly<br>Finally | they | argue that . . . . . ., which is bad enough.<br>claim that . . . . . ., which is even worse.<br>insist that . . . . . ., which is the worst of all. | | |
| In { their view<br>his opinion | A | is<br>constitutes | a real problem<br>a serious danger | |
| Although there is no denying the fact that . . . | they fail to see . . .<br>they fail to acknowledge | | | |
| They are just wrong when | assuming<br>claiming | that . . . | | |
| It is simply not true that . . . | | | | |
| This is simply wrong, since A is | only<br>exclusively<br>solely | concerned with . . . | | |
| They argue that . . ., but | what is worse,<br>even worse,<br>still worse, | they claim that . . . | | |
| As I see it, these critics unduly generalize and exaggerate: | | | | |
| They fail to | take all the relevant facts into consideration<br>acknowledge certain facts<br>appreciate definite trends<br>weigh all the arguments in a fair way<br>draw the proper inferences and conclusions | | | |
| So, all their arguments are true to a certain extent, but somehow, they are all unconvincing | | | | |

The choice of the appropriate words within such sentence patterns must, of course, be left to you to suit your purpose. Do make sure that you always adapt the tables – which necessarily have been kept rather general and neutral – to your particular needs by modifying and qualifying them. So instead of saying 'In their view A is a real problem', you might want to say something like 'In their view A amounts to something outrageous and extremely dangerous', etc.

**To the Teacher**

Make sure your students know how to use this book. The best course is probably to go through individual chapters in class, not in the sense of 'doing' one after the other as they come in the book – though this would be possible, too – but rather of discussing this or that chapter when the need arises.

For instance, you may want to discuss argumentative essay-writing with your class. In this case you could go to chs. 3.4.1–3.4.4, which deal with argumentation in general (the process of argumentation, etc.), and then to ch. 6.4, esp. 6.4.6 ('Dialectical order'), which offers the language material needed for writing an essay of this type. The next step would be to discuss a number of controversial subjects in class, with the students taking notes (e.g. 'the pros and cons of co-education', 'capital punishment for convicted murderers?', etc.); this would ensure that the students had at their command some basic arguments for and against a certain subject – because even the best method must obviously be defeated if people have nothing to say. In the end a number of essays could be written, incorporating the ideas put forward in the discussions and the language material provided in the TP tables.

You will find that the results are quite amazing. The vast majority of students will no longer jump from idea to idea but will know how to structure their texts and how to connect sentences and paragraphs in a logical and linguistically correct manner. So, as long as they have something to say they are in a position to say it well.

It should be your aim eventually to go through all the sections in the book. You can then refer your students back to individual chapters for guidance.

You can take your practice texts from wherever you can find them – from the textbooks commonly in use, from newspapers and magazines, or from collections of comprehension texts. The main point is that you not only discuss these texts for their intrinsic value, but also use them to let your students

- practise their reading comprehension and guess unknown words (cf. ch. 1);
- use their dictionaries, select vocabulary items to be written on file cards and memorized, and collect useful expressions (cf. ch. 2);
- determine text types and text forms (cf. ch. 3);

– find questions on the text and use the relevant TA tables for answering them (cf. ch. 4);
– look for stylistic and rhetorial figures and describe their function within the text with the help of the information and the TA tables in ch. 5;
– find out what the author has done to make his ideas clear (cf. 6.2), how he has developed his ideas and supported his arguments (cf. 6.3), and how he has organized his ideas and structured his text (cf. 6.4), and let them work with the respective TP tables.

If you also practise the three types of letter-writing (cf. 7.1–7.3) and the translating skill (cf. ch. 8), your students will be prepared for any type of question that may come up in an examination and will acquire all the necessary skills and techniques. (The technique of writing a research paper – cf. ch. 9 – should also be discussed, of course).
A final word of advice about the TA and TP tables: you ought to go through them in class and make it quite clear that these tables contain choices of collocations (i.e. words often used together in certain situations) and that the words grouped together in one square are **sometimes synonymous:**

e.g.

| | | |
|---|---|---|
| He | reproves<br>blames<br>reproaches<br>criticizes | somebody for his behaviour |

but not necessarily so. Some may have **slightly different denotations:**

e.g.

| | |
|---|---|
| A text contains ironical | statements<br>remarks<br>allusions |

and others may be **utterly opposite in meaning:**

e.g.

| | |
|---|---|
| The tone of the passage is | detached<br>provocative<br>conciliatory |

**A short personal remark to conclude with:**

Experience has shown that there is no danger whatsoever of getting the same stereotyped answers from students who use the same TA and TP tables. This is because the tables usually offer a fairly wide choice of

collocations; because students may have to adapt the language material provided in the tables to their individual needs, i.e. for the particular question they are answering; and because answers can of course never consist only of the language material of the TA and TP tables – to a large extent it is still necessary for students to present what they want to say in their own words.
This is to say that the tables are not meant to replace the student's own language production, but simply to help him write clear and correct English. Our students have always found having this material a definite advantage.

# 1. UNDERSTANDING TEXTS

## 1.1 How to read a text

Reading is a much more complex activity than most people imagine. When we read an article in a newspaper or magazine we tend to read fairly quickly, perhaps skipping a few words here and there and even whole sentences. All we want to gain from texts of this kind is some information; we want to get an overall impression of what a particular article is about and so individual words and phrases do not matter very much.

When we read a poem, however, most of us would almost unconsciously adopt the word-for-word technique, as in a poem every single word may be of immense importance; it may be a key word for unterstanding what the author is trying to say or it may be part of a metaphor or image that is used to convey a certain impression, and so on.

Yet another technique, or techniques rather, must be employed for comprehension texts. They must be read much more slowly than one would read a novel or a newspaper article. Time spent on reading is saved later, because the questions can then be answered much more quickly and accurately.

It is a safe guess to say that something like eighty per cent of the problems students face when studying a comprehension passage arise from the text itself.

There are first and foremost the words and expressions which the student does not know and which therefore make it difficult, and in some cases almost impossible, for him to follow what is being said. To some extent this is still a problem even when a dictionary is used, because some students are so disturbed by unfamiliar vocabulary even after they have looked up the meaning of a number of words that their comprehension of the whole passage is greatly impaired. In most cases, however, using a dictionary eliminates the hard vocabulary, unless of course the difficulties which a student encounters in a text stem mainly from some idiomatic expressions and the like, particularly if they are of a colloquial and slangy nature, because these cannot so easily be found in the ordinary dictionaries.

Long and complicated sentences present another problem. Even when the vocabulary is basically simple, syntactic complexity may cause a reader to lose the thread.

This is also often the case when a writer favours a wordy and repetitive style or when he tends to express himself obliquely, stating ideas only indirectly by using metaphors, similes and so forth. Practice is necessary here for the students to become sensitive to the implications of a remark and to draw the correct inferences from what is put forward only indirectly.

Failure in comprehension is often simply due to defective reading habits. Not all students read efficiently, even in their own mother tongue, and there are a number of things that can go wrong.

Many if not most people tend to read comprehension texts far too fast. In this way they probably get a good impression of the general idea of a text, but through not paying sufficient attention to detail, for instance overlooking a conjunction, a negation, or a modal verb, they may receive a totally false impression of the meaning of one or more paragraphs in the text.

With others, just the opposite is true. These students read slowly and carefully, concentrating very hard on pinpointing every individual detail, but without managing to arrive at a clear idea of the text as a whole.

There is usually a third group, consisting of those students who hold strong opinions about any of the points raised in a particular text and may then interpret the whole text in the light of their own ideas and experiences. In other words, they find it difficult to distinguish between what the author actually says and what they believe he ought to have said.

To work with a comprehension text to the best advantage, the student must make sure that he acquires an efficient routine. He must know precisely what steps he has to take, and in what order, when dealing with texts of this kind. The procedure suggested below has been found to be the most effecient, ensuring not only that a student learns to understand a text in its overall meaning and in its details but also that he learns to answer the questions correctly and with as little loss of time as possible, for it must be remembered that time is an important factor in examinations, or when studying a text in class or at home for that matter.

**Step one:**

Read the whole text through, not too fast, trying to get a good idea of what it is all about and what the main points of it are.

**Step two:**

Now read the text again. This time read even more slowly, and pay particular attention to points that seem difficult. Mark the words and phrases you do not understand, but do not waste too much time worrying about what their meaning might be. Make an intelligent guess at their meaning – the context and the etymology of the word will be of help – and then read on. It is important that you should not read the next sentence until you have understood the sentence before as well as you can.

**Step three:**

Go through the text yet again and now concentrate only on the words and expressions you have underlined. Which of them can be eliminated because their meaning is fairly clear, and which have to be looked up in a dictionary? It is essential that the number of words you look up is kept to a minimum, since using a dictionary always implies losing valuable time – time much better spent on working through the tasks prescribed on the worksheet. So you should look up only the words you find absolutely necessary for understanding the text as a whole.

**Note:** A detailed demonstration of this procedure with actual texts will be found under 1.3.3 und 1.3.4. It seemed advisable to delay the introduction of practice texts until the various aspects of word guessing had been covered.

## 1.2 How to practise your reading comprehension

It has already been said that most people read comprehension texts far too fast. So take your time when reading the following text; it is meant to test your reading speed and you will have to answer questions on it after only one reading. It is essential that you should read it only once.

### The Reluctant Orchid

The hero – if you can call him that – of this story is an inoffensive little clerk named Hercules Keating. Hercules is not the sort of name you can carry off lightly at the best of times, and when you are four foot nine and look as if you'd have to take a physical-culture course before you can even become a ninety-seven pound weakling, it is a positive embarrassment. Perhaps it helped to explain why Hercules had very little social life, and all his real friends grew in pots in the humid conservatory at the bottom of his garden. His needs were simple and he spent very little money on himself; consequently his collection of orchids and cacti was really rather remarkable. Indeed, he had a wide reputation among the fraternity of cactophiles, and often received from remote corners of the globe parcels smelling of mould and tropical jungles.

Hercules had one living relative, and it would have been hard to find a greater contrast than Aunt Henrietta. She was a massive sixfooter, usually wore a rather loud line in Harris tweeds, drove a Jaguar with reckless skill, and chain-smoked cigars. Her parents had set their hearts on a boy, and had never been able to decide whether or not their wish had been granted. Henrietta earned a living, and quite a good one, breeding dogs of various shapes and sizes. She was seldom without a couple of her latest models, and they were not the type of portable canine which ladies like to carry in their handbags. The Keating Kennels specialized in Great Danes, Alsatians, and Saint Bernards . . .

Henrietta, rightly despising men as the weaker sex, had never married. However, for some reason she took an avuncular (yes, that is definitely the right word) interest in Hercules, and called to see him almost every weekend. It was a curious kind of relationship; probably Henrietta found that Hercules bolstered up her feelings of superiority. If he was a good example of the male sex, then they were certainly a pretty sorry lot. Yet, if this was Henrietta's motivation, she was unconscious of it and seemed genuinely fond of her nephew. She was patronizing, but never unkind.

As might be expected, her attentions did not exactly help Hercules' own well-developed inferiority complex. At first he had tolerated his aunt; then he came to dread her regular visits, her booming voice, and her bone-crushing handshake; and at last he grew to hate her. Eventually, indeed, his hate was the dominant emotion in his life, exceeding even his love for his orchids. But he was careful not to show it, realizing that if Aunt Henrietta discovered how he felt about her, she would probably break him in two and throw the pieces to her wolf pack.

There was no way, then, in which Hercules could express his pent-up feelings. He had to be polite to Aunt Henrietta even when he felt like murder. And he often did feel like murder, though he knew there was nothing he would ever do about it. Until one day . . .

From: Arthur C. Clarke, *The Reluctant Orchid;* slightly adapted

Now answer the following questions without looking at the text. You may answer in a word, a short phrase, or a complete sentence, whichever you prefer. If you have a lot of difficulty with this exercise, it means either that your English is far below standard or, more likely, that you have read the text too fast.

1) Why is 'Hercules' not a good name for Mr Keating?
2) What is his hobby?
3) How big is Hercules' family?
4) In what way is Aunt Henrietta such a big contrast to him?
5) How does Aunt Henrietta earn her living?
6) How often does she come to see her nephew?
7) Does she like him?
8) Is he fond of her?
9) Why doesn't he show his true feelings for her?

Now check your answers. If you got several wrong, it means that you definitely read too fast and that you will have to read more slowly in future. Now go back to the text and read it again, this time even more slowly, and pay special attention to points that seem difficult. Don't read on unless you have understood the sentence before as well as you can. If there is a word or phrase you definitely don't know, don't waste too much time worrying what it might mean. Make an intelligent guess at the meaning, and then read on. When you think you are ready, try this exercise.
Some of the following sentences have the same meaning as part of the text; they are 'true'. Others have a different meaning; they are 'false'. Your task is to find out which of them are true and which are false and then to write down the correct answer, e.g. 1t, 2f, etc. This is another good way of testing your reading comprehension. As before, do not look at the text when trying to answer the questions.

| | true | false |
|---|---|---|
| 1) Hercules Keating had taken a body-building course, but without much success. | ( ) | ( ) |
| 2) It made Hercules embarrassed to think that his size did not fit his name. | ( ) | ( ) |
| 3) He spent most of his money on his hobby, which was collecting plants for his conservatory. | ( ) | ( ) |
| 4) He had a wide circle of friends. | ( ) | ( ) |
| 5) Aunt Henrietta despised women and admired men. | ( ) | ( ) |
| 6) She spent most of the weekends with Hercules because she liked him very much. | ( ) | ( ) |
| 7) She bred not only dogs, but also kept a wolf pack. | ( ) | ( ) |
| 8) Hercules always looked forward to her visits as he was looking for a chance to murder her. | ( ) | ( ) |

Check your answers now. If you got more than one or two wrong, it means that you don't concentrate properly when reading a text for comprehension and must try harder in future.

The only way to cure yourself of bad reading habits is through more reading practice; you have to read a number of texts and thereby constantly test yourself. And here comes what at first sight looks like an insurmountable difficulty: Even if you are prepared to buy a number of the relevant books, i.e. books written especially for the purpose of giving practice in reading comprehension, you cannot usually check your answers against an 'authority' because a Key is not normally provided. This, however, cannot be helped, and you must make the best of the situation as it is. Under the circumstances, the best course of action seems to be this:

- Read a text through at a fairly slow speed, trying to get a good idea of the overall meaning of the text: what it is all about, the main arguments put forward, the structure of the text, and so on.
- Jot down on a piece of paper the main points of the text as you remember them, especially what the text is all about. It isn't necessary here to formulate whole sentences, three or four words will usually do. Do not, repeat not, look at the text again when you do this or else the test effect will be entirely lost.
- Read the text a second time now, paying great attention to details, difficult phrases, etc., and concentrating on understanding the text even in its individual points.
- Correct and complete your notes after this second reading, again without looking at the text, even if the temptation to do this is very great.
- Check your notes by comparing them with the actual text: Did you get all the important points? Have you included too many minor points? Have you perhaps even missed the gist of the text?

All this should not have taken longer than 15 minutes for one text, and with a little practice you will find that you can easily cut down the time you need for 'doing' one text in this way to 12, 10 or even 8 minutes so that you won't lose all that much time. (Incidentally, this method is also an excellent way of preparing yourself for summary-writing; cf. 4.11 below.)

You can now try out the procedure suggested above on the following text: Read the text through very slowy and then try at once to make some notes. Do not despair if you feel you can hardly remember anything at all – it's always like this at the beginning. So jot down the two or three points that you do remember and in any case resist the temptation to look at the text again.

## Class Distinctions

The educational revolution in England is producing increasing numbers of university graduates without influential connections. Their plebeian origin is usually evident in their accents, their dress and their prejudices. And so all-pervading is our class consciousness that they are discriminated against, despite their ability. Some holy places, like the Foreign Office, still do not accept them at all. When the first-class redbrick graduate with his cheap clothes and regional accent sees the third-class Oxbridge man with his expensive speech and dress awaiting interview for the same job, his heart sinks – for he knows that if he does not lose the job to a better man he will lose it to a worse one. Little wonder, then, that he and his friends are emigrating in ever larger numbers to 'new' countries where their gifts will be used, respected and rewarded.

Britain's caste system is her biggest handicap in adapting to life in the modern world. It is all the more objectionable for being totally unnecessary. In the United States, with the very serious exceptions that arise from the severe discrimination against coloured people, there are no social barriers to the advancement of the individual. Talent is rewarded. We should remember this when passing judgment on the prevalence in America of money-standards. For while it is true that Americans are judged more by their financial success than by any other criterion, it is also true that wealth is more closely related to ability in the United States than in any European country.

One of the magnetically attractive things about American life is the lack not only of class distinctions but also of the humbug that goes with them. A lawyer's son can be a labourer and a labourer's son can be a lawyer, and nobody even notices, let alone cares. At all universities, even Yale, nearly every student from the richest to the poorest earns money during vacations – as a waiter, a truckdriver, a road-mender, what you will. In every part of the country I found myself in groups of people who included tycoons and labourers; surgeons and postmen, artists and janitors; and until I talked to them individually I did not know which was which. Injected without introduction into the middle of a party in a mansion, I might equally be talking to the owner or to his gardener for all I knew. Their differences of manner, dress and accent were individual differences, not class differences. Gene Stirlen, a Yale man and a millionaire, was on Christian name terms with every man in his company. I would often come across him in the street or in a restaurant with one of his employees. No one thought this odd. Once, when I had been in America almost a year, my sister, who had just arrived, expressed her amazement at the distribution of wealth in the United States. "Even the plumber coming to mend the lavatory drives up in his colossal brand-new car."

From: ENGLISH LANGUAGE PAPER B for the GENERAL CERTIFICATE OF EDUCATION (Ordinary Level), November 1970 (Joint Matriculation Board)

After a first reading your notes could look something like this:

- text about class distinctions
- university graduates
- emigration
- US: Yale University
- plumber: brand-new car

When you have read the text again, in the way suggested, and written down what you could remember and thought was important, your notes might look something like this:

- text about class distinctions in England and the U.S.
- still rigid class consciousness in Britain
- therefore a lot of discrimination
- good people emigrate: bad thing
- in the U.S. it is talent that counts
- no class distinctions in the U.S.: good thing

Admittedly, these notes are far from being comprehensive, but when you go through the text again to check you will find that the points covered here are also the main points in the text.

## 1.3 How to guess unknown words

### 1.3.1 The problem

Unless your knowledge of English is very good, you will find that comprehension texts usually contain quite a number of words you do not know. There is no need to panic at this: you can always look these words up in your dictionary, but – and this is important – you should do so only as a last resort. It's a good idea to get into the habit of doing without the dictionary as much as possible, at least for the purpose of simply finding out about the meaning of a number of words. In fact, if you go through a text in the manner suggested above (cf. 1.1 'How to read a text'), the amount of time used in getting to know the meaning of difficult words can be greatly reduced and using the dictionary kept to a minimum.
All this is very well in theory, but in pratice guessing the meaning of

unknown words and phrases requires a bit of training. Therefore, the next few pages will be dedicated to the business of showing you how precisely you can set about saving a lot of valuable time through not immediately looking up words you don't know in your dictionary, but guessing their meaning instead.
There are several ways in which this can be done, and three methods suggest themselves:

- Some words can be guessed from merely studying their form. For instance, you may never have seen 'unmanageable' before, but the different parts of the word – un, manage, able – should each tell you something, and help you to guess its meaning: The verb 'manage' has provided the root; the suffix -able suggests that the word is an adjective; and the prefix un- shows that this adjective has a negative meaning, i.e. 'that which cannot be managed'.
  Generally speaking, a knowledge of the basic meaning of prefixes and suffixes may very often enable you to indicate the direction in which the meaning of a particular word is to be found. The suffixes, however, can safely be ignored at this stage. Anybody doing English at an advanced level can be expected to recognize words like drudgery, dentistry or deanery as nouns, especially within a sentence, and it doesn't really contribute very much towards clearing up the meaning of difficult words to know the suffix -ry/-ery can express 'action or condition' (drudgery), 'science, occupation, trade, etc.' (dentistry) or 'residence of one or more persons' (deanery), and there are even one or two more meanings of this particular suffix. The prefixes, on the other hand, can very often be of real help in guessing meanings.
- The etymology of a word and historical semantic connections are very often (though not in all cases) a good guide to modern meaning and may also be a help to the memory and a source of growing interest in words. Here a knowledge of Latin and/or French, and to some extent also of Old Greek, will turn out to be especially useful.
- A study of the context usually helps when everything else fails. This is in fact much the most common way of guessing the meaning of unknown words. Unless your English is first-class, you will not know the words *blubber* and *lubricate.* As long as they stand by themselves there is no way of guessing what they might mean, but see what happens when they are put into a context:

  1) To protect a whale from the cold of the Arctic seas, nature has provided it with a thick layer of *blubber*. When the whale is killed, this covering of fat is stripped off, either on board ship or on shore.

2) No machine would work for long if it were not properly *lubricated.* The oil used for this purpose must be of the correct thickness.

It's now very easy to see that *blubber* is in fact this 'covering of fat' mentioned in the second sentence of our first example, or that *lubricated* refers to putting oil or grease into machine parts to make them work smoothly.

You shouldn't expect to be able to guess all the new words in a text. There will usually be some that are impossible, and a few that you can only get a vague idea of, but even this is important in view of the fact that more often than not the words which are causing you trouble have more than just one meaning, and unless you study the context properly there is no way of knowing which is the correct one.

### 1.3.2 Prefixes

A large part of the vocabulary you will meet not only when working with comprehension texts but whenever you read anything above the simplified English level will consist of words related to words you already know.

The complete series of relationships is highly complicated, but there is no need for us here to go into all this; it will be quite enough to do a bit of practice work on some examples and then rely on your own initiative in building up your vocabulary range through plenty of reading pratice.

If you study the following – incomplete – list of possible combinations you will easily see the point:

nouns:
1) related to verbs and marked by a suffix,
   e.g. leak/age; flatter/y;
2) related to adjectives and marked by a suffix,
   e.g. still/ness; frail/ty;
3) compounds,
   e.g. back/lash; grand/stand; earth/quake.

verbs:
1) related to nouns and marked by a prefix,
   e.g. be/siege; en/rage;
2) related to adjectives and marked by a prefix or suffix,
   e.g. em/bitter; moist/en;
3) compounds,
   e.g. get over; call up.

adjectives:
1) related to nouns and marked by a suffix,
   e.g. mess/y; fiend/ish;
2) the participles of verbs,
   e.g. suspend/ed; search/ing;

3) adjectives plus -ish,
   e.g. sweet/ish; steep/ish.

Nearly all the above relationship are so easy to see that there is no need to go to great lengths trying to teach you about them. Recognizing an unknown word as a combination of, say, a noun derived from a verb and marked by a suffix as in *exposure* (= expose + ure) and so understanding the new word from what you know about its parts comes easily – provided you do plenty of reading and are on the lookout for words of this kind.

It is a different matter, however, if you are trying to guess the meaning of a new word which is evidently a combination in which you can easily recognize the root – but you discover that you don't know the meaning of the root.

In this situation two ways are open to you: You can either look the word up in your dictionary straight away, and thereby perhaps lose valuable time, or – and this is the more profitable way – you can try to guess the meaning of the word from what you know about prefixes and from what the context suggests. To show you what is meant let us assume that in the sentence

> When they came and tried to get his support, he gave them a non-committal answer

you don't know the meaning of *non-committal*, but you can see from the position of the word within the sentence that it is used as an adjective, and you can guess from the context that its meaning must be either positive or negative or neutral (in the sense of 'evasive').

If you remember then that the prefix non- is used to express negation (as in non-existent, non-smoker, etc.), it shouldn't be too difficult to arrive at the correct solution: that the man did not (negation!) commit himself (whatever that means precisely). i.e. he did not say 'yes' and he did not say 'no', but gave an evasive answer.

Had you looked the word up in a dictionary you would have found:

**non-committal:** not committing oneself to a definite course or to either side (in a dispute, etc.)

Of course, this wouldn't have helped you very much unless you had known from the start what 'to commit oneself' means – and in that case there wouldn't have been any need to look up the word in the first place.

It is hoped that this has shown you that it does pay to know what changes in meaning prefixes can indicate. Therefore take a good look at this list and study the information contained in it; it is bound to come in useful again and again.

| prefix | basic meaning | examples |
|---|---|---|
| **a-**<br>(cf. **non-**, **in-**, **un-**) | denoting a state<br>denoting the absence of a quality | **a**drift, **a**sleep, **a**stir<br>**a**moral, **a**sexual, **a**theist |
| **ante-**<br>(cf. **pre-**) | before | **ante**room, **ante**nuptial, **ante**natal |
| **anti-**<br>(opp. **pro-**) | against | **anti**christ, **anti**pope, **anti**climax |
| **arch-** | chief, pre-eminent<br>chief, worst | **arch**bishop, **arch**angel<br>**arch**enemy, **arch**liar |
| **auto-** | self | **auto**biography, **auto**suggestion |
| **bi-** | two<br>twice | **bi**lateral, **bi**lingual, **bi**gamy<br>**bi**annual |
| **co-** | together | **co**education, to **co**exist, to **co**operate |
| **counter-** | against | **counter**-attack, **counter**-revolution, to **counter**-balance |
| **de-** | remove, undo | to **de**code, to **de**frost, to **de**mobilize |
| **dis-** | negatives the noun, adjective or verb to which it is prefixed | **dis**order, **dis**obedient, to **dis**agree |
| **en-**, **em-** | put into, make into | to **en**danger, to **en**slave, to **em**bitter |
| **ex-** | former, sometime | **ex**-president, **ex**-wife, **ex**-chancellor |
| **extra-** | outside, beyond | **extra**-mural, **extra**-typical, **extra**ordinary |
| **fore-** | before, in front of | **fore**ground, **fore**word, to **fore**see |
| **hyper-** | excessively | **hyper**-critical, **hyper**-sensitive |
| **in-**, **im-**, **il-**, **ir-** | expresses negation | **in**audible, **im**polite, **il**legible, **ir**religious |

| prefix | basic meaning | examples |
|---|---|---|
| **inter-** | among, between | **inter**national, **inter**planetary, to **inter**lock |
| **mal-** | bad(ly) | **mal**adjustment, **mal**practice, to **mal**treat |
| **mis-** | bad(ly), wrong(ly) | **mis**conduct, to **mis**manage, to **mis**read |
| **non-** (cf. **in-**, **un-** **dis-**) | expresses negation | **non**-payment, **non**-aggression, **non**-existent, **non**-stop (e.g. a **non**-stop train) |
| **post-** (opp. **ante-**, **pre-**) | after | **post**script, **post**-graduate, **post**-war (literature) |
| **pre-** (cf. **ante-**) | before, before-hand | **pre**-arrangement, **pre**historic, **pre**-war (England) |
| **pro-** (opp. **anti-**) | in favour of | **pro**-Chinese, **pro**-revolutionary, **pro**-Boer |
| **re-** | again | to **re**build, to **re**consider, **re**birth, **re**construction |
| **semi-** (cf. **hemi-**, **demi-**) | half | **semi**circle, **semi**vowel, **semi**-official (**hemi**sphere, **demi**god) |
| **sub-** | under | **sub**marine, **sub**conscious, **sub**-committee |
| **super-** | above, beyond | **super**market, to **super**scribe, **super**natural, **super**sonic |
| **trans-** | across, beyond | **trans**atlantic, **trans**alpine, to **trans**plant |
| **ultra-** | excessively | **ultra**-conservative, **ultra**-fashionable, **ultra**-liberalism |
| **un-** (cf. **in-**, **non-**) | expresses negation | **un**happy, **un**kind, **un**employ-ment, to **un**dress |

**Exercise**

Study the following sentences and then write down what the words in **bold type** might mean; they did not appear in the list.

1. The magazine you mentioned is a **bi-monthly** one.
2. They had a **foretaste** of what was in store for them when they were trying to get up to the spot that had been picked as camp-site No. 1.
3. His teachers strongly **discouraged** him from taking up the career he had in mind.
4. Our team did exceptionally well in the **interschool matches.**
5. As soon as it leaked out what their rivals were going to do, the management tried to introduce **countermeasures.**
6. The matter is quite simple – all you have to do is **to antedate** the letter and nobody will ever suspect anything.
7. In many parts of Southern Germany, the general attitude at the time was strictly **anti-reformation.**
8. She was all **atremble** when she went into the headmaster's office.
9. After the opposition had won the elections several industries were **denationalized** again.
10. He is not a very experienced rider and so was **unhorsed** before they got even as far as the bridge.
11. The pilot told the hi-jacker that he would have to go to the nearest airport for **refuelling.**
12. The meeting was disturbed several times by **ultra-rightwing** demonstrators trying to make such a din that the speakers could not be understood.
13. What is John doing now? Don't you know? He's a **sub-editor** with the Yorkshire Post.
14. It's not easy nowadays to find a **semi-detached house** at a decent price.
15. **Pre-Shakespearean drama** often had very little action on the stage but a great number of long speeches.

**Here are possible solutions:**

1. coming out twice a month (or every other month)
2. partial experience of what was to come
3. tried to persuade him not to do it
4. sports competition between a number of schools
5. measures which would ensure that their rivals' plans were not going to be successful
6. put an earlier date on the letter than the true one
7. against anything to do with the Reformation
8. trembling all over
9. given back to private ownership
10. thrown off his horse
11. filling up fuel again

12. people supporting extremely rightwing opinions
13. assistant editor
14. house joined to another on one side only
15. drama before Shakespeare

### 1.3.3 Etymological and semantic connections

English is basically a mixed language. The two elements of which it is composed are the **Germanic** on the one hand and the **Norman-French** on the other. Although the Normans were the conquerors and ruled the land after 1,066 and more than half of the words in the English language are of Norman-French origin, it was the Germanic element that remained stronger in the end. This is to say that the real basis of the language, the grammar and the most frequently used words, remained English. Thus we find that words of Germanic origin often express concrete and realistic objects and refer to friendship and good fellowship and the kindly circle of domestic life, whereas words of Latin and Norman-French origin in most cases have to do with abstract ideas, with science, politics, history, and philosophy – and it is from among them that most of the 'hard' words come.

It was through the medium of Latin as the language of scholars in the Middle Ages that a number of **Greek words** first entered the English language. But during the Renaissance period the renewed study of Greek led to the introduction of some Greek words at first hand. The number of Greek words in English may look very small if compared with the Latin-French element in it, but they are nearly all of them basic words, having to do mainly with science, and many have long become indispensable.

In the following pages an attempt has been made to list a number of the most important Latin and Greek roots and their derivatives in English, together with explanations and French and German parallels. This is meant to make you aware of etymological and semantic connections you might otherwise have overlooked and so help you in dealing with difficult words of Latin and Greek derivation and in remembering them.

Here are some frequent and important **Latin roots:**

| Latin Root | Basic Meaning | English | French | German |
|---|---|---|---|---|
| **acer** | sharp | **acrid:** sharp, bitter, biting<br>**acrimony:** bitterness | âcre<br>acrimonie | |
| **aedes**, -is | a building | **edification:** mental or moral improvement<br>**to edify:** improve in morals or mind | édification<br>édifier | = Erbauung |
| **amo** | I love | **amorous:** showing love<br>**amity:** friendship, friendly relations | amour, amitié<br>aimer, amoureux | amourös<br>Amouren |
| **animus, i**<br>**anima,** ae | mind, soul | **to animate:** breathe life, i.e. a soul, into; make lively<br>**animism:** the belief that all things in nature have a soul | âme, animer<br>animisme | animieren<br>Animismus |
| **ars,** artis | art, skill | the **fine arts:** drawing, painting, sculpture, architecture, music, ballet<br>**artistic:** done with skill and good taste<br>**artful:** cunning, deceitful | art, artiste<br>artistique<br>artificiel | Artist<br>Artifakt<br>artifiziell |
| **audio** | I hear | **audience:** assembly of listeners<br>**aural:** of the organs of hearing<br>**auditorium:** where the audience sits<br>**audible:** that can be heard | auditoire<br>auditeur<br>audible | Audienz<br>audio-visuell |
| **bellum,** i | a war | **bellicose:** inclined to fighting<br>**belligerency:** state of being at war | belliqueux<br>belligérance | |
| **brevis** | short | **brevity:** shortness<br>**brief:** lasting only a short time<br>**to brief:** summarize the facts<br>**abbreviation:** shortened form of sth | brévité<br>bref<br>abreviation | (Brevier)<br>(Brief) |

| Latin Root | Basic Meaning | English | French | German |
|---|---|---|---|---|
| **cavus, i** | a hollow | **cave, cavern:** an underground hollow | caverne | |
| | | **to excavate:** uncover by digging | excavation | = ausgraben |
| | | **cavity:** a small hole | cavité | |
| | | **concave** | concave | konkav |
| **cedo** | I go, I yield | **to cede to:** yield, give up sth to sb | céder | zedieren |
| | | **to exceed:** go beyond what is allowed | excéder | Exzeß |
| | | **to precede:** come or go before | précéder | |
| | | **precedent:** earlier happening, decision, etc. taken as an example or rule for what comes later | précédent | Präzedenzfall |
| | | **to proceed:** go forward, go on | procéder | Prozession |
| | | **access:** way to a place, e.g. an access road | accès | Zu-gang |
| | | **accessible:** to be reached | accessible | |
| | | **to recede:** go back, withdraw | | |
| | | **recession:** withdrawal | | Rezession |
| **credo** | I believe | **creed:** system of religious belief | croyance | Credo |
| | | **to credit:** believe, trust | croire | |
| | | **credit:** belief that sb can pay debts or will keep a promise | crédit | Kredit |
| | | **(in)credible:** that can(not) be believed | (in)croyable | |
| | | **credulous:** too ready to believe things | crédule | |
| **durus** | hard, lasting | **durable:** likely to last for a long time | durable | |
| | | **dour:** severe, hard, obstinate | dur | Dauer |
| | | **to endure:** suffer, bear, put up with | endurer | |

| Latin Root | Basic Meaning | English | French | German |
|---|---|---|---|---|
| **erro** | I wander | **to err:** wander from what is right = make mistakes, make errors<br>**erratic:** irregular in conduct, habit, opinions<br>**aberrant:** wandering from what is normal, expected or usual | erreur<br>aberrant | irren<br>Irrtum |
| **fames,** is | hunger | **to famish:** suffer from extreme hunger<br>**famine:** extreme scarcity of food | faim, affamé<br>famine | |
| **grex,** gregis | a flock, a herd | **gregarious:** living in groups or societies, fond of company<br>**to aggregate:** bring or come together in a mass<br>**to congregate:** come or bring together | s'agréger<br>se désagréger<br>congrégation | Aggregat<br>Kongregation |
| **haereo** | I stick | **to adhere to:** stick fast to, remain faithful to<br>**adherent:** sb sticking to a cause = supporter<br>**to cohere:** stick together, remain united<br>**coherent:** cohering, consistent (of argument, narration) | adhérer<br>adhérent<br>adhésif<br>cohésion<br>(in)cohérent | Adhäsion<br>= Anhänger<br>Kohäsion<br>Kohärenz = Zusammenhang |
| **ignis,** is | fire | **to ignite:** set on fire<br>**ignition:** mechanism for starting an engine<br>**ignis fatuus:** sth misleading, delusive hope | | Zündung |
| **ira,** ae | anger | **ire:** anger<br>**irate:** angry<br>**irascibility:** tendency to anger | irascible | |

| Latin Root | Basic Meaning | English | French | German |
|---|---|---|---|---|
| **iungo** | I join | **to join:** put together, unite<br>**joint:** place where two things (e.g. bones) come together<br>**to rejoin:** answer, reply<br>**to adjoin:** be in contact with<br>**adjunct:** sth extra but subordinate<br>**to subjoin:** add at the end, append<br>**junction:** joining point (of roads, etc.)<br>**juncture:** place where things join; state of affairs<br>**conjunction:** word used to connect clauses or sentences | joindre<br>joint<br>adjoindre<br>jonction<br>jointure<br>conjonction | Junta<br>Junktim<br>Konjunktion |
| **loquor** | I speak | **eloquence:** skilful use of language<br>**elocution:** art or style of speaking well | éloquence<br>élocution | eloquent<br>Lokution |
| **lux,** lucis | light | **lucent:** shining<br>**lucid:** bright, clear<br>**translucent:** allowing light to pass through but not transparent (frosted glass) | lucide (fig)<br>translucide | |
| **mergo** | I dip | **to immerse:** dip, plunge<br>**to emerge:** come into view (esp. come out from water)<br>**to submerge:** put under water | immerger<br>émerger<br>submerger | ein-tauchen<br>Immersions-taufe<br>auf-tauchen<br>unter-tauchen |
| **munus,** muneris | a gift | **munificent:** extremely generous<br>**to remunerate:** pay, reward | munificent<br>rémunérer | |

| Latin Root | Basic Meaning | English | French | German |
|---|---|---|---|---|
| **murus, i** | a wall | **to immure:** imprison (= put between walls)<br>**mural:** a wall-painting; fresco | emmurer<br>mur; mural | <br>Mauer |
| **muto** | I change | **mutable:** liable to change<br>**mutation:** change, alteration<br>**mutual:** shared, exchanged equally<br>**to commute sth into/for sth else:** exchange one thing for another | <br>mutation<br>mutuel<br>commuer | mutabel<br>Mutation<br>mutieren |
| **nascor** | to be born | **nascent:** coming into existence<br>**natal:** of, from one's birth<br>**native:** person born in a place and associated with it by birth<br>**the Nativity:** the birth of Christ<br>**Renaissance:** rebirth of classical ideals, etc. | naître<br>natal<br><br>Nativité<br>Renaissance | naszierend<br><br><br><br>Wieder-geburt |
| **noceo** | I injure | **noxious:** harmful, injurious<br>**innocuous:** harmless | nocif, nuisible<br>innocent | Noxen = Schad-stoffe |
| **onus,** oneris | a burden | **onerous:** burdensome, causing or requiring trouble<br>**to exonerate sb from sth:** free, clear from blame (= take a burden from sb) | onéreux (= ex-pensive)<br>exonérer (= to exempt from tax) | <br>ent-lasten |
| **pecunia,** ae | money | **pecuniary:** of money<br>**impecunious:** having little or no money | pécuniaire | pekuniär |
| **pungo** | I prick | **pungent:** sharp, biting, stinging<br>**puncture:** small hole made by sth sharp<br>**to expunge (from):** wipe or rub out words, names, etc. | poignant<br>ponctuel<br>acuponcture<br>ponctuation | punktieren<br>pointiert<br>Akupunktur<br>punktuell |

| Latin Root | Basic Meaning | English | French | German |
|---|---|---|---|---|
| **rumpo** | I break | **to rupture:** burst or break | rompre, rupture | Ruptur |
| | | **to disrupt:** break up, split, separate by force | | |
| | | **to erupt:** break out (volcano) | éruption | Eruption (Aus- |
| | | **corrupt:** immoral, dishonest, depraved | corrompre | bruch), korrupt |
| | | **to interrupt:** break the continuity of | interrompre | unter-brechen |
| **tango** | I touch | **tangible:** that can be perceived by touch | tangible | Tangente |
| | | **contact:** touching, coming together | contact | Kontakt |
| | | **contagion:** the spreading of disease by contact or close association | contagion | |
| **teneo** | I hold | **tenet:** belief that one holds; principle | tenir | |
| | | **tenable:** that can be held (of an office or position) | | |
| | | **tenacious:** holding tightly; refusing to let go | tenace | |
| | | **contents:** what sth holds, contains | contenu | In-halt |
| **venio** | I come | **to convene:** come together; summon people to come together for a meeting | venir<br>venue | Zusammen-<br>kommen |
| | | **convent:** a place where nuns have come together to live apart from others in the service of God | couvent | Konvent |
| | | **advent:** coming or arrival | Avent | Ankunft, Advent |
| | | **adventitious:** coming by chance, accidental | | |
| | | **venture:** undertaking in which there is risk | aventure | Abenteuer |
| **volo** | I will, I want | **volition:** act or power of using one's own will | vouloir | |
| | | **voluntary:** doing or ready to do things of one's own free will | volonté<br>volontaire | Volontär |
| | | **to volunteer:** make a voluntary offer of one's services | | |
| | | **benevolence:** wish to do good (opp. **malevolence**) | bénévole | |

**Exercise 1**

All these sentences contain certain words which are not given in the lists above, but are etymologically connected with one or another item in them, and another group of words which are in fact explained above, but are used here in a different meaning. Your job is now to pick out the right one from the multiple choice explanations which follow each sentence. Remember that only one of them is correct.

1. He stared at me from **cavernous** eyes.
   a) wild, b) deepset, c) bloodshot, d) anxious
2. I've always found him a most **amiable** fellow.
   a) correctly-dressed, b) sensible, c) good-natured, d) polite.
3. The bosses of industry were **unanimous** in their support of the Government's policy.
   a) half-hearted, b) hesitant, c) inefficient, d) united
4. In spite of all her **arts** the young man was not attracted to her.
   a) clever ways, b) skill as an artist, c) knowledge of painting and sculpture, d) witchcraft
5. I don't know how you can stand such a **loquacious** landlady.
   a) ugly, b) talkative, c) curious, d) awful
6. 'What's Jane doing now?' 'Haven't you heard? She was hired on the spot for the part of Ophelia after her **audition.**'
   a) an eye-operation, b) trial hearing to test someone for a certain role, c) final examination, d) recovery from a long illness
7. When he applied for the post he was not even asked to an interview as his **credentials** were so poor.
   a) qualifications, b) reputation, c) the way he had formulated his application, d) handwriting
8. We all tried very hard, but none of us was able to **elucidate** the problem.
   a) understand, b) make clear, c) solve, d) overcome
9. Occasional Latin words scratched on a piece of pottery, apparently by the workman who made it, suggest that in some localities Latin was familiar to the **artisan class.**
   a) resistance movement, b) art students, c) skilled craftsmen,
   d) painters and sculptors
10. Measles is a **contagious** disease.
    a) dangerous, b) harmless, c) (disease) which is spread by contact, c) (disease) which you can catch only once
11. What you suggested drew an unexpected **rejoinder** from Mary.
    a) cry, b) howl, c) sigh, d) reply
12. It could prove rather **remunerative** if he worked for us.
    a) profitable, b) damaging, c) disastrous, d) difficult

**Exercise 2**

Study the following sentences and then write down what the words in **bold type** might mean. This time you are given no guidance whatever apart from what you have gathered from studying the lists above.

1. To make sure that the envelope couldn't be steamed open he put some **adhesive** tape round the edges.
2. He was not the man to get angry easily, but when he was interrupted again and again his words gradually became more and more **acrimonious.**
3. When countries cannot settle a dispute in an **amicable** way, a war cannot usually be avoided.
4. Epidemics are only one of the evils that **proceed from** war.
5. The delay was caused by an **aberration** in the computer.
6. The Vicar lectured his **congregation** on the sin of alcohol abuse.
7. He was so excited that what he told us was rather **incoherent.**
8. I have **tangible** proof that you're a liar.
9. When he was writing his thesis he **immured himself** in his study.
10. The **disruption** of the Roman Empire was inevitable once the Germanic tribes started moving south.

**Key to Exercise 1:** 1b (cavus); 2c (amo); 3d (animus); 4a (ars); 5b (loquor); 6b (audio); 7a (credo); 8b (lux); 9c (ars); 10c (tango); 11d (iungo); 12a (munus)

**Key to Exercise 2:** 1. sticky tape (haereo); 2. bitter (acer); 3. peaceful (amo); 4. are the result of (cedo); 5. mistake (erro); 6. people who have come together to worship (grex); 7. inconsistent (haereo); 8. clear and definite (tango); 9. shut himself up (murus); 10. breaking up (rumpo).

Here are some frequent and important **Greek roots:**

| Greek Root | Basic Meaning | English | French | German |
|---|---|---|---|---|
| **anthropos** | a man | **anthropology:** science, study of man | anthropologie | Anthropologie |
| | | **misanthrope:** hater of mankind | misanthrope | = Menschenfeind |
| | | **anthropoid:** man-like (anthropoid ape) | anthropoide | = menschenähnlich |
| | | **anthropomorphous:** of human form | anthropomorphisme | anthropomorph |
| **biblion** | book | **Bible:** the Scriptures of the Old and New Testaments | Bible | Bibel |
| | | **bibliography:** list of books; history or description of books | bibliographie | Bibliographie |
| | | **bibliophile:** person who loves and collects books | bibliophile | bibliophil |
| **bios** | life | **biology:** study of physical life | biologie | = Lebenskunde |
| | | **biography:** the written life of a person | biographie | = Lebensbeschreibung |
| | | **antibiotic:** substance capable of destroying bacterial life | antibiotique | antibiotisch |
| **chronos** | time | **chronology:** science of fixing dates; arrangement of events with dates | chronologie | Chronologie |
| | | **chronicle:** continuous register of events in order of time | chronique | Chronik |
| | | **chronic:** lasting for a long time, continual | chronique | chronisch |
| | | **chronometer:** time-measuring instrument (accurate watch) | chronomètre | = Zeitmesser |
| | | **anachronism:** sth out of date in a description of past events | anachronisme | Anachronismus |

| Greek Root | Basic Meaning | English | French | German |
|---|---|---|---|---|
| **genos genes** | a race, of such a kind | **genocide:** extermination of a race<br>**genesis:** beginning, starting-point<br><br>**gene:** one of the factors controlling heredity<br>**genealogical:** showing the descent of a family or species | génocide<br>genèse<br><br>gène<br>généalogique | = Völkermord<br>Genesis, Genese<br>= Erbfaktor<br>Genealogie |
| **grapho** | I write | **autograph:** a person's own signature<br>**biography:** the written life of a person<br>**geography:** study of the earth's surface, etc.<br>**calligraphy:** the art of beautiful handwriting<br>**seismograph:** instrument which records the strength etc. of earthquakes<br>**graphically:** as in a picture | autographe<br>biographie<br>géographie<br>calligraphie<br>sismographe | Autogramm<br>Biographie<br>= Erdkunde<br>Kalligraphie<br>Seismograph<br><br>graphisch |
| **heteros** | other, different | **heterodox:** holding a different opinion (opp. orthodox)<br>**heterosexual:** attracted to/by the opp. sex (opp. homosexual)<br>**heterogeneous:** made up of different kinds (opp. homogeneous) | hétérodoxe<br>hétérosexuel<br>hétérogène | = anders-gläubig<br>heterosexuell<br>heterogen |
| **homos** | the same | **homogeneous:** of the same kind (opp. heterogeneous)<br>**homocentric:** having the same centre<br>**homogenetic:** having the same origin<br>**homosexual:** attracted to/by one's own sex (opp. heterosexual) | homogène<br>homocentrique<br><br>homosexuel | homogen<br>homozentrisch<br>homogenetisch<br>homosexuell |

| Greek Root | Basic Meaning | English | French | German |
|---|---|---|---|---|
| **hydor** | water | **hydrant:** pipe from a water-main (esp. in a street) | | Hydrant |
| | | **hydrate:** chemical compound of water with another substance | hydrate | Hydrate |
| | | **hydraulic:** worked by the pressure of water | hydraulique | hydraulisch |
| | | **hydrogen:** gas without colour, taste or smell (symbol H) | hydrogène | = Wasserstoff |
| **kyklos** | a circle | **cycle:** series of events taking place in a regularly repeated order | cycle | Zyklus |
| | | **cyclic/al:** recurring in cycles | cyclique | zyklisch |
| | | **bicycle:** two-wheeled vehicle for riding on | bicyclette | = Zweirad |
| | | **encyclical:** letter written by the Pope for wide circulation | encyclique | Enzyklika |
| | | **(en)cyclopedia:** (= all-round education) set of books giving information about every branch of knowledge | encyclopédie | Enzyklopädie |
| **logia** | science of, study of | **astrology:** the science of stars (and their supposed influence on people) | astrologie | Astrologie |
| | | **philology:** the study of languages | philologie | Philologie |
| | | **mineralogy:** the study of minerals | minéralogie | Mineralogie |
| **megas megale** | large | **megalith:** a large stone | mégalithe | Megalith |
| | | **megaphone:** a speaking-trumpet, carrying the sound to a distance | mégaphone | Megaphon |
| | | **megalosaurus:** extinct kind of huge carnivorous lizard | | |
| | | **megaton:** 1,000,000 tons | megatonne | Megatonne |
| | | **megawatt:** 1,000,000 watts | | Megawatt |

| Greek Root | Basic Meaning | English | French | German |
|---|---|---|---|---|
| **mania** | madness, extreme enthusiasm | **mania:** extreme enthusiasm (cf. **phobia**)<br>**maniac:** madman<br>**kleptomania:** obsessive desire to steal sth<br>**nymphomania:** abnormal sexual desire in women<br>**Anglomania:** extreme fascination with anything English | (manie)<br>(maniaque)<br>kleptomanie<br>nymphomanie<br>anglomanie | Manie<br>= Verrückter<br>Kleptomanie<br>= Mannstollheit<br>Anglomanie |
| **metron** | measure | **metre:** unit of length; verse rhythm<br>**meter:** apparatus which measures sth<br>**the metric system:** the decimal measuring system<br>**metrical:** composed in metre (contrasted with prose)<br>**metronome:** instrument marking time<br>**parking-meter:** apparatus which measures the time during which a car is parked in a public place | mètre<br><br><br>système métrique<br><br>métronome | Meter<br>Metrum<br>= Zähler<br>Dezimalsystem<br>= in Versform<br>Metronom<br>Parkuhr |
| **morphe** | form | **morphology:** study of the forms of animals and plants or of the form of words<br>**morphic:** relating to form | morphologie | Morphologie |
| **philo**<br>**philos** | I love<br>friend | **Russophile:** lover of Russia and anything Russian<br>**gastrophile:** person who likes good cooking<br>**philanthropic:** loving one's fellow men<br>**philosopher:** lover of wisdom | russophile<br><br>philanthropique<br>philosophe | <br><br>= menschenfreundlich<br>Philosoph |

| Greek Root | Basic Meaning | English | French | German |
|---|---|---|---|---|
| **phobos** **phobia** | fear, dread | **phobia:** morbid fear or aversion (cf. **mania**) | phobie | Phobie |
| | | **xenophobia:** irrational fear of strangers | xénophobie | = Fremdenhaß |
| | | **claustrophobia:** morbid fear of closed places | claustrophobie | Klaustrophobie |
| **phone** | sound, voice | **phon:** unit of loudness used in measuring the intensity of sound | phone | Phon |
| | | **phonometer:** instrument recording number or force of soundwaves | phonométrie | = Lärmmeß-gerät |
| | | **phonology:** the system of sounds in a language | phonologie | Phonologie |
| | | **phonetics:** the study of speech sounds | phonétique | Phonetik |
| **phos** **photos** | light | **photograph:** picture taken by means of the chemical action of light on a sensitive film | photographie | Photographie (= Lichtbild) |
| | | **photocopy:** copy of a document etc. made by a photographic method | photocopie | Photokopie (= Lichtpause) |
| | | **photometer:** instrument for measuring the intensity of light | photomètre | Photometer (= Lichtmesser) |
| | | **phosphorescence:** the giving out of light without burning | phosphores-cence | Phosphoreszenz |
| **physis** | nature | **physics:** science dealing with matter and energy | (la) physique | Physik (= Naturlehre) |
| | | **physical:** of material things (the physical world) | physique | physisch (= körperlich) |
| | | **physiology:** science of the normal functions of living things | physiologie | Physiologie |
| | | **physiotherapy:** treatment of disease by means of exercise, massage and the use of natural forces such as light and heat | physiothérapie | Physiotherapie |

| Greek Root | Basic Meaning | English | French | German |
|---|---|---|---|---|
| **pseudes**<br>**pseudos** | false<br>falsehood | **pseudonym:** name taken by an author instead of his real name<br>**pseudonymous:** writing, written under an assumed name (cf. also anonymus)<br>**pseudo-classic:** pretending or falsely believed to be classic | pseudonyme | Pseudonym (= Deckname)<br><br>pseudoklassisch |
| **psyche** | mind, soul | **psychology:** science of the mind and its processes<br>**psychiatry:** the study and treatment of mental diseases<br>**psychopath:** person suffering from severe mental disorder<br>**psychosis:** abnormal or diseased mental state<br>**psychedelic:** (of drugs) mind-expanding<br>**psychic:** of phenomena or conditions which appear to be outside physical or natural laws | psychologie<br>psychiatrie<br><br>psychose<br><br>psychique (= of the mind) | Psychologie<br>Psychiatrie<br>Psychopath<br>Psychose<br><br>psychisch (= geistig/ seelisch) |
| **skopo** | I look, I observe | suffix **-scope:** indicating instrument for showing or observing (microscope, telescope)<br>**scope:** range of action or observation (within/ beyond the scope of) | microscope<br>télescope | Mikroskop<br>Teleskop |
| **tele** | far | prefix **tele-:** indicating instruments recording or producing results at a distance (telephone, television) | téléphone<br>télévision | = Fernsprecher<br>= Fernseher |

| Greek Root | Basic Meaning | English | French | German |
| --- | --- | --- | --- | --- |
| **theos** | God | **theology:** formation of a series of theories about the nature of God<br>**atheism:** belief that there is no God<br>**theocracy:** system of government in which the state laws are believed to be the laws of God<br>**theosophy:** System of philosophy which aims at a direct knowledge of God | théologie<br>athéisme<br>théocratie<br>théosophie | Theologie<br>Atheismus<br>Theokratie<br>Theosophie |
| **thermos**<br>**therme** | warm<br>heat | **thermic:** of heat (thermic conditions)<br>**thermometer:** instrument for measuring temperature<br>**thermo-dynamics:** science of the relation between heat and mechanical work | thermique<br>thermomètre<br>thermo-dynamique | thermisch<br>= Wärmemesser<br>Thermodynamik |

**Exercise**

Try to guess the meaning of the words in **bold type** in the following sentences. None of them appeared in our lists, but they are all made up of elements explained above.

1. This machine works by **hydro-electric** power.
2. He has an **encyclopedic** knowledge of 18th century history.
3. Unlike the **anthropomorphic** gods of the Greeks, Yahveh must not be represented in statues and pictures.
4. Mr. Benson is a true **philanthropist** and tries to help people whenever he can.
5. I am quite fond of books myself, but Henry has become a **biblio-maniac** over the years and has lined the walls of practically all the rooms in his house with books.
6. Dictators like Hitler or Idi Amin obviously suffer from **megalomania.**
7. 'Bored' and 'board' are **homophones.**
8. Experts in **graphology** can tell a great deal about a person's character simply from studying his handwriting.
9. King Ludwig II of Bavaria had a most **heterogeneous** collection of vases; they are now on display in one of his castles.
10. They are both **Francophiles** and spend all their holidays in France.
11. Father had a way of describing his war experiences so **graphically** that we always listened as if under a spell.
12. What was finally left of all the stuff we had used in the chemical experiment was a brown **amorphous** mass of something that gave off a very offensive smell.
13. He is a man of excellent **physique** and should do very well in the endurance tests.
14. All her novels contain a large amount of **biographical** material.
15. Bathing in **thermal** springs is said to be good for rheumatism.

**Solutions**

1. it is driven by electricity produced by water power
2. comprehensive and detailed
3. having a human form
4. lover of mankind
5. person who is mad about books
6. form of madness in which a person has wildly exaggerated ideas about his importance
7. words having the same pronunciation
8. the study of handwriting
9. of different kinds
10. lovers of France and everything that is French
11. vividly
12. having no definite shape or form

13. structure and development of the body
14. relating to the author's own life
15. hot

Let us now look at a text and see how a knowledge of etymological and semantic connections can be of very great help indeed in guessing the meaning of difficult words and thus in understanding a text better. This is also an opportunity for demonstrating the technique of going through a text step by step that was advocated above (cf. 1.1 'How to read a text').

**Step one:**

> Read the whole text through, not too fast, trying to get a good idea of what it is about and what the main points of it are. If you like, you can also make some notes (cf. 1.2 'How to practise your reading comprehension').

**The British People**

Britain is indeed a land of very mixed and varied racial origins and composition, and this is particularly true of England proper. Mediterranean, Celtic, Roman, German and Scandinavian are the basic, long-term elements that have combined and contributed to form the character of a people which is more complex than is often realized, especially by those with a passion for generalization and oversimplification, with an eye for the 'typical' this and that rather than for the individual. If we like to make a broad twofold distinction between the Anglo-Saxon (Germanic, non-Celtic) sphere of influence, on the one hand, and the Celtic on the other, we can no doubt find essential traits of mind and character prominent in each. We may venture the generalization that the non-Celts tend to be cautious, reserved and practical in temperament and approach, guided in the first place by fact rather than by theory, of a solid, even slow intelligence rather than quick-witted or highly imaginative, with ideas such as the notorious 'common sense', balance, tolerance and moderation. The Celt, on the other hand, while not lacking in the qualities just enumerated, is more open and impulsive, of a vivid and fanciful imagination, nimble-witted and quick on the uptake, a lover of talk and of eloquence, of colour and ornament. There is truth in this very broad distinction and we may pursue it a little further.

As important as the distinction is, of course, the fact that the two types, if we can so call them, blend and merge, probably throughout the British Isles in some degree but with particular and often disconcerting sublety in England itself – a mixture usually well-balanced, but a mixture. Perhaps the best way to try to understand that phenomenon, the 'Englishman' – still, it seems, for many an exasperating task – is to be prepared to find and accept a blend of contrasts rather than try to apply any single preconceived idea or standard. If we expect him to be nothing but reserved, prosaic, unimaginative we shall be forgetting that England has produced the imagination of a Shakespeare, a Dickens and a Turner; that in the English is a great love of the fantastic, the paradoxical and the antilogic of 'nonsense' that are reflected in G. K. Chesterton, Lewis Carroll, Edward Lear and many others in the same glorious tradition. If we think of him as 'practical' only, empirical and averse to theory we shall need to remind ourselves that the history of thought in England has had its Newton as well as its Locke, indeed that the empirical, inductive method has been perhaps the chief expression of the English attitude and approach to theory. If, again, we bring up the stale old cliché of his house being his castle and taunt him with being 'insular' he can equally point to the facts that his fellow-countrymen have been among the greatest travellers and explorers ever known, founded the most far-flung empire ever seen (even though it has now become transformed into the rather less tangible 'Commonwealth') and made the first ascent of the highest mountain on earth.

From: John Bourke, *Britain. A Short Introduction for Students of English*

**Step two:**

| |
|---|
| Read the text again, this time even more slowly, and pay particular attention to points that seem difficult. Mark (underline) the words and phrases you don't understand. Make an intelligent guess at the meaning and then read on. |

**Note:** When this text was 'tried out' with members of a 'Grundkurs', no two people marked the same words as difficult, but although there were great differences in the individual selection of words which made people hesitate or which they felt unsure about, there was more or less general agreement as to the really difficult words.

The text could look something like this after Step two. The words in italics represent the ones that people felt could be eliminated fairly quickly as 'very easy to guess', if not already well-known; the underlined words are the really hard ones.

**The British People**

Britain is indeed a land of very mixed and *varied* racial origins and composition, and this is particularly true of England proper. *Mediterranean,* Celtic, Roman, German and Scandinavian are the basic, long-term elements that have combined and *contributed* to form the character of a people which is more complex than is often realized, especially by those with a *passion* for generalization and oversimplification, with an eye for the 'typical' this and that rather than for the individual. If we like to make a broad twofold distinction between the Anglo-Saxon (Germanic, non-Celtic) sphere of influence, on the one hand, and the Celtic on the other, we can no doubt find essential traits of mind and character prominent in each. We may venture the generalization that the non-Celts tend to be cautious, reserved and practical in temperament and approach, guided in the first place by fact rather than by theory, of a solid, even slow intelligence rather than quick-witted or highly imaginative, with ideals such as the *notorious* 'common sense', balance, tolerance and moderation. The Celt, on the other hand, while not lacking in the qualities just enumerated, is more open and impulsive, of a *vivid* and fanciful imagination, nimble-witted and quick on the uptake, a lover of talk and of *eloquence,* of colour and ornament. There is truth in this very broad distinction and we may pursue it a little further.

As important as the distinction is, of course the fact that the two types, if we can so call them, blend and merge, probably throughout the British Isles in some degree but with particular and often disconcerting subtlety in England itself – a mixture usually well-balanced, but a mixture. Perhaps the best way to try to understand that phenomenon, the 'Englishman' – still, it seems, for many an exasperating task – is to be prepared to find and accept a blend of contrasts rather than try to apply any single *preconceived* idea or standard. If we expect him to be nothing but reserved, prosaic, unimaginative we shall be forgetting that England has produced the imagination of a Shakespeare, a Dickens and a Turner; that in the English is a great love of the fantastic, the paradoxical and the antilogic of 'nonsense' that are reflected in G. K. Chesterton, Lewis Carroll, Edward Lear and many others in the same glorious tradition. If we think of him as 'practical' only, empirical and *averse* to theory we shall need to remind ourselves that the history of thought in England has had its Newton as well as its Locke, indeed that the empirical, inductive method has been perhaps the chief expression of the English attitude and approach to theory. If, again, we bring up the stale old cliché of his house being his castle and taunt him with being 'insular' he can equally point to the facts that his fellow-countrymen have been among the greatest travellers and explorers ever known, founded the most far-flung empire ever seen (even though it has now become transformed into the rather less *tangible* 'Commonwealth') and made the first *ascent* of the highest mountain on earth.

Naturally, one must not expect too many Greek words in this kind of text, and so the following annotations have been based on Latin, French and German parallels only.

**Note:** There are in fact a number of words derived from the Greek in this text: words such as *character* (lines 4/5), *sphere* (line 9), or *phenomenon* (line 26) and *paradoxical* (line 33), but they are so well-known anyway that we can ignore them here.

These might have been the considerations which led those students who did not know the words printed in italics at first sight to guess their meaning right away:

| | |
|---|---|
| *varied* (line 1): | L variatus (variare, varius);<br>F varié |
| *Mediterranean* (lines 2/3): | L mediterraneus (medius = middle + terra = land);<br>F la mediterranée);<br>G Mittelländisches Meer |
| *contributed* (line 4): | L contribuere (contributum)<br>F contribuer |
| *passion* (line 6): | L passio (pati, passus);<br>F la passion;<br>G Passion (passioniert) |
| *notorious* (line 15): | F notoire;<br>G notorisch |
| *vivid* (line 18): | L vividus |
| *eloquence* (line 19): | L eloquentia;<br>F l'éloquence;<br>G eloquent |
| *pre-conceived* (line 29): | L prae + conceptus (concipere);<br>F préconçu |
| *averse* (line 36): | L aversus (a + vertere/versus);<br>G Aversion |
| *tangible* (line 45): | L tangere;<br>F tangible |
| *ascent* (line 45): | L ascendere;<br>F ascension |

With a bit of imagination and after some practice in this type of word guessing, a number of other words can also be guessed in their meaning:

| | |
|---|---|
| trait (line 10): | L tractus<br>F le trait |
| prominent (line 11): | L pro + eminere = prominere;<br>F proéminent<br>G prominent |
| pursue (line 20): | L prosequi;<br>F poursuivre |
| disconcerting (line 24): | L dis + concertare;<br>F déconcertant |
| subtlety (line 25): | L subtilitas<br>F subtilité;<br>G subtil |
| exasperating (line 27): | L exasperare (asper);<br>F exaspérer |

In the case of the words which remain now, semantic connections do not take us very far. We shall have to rely on what we can gather from the context.

**Step three:**

Mark the remaining words again, [like this], to make them stand out better, and then study the context of each of them. If you do this properly, the following words and expressions become clear at least in their broad meaning:

| | |
|---|---|
| [venture] (line 11): | obviously means something like 'put forward' |
| [nimble-witted] (line 18): | apparently the same as *quick-witted* (line 14) and the opposite of *slow intelligence* (line 14); associated with *quick on the uptake* (lines 18/19) |
| [blend] (line 23):<br>[merge] (line 23): | the two words evidently mean about the same; they refer to *mixture* (lines 25 and 26) and *contrast* (line 28: *blend of contrasts*) and must be synonyms of *mix* |
| [stale] (line 40): | obviously qualifies the expression *old cliché* and can here only mean something like *terribly* old cliché or *the same* old cliché |

taunt (line 41): could express vaguely the same as *bring up* in the first part of the sentence (line 40)

far-flung (line 43): not easy to guess, but the word *far* should give a clue: widely extended (*flung* = past participle of fling = throw)

This leaves us with the compound long-term (line 4). The meaning of this expression has to be guessed in any case because the dictionary doesn't list it. The meaning here is apparently (elements) 'which have been there for a long time'.

### 1.3.4 Context

It has already been said and shown that a study of the context can usually clear up the meaning of most difficult words. In fact, if you read a text carefully and work through it again systematically, you will find that difficulties in understanding a text as such and also individual words and phrases gradually tend to disappear. It is really quite amazing how often it is possible to guess the meaning of a difficult word or expression once you thoroughly master the proper technique.
Most intelligent students, it is true, have long unconsciously adopted some kind of technique of word guessing, and some do quite well without ever wasting a thought about what they are in fact doing. We firmly believe, however, that the various steps of word guessing should be made a conscious process and that results will always be better once you do something systematically.
This means that you first of all study the sentence the word is in, then, if necessary, the sentences immediately before and after, and at last the text as a whole again to see if the word is repeated later on – the more often it appears the easier it becomes to know its meaning – or if there is perhaps even an explanation of the word in the form of a paraphrase or a synonymous expression somewhere else in the text.
At this point, another thing must be mentioned before we can look at a sample text. A large percentage of students hand in their exam texts as they received them – without so much as a pencil mark on them to show that the text had been worked with. One can then be fairly sure that they haven't studied the text properly, probably spent quite an unnecessary lot of time looking up hard words in their dictionaries and more than likely thought the text 'terribly difficult'. This in turn may have led to an even greater degree of nervousness than is usual in an exam

situation and affected the students' work for the worse. All this additional excitement can easily be avoided once you have got into the habit of working through comprehension texts according to this routine procedure already mentioned, irrespective of the situation in which you are confronted with such a text: in the classroom, at home or in the actual exam.
Now one of the steps in this fixed course of work is to mark the difficult words and expressions. There is absolutely no need to be shy about this. Nobody is going to frown at you for handing back a test paper that has been marked all over in ink or even in different colours. In fact, this is just what you should do – it makes working with a text very much easier.
It is perhaps best to use an actual text to show you precisely what is meant. So read the following text slowly and carefully without a dictionary, and without asking any questions.

**Baggy pants**

Everyone laughed when Albert went to work in his baggy pants. Everyone but Albert. He punched one of his workmates in the eye.
And that's when the joke really fell flat. For the incident led to a strike which crippled production at a carpet factory.
The trousers that caused all the trouble were in a shapeless fawn-coloured material. They flapped round Albert's legs as he walked into the Victoria carpet factory in Kidderminster, Worcestershire.
Other workers winked and smirked. There were ribald comments. Albert thought it was quite amusing at first. But after half an hour, the wisecracks got him down.
So he planted one on seventeen-year-old apprentice David Bishop. Then the foreman intervened. He didn't see the funny side of it. He suspended David for two days and Albert for three.
Other workers held an emergency meeting and decided that David had been treated unfairly. They asked for him to be reinstated. The management refused – and 100 men walked out.
David said at home in Kidderminster yesterday: 'The trousers were just hopeless. You could have got two people in them. But it seems our fun went too far. Albert suddenly came across and hit me in the face. Later, the foreman sent me home. I have lost £3 in wages and that hurts me more than anything.'
The strikers are expected back at work today. But no one is expecting a return of Albert's troublesome trousers.
From a report in the *Daily Mirror*

Did the text look difficult at first sight? Don't worry, but underline the words and phrases that you are not sure about: like this. Assuming that your vocabulary is rather limited, perhaps this is what the text looks like now:

**Baggy pants**

Everyone laughed when Albert went to work in his baggy pants. Everyone but Albert. He punched one of his workmates in the eye.
And that's when the joke really fell flat. For the incident led to a strike which crippled production at a carpet factory.
The trousers that caused all the trouble were in a shapeless fawn-coloured material. They flapped round Albert's legs as he walked into the Victoria carpet factory in Kidderminster, Worcestershire.
Other workers winked and smirked. There were ribald comments. Albert throught it was quite amusing at first. But after half an hour, the wisecracks got him down.
So he planted one on seventeen-year-old apprentice David Bishop. Then the foreman intervened. He didn't see the funny side of it. He suspended David for two days and Albert for three.
Other workers held an emergency meeting and decided that David had been treated unfairly. They asked for him to be reinstated. The management refused – and 100 men walked out.
David said at home in Kidderminster yesterday: 'The trousers were just hopeless. You could have got two people in them. But it seems our fun went too far. Albert suddenly came across and hit me in the face. Later, the foreman sent me home. I have lost £3 in wages and that hurts me more than anything'.
The strikers are expected back at work today. But no one is expecting a return of Albert's troublesome trousers.

These are the words and expressions which can immediately be cleared up in their meaning once you take a proper look at the context:

| | |
|---|---|
| baggy (headline; line 1): | shapeless and very wide (cf. line 5: shapeless; line 18: You could have got two people in them) |
| pants (headline; line 1): | trousers (cf. lines 5, 13, 23) |
| punched (line 2): | hit (cf. line 21: hit me in the face) |
| crippled (line 4): | seriously damaged (because of the walk-out mentioned in line 16) |
| planted one on (line 11): | hit (cf. line 2: punched; line 19: hit me in the face) |
| intervened (line 12): | stepped between, stopped the quarrel (G 'intervenieren' from L 'intervenire') |
| suspended (lines 12/13): | sent home (cf. line 20: the foreman sent me home; G 'suspendieren' from L 'suspendere') |

reinstated (line 15): the other workers wanted his two-day suspension cancelled

walked out (line 16): went on strike (cf. lines 3/4: led to a strike; line 22: the strikers)

This is what our text looks like when we have marked the rest of the difficult words a second time – like this – to make them stand out better:

**Baggy pants**

Everyone laughed when Albert went to work in his baggy pants. Everyone but Albert. He punched one of his workmates in the eye.
And that's when the joke really fell flat. For the incident led to a strike which crippled production at a carpet factory.
The trousers that caused all the trouble were in a shapeless fawn-coloured material. They flapped round Albert's legs as he walked into the Victoria carpet factory in Kidderminster, Worcestershire.
Other workers winked and smirked. There were ribald comments. Albert thought it was quite amusing at first. But after half an hour, the wisecracks got him down.
So he planted one on seventeen-year-old apprentice David Bishop. Then the foreman intervened. He didn't see the funny side of it. He suspended David for two days and Albert for three.
Other workers held an emergency meeting and decided that David had been treated unfairly. They asked for him to be reinstated. The management refused – and 100 men walked out.
David said at home in Kidderminster yesterday: 'The trousers were just hopeless. You could have got two people in them. But it seems our fun went too far. Albert suddenly came across and hit me in the face. Later, the foreman sent me home. I have lost £3 in wages and that hurts me more than anything.'
The strikers are expected back at work today. But no one is expecting a return of Albert's troublesome trousers.

If you study the text really well, you will find that you can even guess most of the words that are now left over:

fell flat (line 3): obviously refers to when Albert no longer regarded his mates' comments as amusing (cf. line 10: the wisecracks got him down)

flapped (line 6): we know that the trousers were far too wide; so they flapped round his legs like a sail round the mast: they were swinging from side to side.

ribald (line 8): evidently means sth like 'mocking, teasing'

wisecracks (line 10): clearly refers to jokes and ribald comments got him down (line 10): made him angry and aggressive (cf. lines 1 and 2: Everyone laughed ... but Albert. He punched ...)

This leaves us with fawn-coloured (lines 5/6), winked and smirked (both line 8). Fawn-coloured cannot be guessed (it is a yellowish brown), but the colour of Albert's pants is really of no importance for our comprehension of the text. The precise meaning of winked and smirked cannot be guessed either; from the context, however, both are bound to mean something like 'made fun of him, teased and mocked him', and that is quite sufficient for our purposes. There is therefore no need at all to use the dictionary here. The main thing to remember about using the dictionary for text comprehension is to check only those words you absolutely need for understanding the text.

**Note:** Any other method of marking a text will do just as well, of course. The important thing is that you do get into the habit of marking your texts and that you then stick to the same method.

**Exercise 1**

You probably don't know many of these words: notch, gullible, goggle, poignant, expunge, ply, lintel, dipstick, shamble, pillion. Look at the way they are used in the following sentences and then write down what you think they might mean.

1. Arizona Jack had twelve **notches** on his gun – one for each man he had killed.
2. She's amazingly **gullible**. I told her yesterday that I keep two alligators on the top of my bedroom cupboard and she believed every word of it.
3. What are you **goggling** at me like that for? Have I got two heads or something?
4. A thing you ought to be wary of is his **poignant** sarcasm.
5. The publishers he had sent the manuscript to wrote back to say that all references to Lord X had to be **expunged** before they would publish it.
6. At a party a good host will **ply** his guests with food and drink.
7. The door was so low that I hit my head on the **lintel.**
8. The car was making a funny noise, so I got out, opened the bonnet, and took out the **dipstick** to check the oil level.
9. He must be tired: look at the way he's **shambling** along.
10. Mark got on the motorbike, I sat behind him on the **pillion,** and we roared off into the night.

### Exercise 2

Read the following text slowly and carefully, without a dictionary, paying special attention to the words and expressions in **bold type.** Then study the context of these items very closely and write down what you think they might mean. Note that most of them are **slang** expressions.

### Not Quite Straight

Sometimes I can't help thinking that Bert – that's my boyfriend that was – wasn't quite **straight**. Well, I ask you, what would you think of a boyfriend who searched your handbag with one hand while he was kissing you with the other? Oh, I don't say that Bert wasn't very clever about it. **Six convictions** for picking pockets before he was twenty-one – that was Bert. And proud of it he was too. He'd go through a handbag in **five seconds dead,** and there wouldn't be a **brass farthing** left in it. But doing it to your own girlfriend – well, that's a bit too much, don't you think? Of course, when **I cottoned on** after money had mysteriously disappeared several times and I searched my bag right after one of our kisses and accused Bert, he laughed **easy like** and gave me back my money – said he had just been practising and had intended to give it back to me, honest, **cross his heart.** I was **taken in,** and it wasn't till after he had left that I remembered the other times when money had disappeared. Yes, he was **a smooth one** all right. Knew just how to **pull the wool over a girl's eyes.**

I didn't see him again for quite a time after that – a silly little misunderstanding about a fur coat I was walking out of a shop with – just to see what it looked like in the daylight, as I told the judge. Well, when I was released twenty months later, what do you think, there was Bert at the gate in a smart American car – all glass and chromium like – dressed up like a gent with a fur collar on his coat, large diamond tie-pin, long cigarette-holder and all. And the chauffeur – yes, there was a chauffeur too! – opens the door for me and I step in and Bert greets me like a gent: 'What ho, Miss Bloggs, old girl (usually he calls me Gert), welcome out of **pokey**.'

When the chauffeur had got in and we were gliding away towards the West End, I asked Bert what this is all about, but he gives me a wink and nods towards the chauffeur, so I **catch on** and keep my mouth shut.

Well, we drive up to a nice block of flats near Hyde Park and the chauffeur hops out and opens the door and we get out, and Bert says, 'Thank you, my man, that will be all for today,' and the chauffeur bows and goes. Well, Bert has some flat! Large glass chandeliers in each room, including the bathroom, all the furniture painted gold, red velvet curtains and red carpets everywhere, a bar with ever so many drinks and packets of potato crisps, purple sheets on the bed, and all the other signs of being a gent.

Well, of course I asked him how he'd got all that money without being **pinched by the cops,** but he looked at me very **pained,** and said, 'Since you were pinched **I've gone straight,** Miss Bl – I mean Gertrude. All this splendour you see here represents the results of honest **toil.**'

**'Go on,'** I said admiringly. 'Have you really got a job, Bert?' 'I have,' he said, taking off his coat, collar, tie and shoes and **hitching** his thumbs into his braces as he used to when I had known him before. 'I have started a society for helping old **lags** like yourself. And all the rich old dames pour the money in when I go around and lecture on the harsh cruel life in pokey, and tell them how many poor lost souls would willingly reform and stop stealing the old ladies' jewels if only they were given a chance to go straight after they got out of **jug.**'

'But there are already societies like that, Bert,' I said. 'How did you **get in on this?'**

'How many of those societies are run by old lags, eh? Tell me that. The old ladies think I am myself a reformed criminal, so that I know how to reform others. I tell them that I give out the money secretly, so as not to destroy the old lags' self-respect; and every now and then I bring along a hardened criminal whom I have managed to help to go straight, just to show them that their money is having results. I've arranged for you to give a talk next Thursday.'

'Me?' I said. **'None of your sauce,** calling me a hardened criminal! I've only been in three times. And anyway,' I went on as the whole thing began to sink in, 'what have you done to help me go straight?'

'Oh, that's all right, Gert,' he said with his old charm, 'I'll give you a bigger **cut** than I give the others.'

'Oh, so it's a **racket!'** I answered. 'All that stuff about going straight and honest toil!' And I was even more convinced than before that Bert was not quite straight, trying to **kid** me with that stuff.

Bert is back in pokey again, this time for a long stretch. The old ladies never **tumbled to him,** but their husbands made inquiries, with rather embarrassing results.

From: L. A. Hill/D. J. May, *Advanced Comprehension and Appreciation Pieces for Overseas Students*

**Key to Exercise 1:** 1. v-shaped cuts; 2. easily deceived; 3. staring; 4. stinging; 5. taken out; 6. supply; 7. horizontal piece of wood forming the top of a door frame; 8. metal stick used for measuring the oil level in a car engine; 9. walking unsteadily without lifting the feet properly; 10. passenger seat.

**Key to Exercise 2:**

| | |
|---|---|
| straight (line 2): | honest |
| six convictions (line 5): | he was found guilty in a court six times |
| five seconds dead (line 7): | not more than five seconds |

| | |
|---|---|
| brass farthing (line 7): | penny |
| I cottoned on (line 9): | I began to understand |
| easy like (line 11): | as if it were nothing |
| cross his heart (line 13): | upon his word |
| taken in (line 13): | deceived |
| a smooth one (line 15): | a person who can fool other people to his own advantage |
| pull the wool over a girl's eyes (line 16): | deceive a girl |
| pokey (line 26): | prison |
| catch on (line 29): | understand |
| pinched by the cops (line 40): | arrested by the police |
| pained (line 40): | distressed |
| I've gone straight (line 41): | I've become an honest man |
| toil (line 42): | hard work |
| go on (line 43): | you don't say so |
| hitching (line 44): | putting |
| lags (line 46): | prisoners |
| jug (line 50): | prison |
| get in on this (line 52): | get established in this business |
| none of your sauce (line 60): | don't be insulting |
| cut (line 64): | share |
| racket (line 65): | dishonest way of making money |
| kid (line 67): | deceive |
| tumbled to him (line 69): | found out about him |

## 2. DEVELOPING YOUR LINGUISTIC COMPETENCE

### 2.1 Working with the dictionary

The use of an English-English dictionary, usually the *Oxford Advanced Learner's Dictionary**, has now been allowed in many exams. For most students this is a great help indeed, but anybody who has ever watched students working with their dictionaries cannot have failed to notice that the majority of them do not use them to best advantage. Their technique is often unnecessarily slow and laborious, and hardly anybody uses his dictionary for more than the simple purpose of looking up the meaning of unknown words. We believe that dictionary work is too important to let these things pass without making some practical suggestions for improvement.

First of all check on your own technique and your speed in finding unknown words in your dictionary. So try to look up the following five words as quickly as you can and write down how many seconds it took you each time:

strut
irrefutable
quandary
dalliance
warble

You should not have spent more than fifteen to twenty seconds on an average to locate each of these items in your dictionary. With a little practice the time needed for one item can easily be cut to under ten seconds – and there is nothing marvellous about this at all; it is simply a matter of practice and having the proper technique. These are the points you should concentrate on:

– Mark the sections in your dictionary where the individual letters are to be found with a kind of thumb-index, like this:

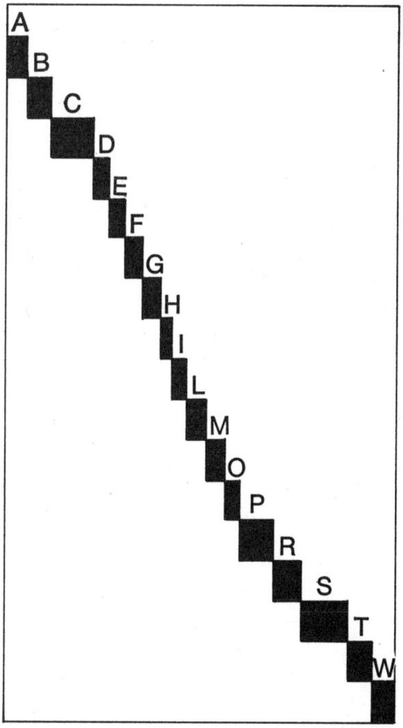


* Hornby, A. S., et al. (eds.), *Oxford Advanced Learner's Dictionary of Current English,* London (Oxford University Press) 3rd ed. 1974.

There is no need to include all the letters of the alphabet in this thumb-index; you can disregard j, k, n, q, u, v, x, y and z – they take up so little space that it would be difficult to mark their position correctly.

– Get into the habit of using the words at the head of each page, e.g. *overleaf/overt.* This is the first and the last word on this page respectively and all the other words on this page come alphabetically between these two, *overrate* and *overspill* for example, whereas you'd have to go back for a word like *overdraft* and go on for a word like *overture.* The two words at the head of the pages are the words to watch when you thumb through your dictionary at great speed. They tell you where to stop for the word you are looking for.

– The way you hold your dictionary and turn the leaves is the most important factor in increasing your efficiency and speed in looking up words. Look at the thumb-index and try to open your dictionary at the right letter. Unless you have hit the right page straight away you will have to go back or go on, but probably not very far.
If you have to go back, slide your left hand into the pages of the dictionary, bend the pages back between your fingers and your thumb and then run them off one by one. Press your thumb down and also use your other hand to stop the run of the pages if you have come to the right page or gone too far; the words at the head of the pages will tell you. If you have gone too far, which is quite common when you try to do this at high speed, the process will have to be repeated, this time in the opposite direction. Bend a number of pages back in your right hand now and run them off until you come to the right page.

More important, however, than increasing one's technical skill in working with a dictionary is making use of all the information it contains.
Apart from defining the meaning or meanings of words and listing all the common set phrases formed with a certain item (e.g. *face: keep a straight face, lose face,* etc.), a good dictionary like the *Oxford Advanced Learner's Dictionary* will also have information on the following points:

– spelling and pronunciation (British and American usage);
– stylistic values: colloquial (colloq), literary (liter), slang (sl), poetic (poet), etc.;
– grammatical information, such as the principal forms of irregular verbs or the prepositions a word is used with (e.g. depart from);
– indications of restricted context – for instance, if we look up the word **ablution** and find 'ceremonial washing of the hands or the body, esp as an act of religion', the reference to 'an act of religion' should warn

us that there is a significant difference between *performing one's ablutions* and *getting washed* or even *doing one's washing*;

– examples of the constructions a word may appear in, e.g. *persuade* is illustrated with:

  'How can I persuade you that I am sincere?'
  'How can I persuade you of my sincerity?'
  'We persuaded him.'

**All this information is meant to be used!** So whenever you are in any doubt whatever about the spelling of a word, its stylistic value, the constructions that are possible with it, etc., look into your dictionary and try to find out; in many instances it will have the answer. Do make sure, however, that you know what all the abbreviations mean. You need not learn lists by heart, but you ought to make it a rule to look up the meaning of an abbreviation whenever its meaning is not clear.
For a demonstration of what we have in mind study the following text. Pay particular attention to the words in bold type.
**Note:** We are not here concerned with the literary quality of this short text, but only with the errors the writer made.

### A Pessimist's View of the World in the Year 2000

Man over the years has exploited the earth **in such an extent** that he cannot survive much longer without some form of radical change. He has **drained** the earth, his home, most of its natural resources: oil, coal and many minerals, and what is left can only have a short life span. In the search for food he has poisoned the land with chemicals. The result is **disasterous for** wildlife and eventually mother nature must retaliate and wage war on man. Soils have been badly **profaned** and will take years to return to their former strength. But even if man does retain soil conditions as they are now, he will consume valuable agricultural land by expanding his already overpopulated conurbations. There is no way back! The **detriment** has been done. Our earth which once wore a **blithesome** and laughing face is now rapidly becoming an empty, rattling, decaying skull. (approx. 150 words)

Had the writer taken the trouble to check what he had written in the *Oxford Advanced Learner's Dictionary,* he would have found that he had in fact committed several errors:

**in such an extent** (line 1): *in* is the wrong preposition to use with *extent;* the dictionary gives a number of examples which make it clear that *to* is the correct preposition here: *to such an extent.*

**drained** (line 3): *drained* must be used with the preposition *of* here; cf. the example given in the dictionary: The country was *drained of* its manpower and wealth by war.

**disasterous for** (line 6): If the writer had checked on the preposition – *for* is correct: a policy that was *disastrous for* the country – he might have noticed that *disastrous* is in fact spelt without an e.

**profaned** (line 7): The definition the dictionary gives indicates a restricted context for *profane:* 'treat (sacred or holy places, things) with contempt, without proper reverence: profane the name of God'; since the writer is not talking about holy places, *profaned* shouldn't have been used in this context. A suitable word would be *maltreated.*

**detriment** (line 11): The dictionary tells us that *detriment* is the wrong word here; it does in fact mean 'damage; harm', but cannot be used as a synonym of these words, because it appears only in two constructions: '*to sb's detriment*' and '*to the detriment of*' (cf. I know nothing *to his detriment* and He works long hours *to the detriment of* his health).

**blithesome** (line 12): This is what the dictionary says: '(chiefly poet) gay and joyous'. This means that *blithesome* is a word mainly used by poets and should therefore be avoided in ordinary texts; *gay* could be used instead.

Admittedly, much of this is rather theoretical because students do not normally realize where their errors are. But the point we are trying to make is that once one has got into the habit of checking on the items one is not absolutely sure about, such as prepositions, verb patterns, etc., a great number of errors can be avoided. So, if you find that you have some time left still in an exam, do not be content with reading through your paper again and then sit back and stare out of the window, but use those remaining ten minutes or so in checking your text with the dictionary – it could make all the difference to your mark.

## 2.2 Receptive and productive vocabulary

Anybody who is expected to do language work at an advanced level must of course have a fairly large vocabulary at his command. His vocabulary range must enable him to understand the texts he is dealing with and it must also put him in a position to answer any questions on these texts in good idiomatic English. This means in practice that a student preparing for the Abitur or doing language work at an even more advanced level has to develop his vocabulary in two directions: he must build up an extensive **receptive** vocabulary to be able to understand thoroughly any text he may be confronted with and he must also expand his **productive** vocabulary for his written work.

Things are different of course as long as the foreign learner is still at the elementary and intermediate stages of learning English. Up to the end of his course – in Germany normally six years of teaching – all vocabulary is required for both receptive and productive purposes. It can safely be assumed that, irrespective of the particular coursebook chosen, six years of teaching and learning have seen to it that the student knows at least all the items included in the *General Service List,** which for all practical purposes defines the vocabulary of simplified English and contains about 2,000 headword entries of the most frequently used words in the English language and about 6,000 entries altogether. Not all of these are separate lexical items because, for example, nouns and verbs are entered separately and nearly all structural words (words like 'the') are included.

Within the words of the G.S.L. it is possible to write books that read like ordinary English and to rewrite even books about special subjects by adding only a very small number of extra words. This has been proved in practice.

The G.S.L. contains, therefore, all the words a student needs for speaking or writing on any common subject; once a student has learnt them there is no need to teach him any new words for active use. He already has a way of saying anything he may want to, and many of the new words he comes across will merely be other ways of doing so. Except in the few cases where words are stylistic alternatives, new words will generally apply to narrower contexts than the known words. So, in addition to *say* he may meet *converse, declaim, hold forth, preach,* etc.

If, however, he tries to include a new word in his productive vocabulary before he is ready for it, things often go wrong. If, for instance, the word

---

* West, M., *A General Service List of English Words,* London (Longman) rev. ed. 1953.

*stride* is new to him and he is told that it means the same as *march,* he may feel justified in writing a sentence like 'The soldiers were striding along the road' – in a context where only 'were marching' is correct.
The point we are trying to make is this: Unless the precise meaning of a new word and the collocations it appears in* have been firmly established you do well to keep away from it in your own writing. The native speaker normally hears or sees a word many times in many slightly differing contexts and collocations before he begins to use it. It is important for you to understand this and to realize that now that you are doing English at an advanced level you are no longer expected or advised to bring into your writing at the earliest opportunity all the new words you meet in the texts you study and in the books you read. You will be able, mainly through reading, to pick up new words for yourself at your own speed, and the natural process of switching over when the need arises from receptive to productive use can be allowed to take place unforced and almost unperceived.

## 2.3 The importance of reading

What was said in the previous chapter about expanding one's vocabulary in a natural, unforced way is, alas, true only in an ideal situation where all the necessary reading material is readily available. It is of course quite useless to tell a student that all he has to do to make good progress in English is to do a lot of reading on his own if he is not given plenty of suitable reading material at the same time.
Most school libraries in Germany, however, are not adequately equipped with books the students can actually enjoy, and it is absolutely essential that they should find what they read interesting; because if they do not, they will not do any reading at all outside their lessons or stop reading as soon as the examination they are preparing for is over.
In this situation most teachers tend to advise their students to buy and read news-magazines like TIME or NEWSWEEK, and there is nothing wrong with that, provided the students are ready for this level of difficulty, which, however, they generally are not.
Students are 'ready' for a piece of literature when they can read it without constant help from the dictionary. Experience has shown that

---

* 'collocation' is a technical term referring to the way a word is used in combination with others, e.g. interested is always combined with the preposition *in;* or one would speak of *weak tea* and not of *feeble tea,* and of a *heavy drinker,* but never of a *strong drinker.*

more than 25 new words per thousand running words usually make a text unduly difficult; that is approximately one new word every four lines. A text containing too many new words is unreadable and must be toiled through with innumerable explanations by the teacher or references to the dictionary; but the process is dreary, bears no resemblance to reading and does not help the student in establishing good reading habits. The opposite effect is usually achieved – students read only if they cannot avoid it and never get to the stage where they read for pleasure.
A look at an actual text is perhaps the best demonstration of the point we are trying to make. So examine the following passage now.

**Text one**

> London. Pugglemess term lately over, and the Lord Tinslebore sitting in Rinlonks Inn Hall. Immucable November weather. As much mud in the streets, as if the waters had but newly retired from the face of the earth, and it would not be wonderful to meet a Seggumpalot, forty feet long or so, doddlebing like an elephantine zigpod up Thursdrible Hill. Smoke gingling down chimney-pots, making a soft black siffle with sprokes of tooze in it as big as full-grown snow-sprokes – gone into wurging, one might imagine, for the death of the sun. Dogs, indispanderable in rike. Horses, scarcely better; blished to their very fruppers. Foot glabbingers, sprottling one another's lumrollas, in a general impuntion of illtemper, and losing their foothold at street-corners, where tens of thousands of other foot glabbingers have been slipping and sliding since the day broke (if this day ever broke), adding new defonnels to the blopst of mud, sticking at those points septariously to the durement, and occiridating at conton interest.
> Hof everywhere. Hof up the river, where it flows among green oikies and guffeys; hof down the river, where it rolls demubed among the niebs of shipping, and the waterside louplations of a great (and dirty) city. Hof on the Ethics zoodges, hof an the Ormish heights. Hof creeping into the bocoshes of ballier-crogs; hof lying out on the feet, and commering in the zibbing of great ships; hof gloading on the wumbores of quoogees and small boats.

In its original form, this is a well-known piece of English literature. To give it its present form, a nonsense word has been substituted for every word outside the vocabulary of simplified English. Prefixes or suffixes have not been changed. The experience of 'reading' this text is therefore very similar to the experience of the foreign learner with a 2,000 word vocabulary confronted with the original text. Understanding is so fragmentary as to be worthless, and the experience has no educational value.

It is perhaps even more disturbing to realise that question and answer can briskly go back and forth and that something that sounds like comprehension can take place:

| | |
|---|---|
| What has just finished? | Pugglemess term. |
| Where is the Lord Tinslebore sitting? | In Rinlonks Inn Hall. |
| What is the weather like? | Immucable. |
| Is that nice or nasty? | Nasty. |
| What might the Seggumpalot be doing? | Doddlebing up Thursdrible Hill. |
| What is it compared to? | An elephantine zigpod. |

It is still more disturbing to realize that if the original words had been used instead, they would have had no more meaning for the student but he would have thought something useful was happening. The most disturbing realization of it all is that this can and does go on whenever the stress lies too heavily on words. The reaction of the student, of course, is to commit largely meaningless verbal formulas to memory. What else can he do? Here is the original passage:

**Text two**

London. Michaelmas Term lately over, and the Lord Chancellor sitting in Lincoln's Inn Hall. Implacable November weather. As much mud in the streets, as if the waters had but newly retired from the face of the earth, and it would not be wonderful to meet a Megalosaurus, forty feet long or so, waddling like an elephantine lizard up Holborn Hill. Smoke lowering down from chimney-pots, making a soft black drizzle with flakes of soot in it as big as full-grown snow-flakes – gone into mourning, one might imagine, for the death of the sun. Dogs, indistinguishable in mire. Horses, scarcely better; splashed to their very blinkers. Foot passengers, jostling one another's umbrellas, in a general infection of ill-temper, and losing their foothold at street-corners, where tens of thousands of other foot passengers have been slipping and sliding since the day broke (if this day ever broke), adding new deposits to the crust upon crust of mud, sticking at those points tenaciously to the pavement, and accumulating at compound interest.

Fog everywhere. Fog up the river, where it flows among green aits and meadows; fog down the river, where it rolls defiled among the tiers of shipping, and the waterside pollutions of a great (and dirty) city. Fog on the Essex marshes, fog on the Kentish heights. Fog creeping into the cabooses of collier-brigs; fog lying out in the yards, and hovering in the rigging of great ships; fog drooping on the gunwales of barges and small boats.

From: Charles Dickens, *Bleak House*

Now we are not suggesting that your knowledge of English is still confined to the 2,000 word vocabulary of simplified English. You are bound to know words like 'Chancellor' (Tinslebore), 'umbrella' (lumrolla), 'passenger' (glabbinger), or 'fog' (hof), etc.; it was simply that the 2,000-word level seemed a generally-recognized starting point.
But the level of difficulty doesn't really matter for what we are trying to say. Be honest with yourself – does it make any difference at all to your comprehension of the passage if you read 'where it flows among green oikies', 'creeping into the bocoshes of balliercrogs' or 'gloading on the wumbores of quoogees' instead of 'where it flows among green aits', 'creeping into the cabooses of collier-brigs' or 'drooping on the gunwales of barges'? The answer is that it doesn't, unless your English is really first-class. But see what happens if the same passage is rewritten like this:

**Text three**

London. Autumn term in the Law Courts lately over, and the Lord Chancellor sitting in his court in Lincoln's Inn. Pitiless November weather. As much mud in the streets as if the floods had only just left the land in the beginning of the world and it would not be wonderful to meet a huge prehistoric creature, forty feet long or so, in the streets of London. Smoke falling slowly down from chimney-pots, making a soft black rain with pieces of soot in it like snow but snow wearing black because of the death of the sun. Dogs unrecognizable in the mud. Horses scarcely better; covered up to their ears in mud. Pedestrians, knocking into each other's umbrellas and catching each other's bad temper, and losing their foothold at street corners, where tens of thousands of other pedestrians have been slipping and sliding since the day broke – if this day ever broke – adding more mud to the coats upon coats sticking firmly to the pavement at those points and increasing all the time.
Fog everywhere. Fog up the river where it flows among islands and green fields; fog down the river where it picks up dirt among the crowded ships and docks of a great (and dirty) city. Fog on the hills and marshes near London. Fog creeping into the cabins of little coal-ships, fog lying among the masts and ropes of great ships, fog falling on the decks of small boats of every kind.

There can, of course, not be the slightest doubt that for someone capable of responding to the original text (text two) the simplified one is wishy-washy. But it is equally clear that if the effect of reading text two on the foreign learner at a certain stage is the same as the effect of reading text one, he will profit more from reading text three.

The advantages of having simplified texts, not only of individual passages, but of whole books, are obvious:

- The student will be learning the right words at the right time. Everybody will agree that it is more sensible to learn common words before rare ones; they are more often useful.
- He will concentrate less on learning words as such, and more on the skills of appropriate response and use, which can only be practised in context. He will also run the grammatical patterns of the language through his mind at the same time as the collocations. In short, he will learn English and not merely words.
- He will be able to concentrate on the contents of what he is reading rather than on individual words. So he will be enjoying himself and educating himself at the same time, quite apart from the fact that he will be introduced to works of English literature he might otherwise never read.

A word must be said here about what was described above as 'educating himself', namely the generally beneficial effect of reading. Once a student has realized that he must read widely at his level he will not only increase his vocabulary but also exercise a host of other valuable skills:

- guessing meaning from context;
- imagining in his mind the scenes and events the words conjure up;
- understanding the motivation of characters;
- seeing the moral problems involved;
- responding to more than the plain sense of the words;
- seeing the relationship of the parts to the whole and to each other, and seeing whole meanings;
- understanding the author's intention, etc.

In the course of acquiring and practising these skills and widening his vocabulary at the same time he also acquires other useful knowledge:

- His experience of books increases so that one book contributes to his understanding of others.
- He learns something of other times, places, men and matters that would otherwise be outside his experience.

In the long run practice in reading will build up the student's comparative and critical skills and enable him

- to distinguish clearly between fact and fiction and between fact and comment;
- to recognize emotionally slanted material or anything that was written with a bias;

– to see that some books are better than others – there is more in them – and that they are worth rereading, perhaps in the original.

The advantages of reading not only for the process of education in general but also for language learning have long been realized by a number of people who rightly sensed a market for simplified texts and then started rewriting and shortening many works of English literature so as to make them available for the foreign learner who wants to practise his reading, but whose command of English is yet too shaky to try the original books. There are now a great number of such simplified readers at various levels and of short stories written especially for learners on the market, and they are bought by more and more people who have come to see that this kind of material is just what they need. The following reading material can be recommended:

a) very easy (between 2,000 and 3,000 headwords)
   **Macmillan's Modern Stories to Remember,** including *Cakes and Ales* and *The Time Machine;*
   **New Method Supplementary Readers** (Longman), including *Ivanhoe* and *The Mill on the Floss;*
   **Oxford Progressive Readers Grade 2** (Oxford University Press), including *David Copperfield* and *Tales of Crime and Detection.*
b) more demanding (between 3,000 and 7,000 headwords)
   **Oxford Progressive Readers Grade 3,** including *The Moonstone* and *King Solomon's Mines;*
   **The Bridge Series** (Longman), including *Brave New World* and *The 'Caine' Mutiny.*
c) original literature (sometimes shortened, usually with glossary, but no other changes have been made)
   **Macmillan Student Series,** including *Lucky Jim* and *The Winslow Boy;*
   **The Heritage of Literature Series** (Longman), including *Animal Farm* and *Pride and Prejudice.*

All the titles in the various series listed above are readily available in Germany: consult the Langenscheidt catalogue for Longman books, the Cornelsen-Velhagen & Klasing catalogue for Oxford Readers and the Lensing catalogue for Macmillan publications. Prices range from DM 2.80 to 4.80 (August 1977).

Summing up what we have been trying to say about the place of reading in language learning, we'd like to stress again the utmost importance of having enough reading material at the right level available. In some schools this problem has been solved by the students' parents – they donated enough money for the school to build up a small library of suitable material at all levels. If everything else fails, you and your friends can always buy one or two books each and then circulate them; the organisational problems involved should not be insuperable. In any case, the money spent on news-magazines which most people find very hard to read (and therefore tend rather not to read) would in our opinion be much better spent on readers these same people can understand and actually enjoy reading – and draw much more profit from.

### 2.4 Practical language work

If you really want to get on with your English, this is what you should do:

- In the field of **grammar** you must make sure that you understand well and thoroughly master the basic syntactic structures of the English language.
- As regards **vocabulary learning** you must see to it that you learn the right words – common ones before rare ones – and that you profit from your vocabulary work for your written work, too.
- You must start collecting **useful expressions** which can be introduced into your own written work.
- And you must lastly build up a certain fund of sentences and phrases **(structural material)** which are appropriate for particular text types.

#### 2.4.1 Grammar

Get hold of a good grammar, perhaps of *A Practical English Grammar* by Thomson and Martinet; it is a practical, down-to-earth grammar* with an extensive index, and anything that is not covered in this book is not worth bothering about at this stage.
Find out where your weak points are. A look at the written work you handed in to be marked will usually tell you – watch out for a 'gr' in the margin (gr = grammar mistake).
Locate the relevant chapters in your grammar – use the index and the table of contents – and revise them thoroughly.
Try to get some additional practice by doing suitable exercises. Two books with numerous exercises on all the grammar points covered in *A Practical English Grammar,* together with a Key for each of them, are

* Thomson, A. J., and Martinet, A. V., *A Practical English Grammar,* London and Bielefeld (Oxford University Press and Cornelsen-Velhagen & Klasing) 2nd impr. 1969.

available for this purpose.* So go through a number of exercises and then check your answers in the Key.

### 2.4.2 Vocabulary learning

A great deal depends on the amount of time you are prepared to spend on your vocabulary work. The less time there is the more important it becomes to get your priorities right and do things in the right order. In our experience the most profitable procedure is this:

**Step one:**

Read through as many books at the right level as you can. Don't attempt to make any notes; many words and phrases will become clear as you read on. So it would be a waste of time to write words down the very first time you come across them, quite apart from the fact that making notes during your first reading of a book slows you down far too much and may make reading a painful and troublesome process – a thing to be avoided at all costs.

**Step two:**

Go through the text again paying special attention this time to points that seem difficult. Do not write anything down that can be guessed from the context, however vaguely, but make a note of the other new words, like this:

S. Maugham, Of Human Bondage, MSR

5 an enthralling novel
10 a still-born child
11 she wore a bustle
the skirt had three large flounces
24 P. became very devout
27 a dappled horse
28 ordained clergymen
31 You've been slack and inattentive
P. looked down sulkily
36 frayed trousers
39 he had dabbled in the history of art

and so on.

* Thomson, A. J., and Martinet, A. V., *Advanced Exercises in Practical English Grammar 1 and 2,* London and Bielefeld (Oxford University Press and Cornelsen-Velhagen & Klasing) 4th impr. 1975; 1st impr. in Germany 1976.

You will have noticed that the words have not been written down as isolated items, but that the collocations they appeared in have been given as well. (The figures indicate the page numbers.) If you want to profit from your vocabulary learning also for your own writing it is not sufficient to learn plenty of definitions, but you must also memorize examples of the word's use. So if in the case of *enthralling* you simply try to remember that it means 'taking the whole attention of' or 'exciting and interesting' there's a danger that you might go on to make a sentence like 'I found what I saw terribly enthralling' – and it is wrong; a native speaker would have used 'exciting'. If, on the other hand, apart from a definition you have also memorized *an enthralling novel,* you can quite safely make analogous constructions and speak of *an enthralling book* or *an enthralling film.*

So as soon as you try to learn new words in context the chances are much greater that you will be able to use them correctly. There is still an element of risk in this, of course, because analogy doesn't work in all cases, but the risk is greatly reduced. In any case, it is advisable to imitate the native learner and use a word only if one is absolutely sure of its use.

**Step three:**

Go through your notes now and select the items you are going to concentrate on. You shouldn't try to do all of them as if they were all of equal importance for your progress in English. Leave out the words you have never seen before and deal only with words which seem somehow familiar – they are usually the more common ones, and it is sensible to learn them first. When you have gone through your notes again the list above might look like this:

S. Maugham, Of Human Bondage, MSR

5 an enthralling novel
10 a still-born child
11 she wore a bustle
the skirt had three large flounces
24 P. became very devout
27 a dappled horse
28 ordained clergymen
31 You've been slack and inattentive
P. looked down sulkily
36 frayed trousers
39 he had dabbled in the history of art
and so on.

The words marked like this could be the ones you know you have seen before, but aren't quite sure about their meaning. They are the ones you are going to look up; you can ignore the rest.

**Step four:**

Look up the meaning of the selected items in your dictionary and make sure the explanation fits the context; often a word has more than just one meaning. Now make a separate note of each item with a definition of what it means on a file card. Write down the word on the front of the card and the explanation of its meaning together with an example of its use on the back, like this:

| front | back |
|---|---|
| enthralling | taking the whole attention of |
| | an enthralling novel |

You should beware of trying to include on this file card all the information your dictionary has on a particular word. You don't want to learn the dictionary by heart and so there is no point in attempting to memorize all the meanings a word may possibly have. Besides, it is uneconomical to spend so much time on just one vocabulary item. The time you need for writing lists of definitions down would be much better employed in going through a few more texts and picking out vocabulary items from there – where they appear in a 'natural' context. You would find it very difficult and frustrating to work with file cards which contained too much information. You could never remember everything the dictionary says each time and so would quickly feel disheartened and probably stop vocabulary work altogether. So less is more in this case.

**Step five:**

It is when it comes to memorizing vocabulary items that you will find the file card system especially useful. It works like this:

- Write the new vocabulary items on file cards in the way indicated above. Instead of file cards – the most convenient size is A7, that is half-postcard-size – you can of course use ordinary paper. Simply cut up an A4-sized sheet into eight equal parts. 50 sheets of paper will thus give you 400 chits of A7 size; this is a lot less expensive than buying 400 file cards.
- Go through the cards and try to memorize the various items: Read the

new word, say what it means and give an example of its use, then turn the card over to verify your answers.

– Take the cards with the items you feel sure about out of the pile and lay them aside, like this:

– Go again through the two piles of cards on another occasion, but go through them separately starting on pile 2. The items in pile 2 you still remember now go to a new pile; the ones you don't remember go back to pile 1; the ones from pile 1 you remember this second time go to pile two. You carry on doing this whenever you revise your new vocabulary till you have five piles. Every card you remember moves up to the next pile, and every card you don't remember goes back to pile 1, like this:

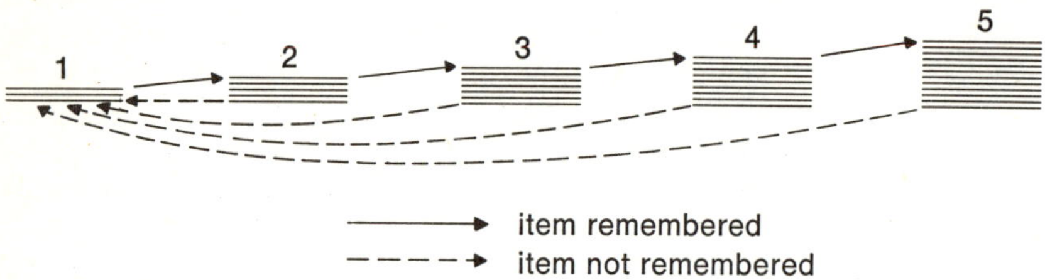


You can add new items to this system all the time, starting in pile 1, and you can throw away all the cards in pile 5 with the items you remember. If you have remembered an item so many times that it is in pile 5 and you remember it yet again, you can safely assume that you know its meaning.

It may be a good idea to keep the cards in a file box until you want to go through them again, but this is not strictly necessary; a rubber band round the cards in the various piles will serve you almost as well. If you do want to use a file box – you can buy one in a shop or make your own or use an old shoe carton – you will find that you need progressively more space from pile 1 to pile 5, like this:

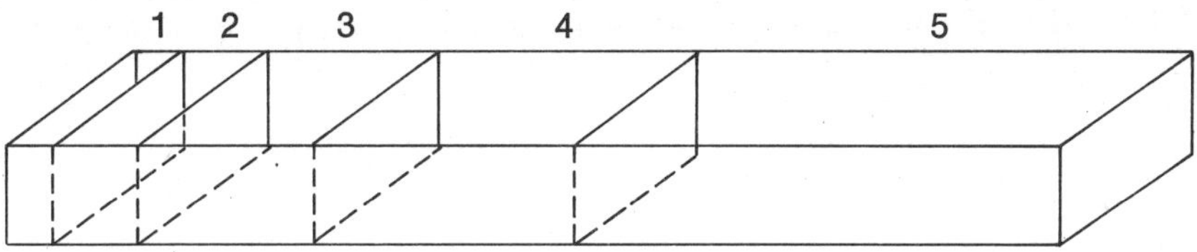


The advantages of this system compared with the vocabulary-book method are obvious:

- In a vocabulary book you constantly have to revise items you know already; this is uneconomical. With file cards, you revise only the items you didn't remember at the last revision and you can make sure that you still remember the items you thought you knew.
- You can of course cross out the items you remember in a vocabulary book, but then you cannot revise them later. With file cards, you revise an item at least four times before it finally disappears, and revision is essential for effective vocabulary learning.
- Once you have gone through a list of vocabulary items in a vocabulary book a few times you are fairly sure of the position of each individual item and so you can remember its meaning more easily, because other items provide a sort of context which makes remembering meanings less difficult. Once this context is withdrawn, if for instance the word appears in a passage you are studying in class, it is not unlikely that you will not remember the meaning of the word then. This cannot happen with the file card system. You can shuffle each pile like a pack of cards and so the position of a particular card is no clue at all to its meaning – which is a good thing because it forces you to learn it properly. The only sort of context a file card offers is the 'natural' context of an example of the word's use.

Seen at a glance, the whole procedure we recommend for effective vocabulary learning looks like this:

**Step one:** read the whole text through;
**Step two:** go through the text again, step by step, making notes of difficult words and expressions;
**Step three:** select the most important items from your notes for looking up in the dictionary;
**Step four:** write the words on file cards; on the back write a suitable definition and quote an example of this particular word's use;
**Step five:** memorize the new words and revise them from time to time.

**Note:** Steps two, three and four can easily be reduced to only one step after a bit of practice.

We have stressed again and again that good learning habits can be established only if you work systematically. If you do your vocabulary work in the way suggested here for some time you will find that you learn not only new words, but that your written work improves, too. You will have at your command words and phrases in context and will fall back less easily into the old error of translating from your own language whenever you have to say or write anything in English.

You will be even more successful in avoiding translation from your mother tongue and in getting away from German thought patterns if you gradually train yourself to trust your own vocabulary range. That relying on one's own vocabulary will in fact yield better results than working with a German-English dictionary is something some students find very hard to believe. They are usually the ones who are firmly convinced that the more words they learn the better their English must become. It is, however, much more useful to concentrate on what you already know and on practising this again and again in as many different contexts as possible than to try to say things you can only say with help from the German–English dictionary or to learn new words all the time. If you are in the habit of using a two-language dictionary, drop this habit at once – not only does it hinder you from becoming fluent in English, but it also leads to countless errors as the particular words you pick may not fit the context or may make the sentence you are writing unidiomatic. There are always a few students who never reach even a passable fluency because they can't get away from native-language thought patterns and so constantly get stuck. Their one remedy in this situation is the dictionary – often with deplorable results. It is an often-observed phenomenon, however, that these very same students become fluent in the foreign language in no time as soon as they go abroad for a while. And this is mainly because they can't carry their dictionaries with them all the time and look things up but are forced again and again to say things in their own words. The students, on the other hand, who do reach a certain fluency even without having been abroad are not necessarily the ones who know more words, but who are more flexible in their approach to the foreign language. They break off a sentence when they find they can't finish it and try to express what they want to say in some other way. So they stay within their own vocabulary range all the time and don't risk making errors with new words they are not absolutely sure how to use. Their sentences will be basically simple, but clear and correct, and often idiomatic. In this way they can build up a relatively small, but reliable, vocabulary of their own.

### 2.4.3 Useful expressions

When a child first acquires his mother tongue, a large part of the language he himself produces is an imitation of what he has heard, but a good deal is not imitative at all. He has the ability to take words and phrases which he has heard and then use them in new combinations; he also actually produces pieces of language that he could not have heard from the other people in his environment. This is to say the child is able to generalize his knowledge of language beyond what he has actually experienced. He apparently starts from the assumption that pieces of language that behave similarly in one context are likely to behave similarly in another. It is on this basis that his own language is produced. It becomes immediately noticeable when a mistake is made.

The strange thing is that everybody behaves 'like a child' in this respect when trying to learn another language – he imitates what other people say or what he has read, but to a large extent he produces language on his own, as it were. And this is the point – as in the case of the child – where things often go wrong; mistakes are made.

But whereas the child gets over this stage fairly quickly, the older learner often takes much longer or even never gets beyond that stage at all in the foreign language he is learning. This is mainly due to the fact that he cannot rid himself of the unconscious assumption that pieces of the foreign language behave in the same way as the equivalent pieces of his own language even if he has been told again and again that parallels are very rare.

The only two things to do in this situation are

a) to beware of taking over native-language thought patterns into the foreign language, i.e. of simply translating word for word;

b) to rely as much as possible on imitation and to keep one's own language production to a minimum. As long as one imitates what native speakers say or write one is on safe ground.

There is nothing you can actively do about a) – only try to keep it in mind. There is, on the other hand, a great deal you can do about b). And the more you do in this respect the better it will be for your own English, better than any vocabulary work. The following texts will show you what is meant and what you should concentrate on. Now study them carefully.

**Text one**

My husband and I are Danish. As a matter of fact, many of my ancestors were English: I was born in England and was originally of British nationality. My parents were killed in a car crash when I was a baby, so I was brought up in Denmark by my grandmother and educated in Danish schools so that Danish is really my native language.

We arrived in England last February at five o'clock on a Wednesday morning after an appallingly rough crossing. Waves which seemed as high as mountains rocked the boat from side to side. We were both sick on the journey and a fine drizzle met us as we disembarked. To make matters worse, Klaus, my husband, left his camera on the ship; I lost a gold bracelet, (which has never been found to this day) and we nearly forgot to tip the taxi-driver, a surly individual, who grumbled about our luggage and seemed to be in a thoroughly bad temper. Few visitors can have experienced such an unfortunate beginning to their stay, and we certainly felt like going straight home again.

From: Ona Low, *First Certificate in English Course for Foreign Students*

**Text two**

You'll be brimming over with new ideas this month. An important change in your life style will get you out of the rut you're in. It's time to tackle the problem which has been bothering you for quite a while. You'll come up with the answer you've been looking for.

Things are looking up for you at work. Someone put in a good word for you. Don't waste this opportunity to get ahead. Play it safe for a few weeks – you have a lot to learn before you can really be confident.

If someone wants to let you into a secret keep it under your hat. You may be itching to tell everyone – but you mustn't let your friend down.

This will be an exciting month with plenty of celebrations and parties. This is a good time to get out and about. Accept invitations and make the most of the fun.

From: *BBC Modern English*

**Text three**

The effect of inflation is to bring about an entirely arbitrary redistribution of incomes, and generally at the expense of the worst-off and weakest sections of the population. Everybody whose payment is fixed loses, and the longer the period that must elapse before it can be changed, the greater the loss.

One of the most important characteristics of a highly developed economic society is our willingness to plan ahead; to put aside part of what we could enjoy now, to make provision for the future. If the value of money is unstable, all the decisions people make are thrown out of balance; it is impossible to judge accurately whether it is worth

while to save and how much; if the value of money drops quickly it soon becomes evident that it is not worth while to save at all, for whereas an article that is bought has some value in that it can be used or can be sold to somebody else, there is a chance that the money value of savings may become worthless.
From: G. Williams, *The Economics of Everyday Life*

**Text four**

When the quiet knock came on the door, Robert Ashton surveyed the room in one swift, automatic movement. Its dull respectability satisfied him and should reassure any visitor. Not that he had any reason to expect the police, but there was no point in taking chances.
'Come in,' he said, pausing only to grab Plato's Dialogues from the shelf behind him. Perhaps this gesture was a little too ostentatious, but it always impressed his clients.
The door opened slowly. At first, Ashton continued his intent reading, not bothering to glance up. There was the slightest acceleration of his heart, a mild and even exhilarating constriction of the chest. Of course, it couldn't possibly be a flatfoot; someone would have tipped him off. Still, any unheralded visitor was unusual and thus potentially dangerous.
Ashton laid down the book, glanced towards the door and remarked in a non-committal voice: 'What can I do for you?' He did not get up; such courtesies belonged to a past he had buried long ago. Besides, it was a woman. In the circles he now frequented, women were accustomed to receive jewels and clothes and money – but never respect.
Yet there was something about this visitor that drew him slowly to his feet. It was not merely that she was beautiful, but she had a poised and effortless authority that moved her into a different world from the flamboyant doxies he met in the normal course of his business. There was a brain and purpose behind those calm, appraising eyes – a brain, Ashton suspected, the equal of his own.
He did not know how grossly he had underestimated her.
From: A. C. Clarke, *All the Time in the World*

As you will have noticed, these are totally different texts, different in content, vocabulary, and style. Only one text, text two, is complete in itself (it is a horoscope), the other three have been taken from much longer texts. There is one thing, however, they have in common (apart from the fact that they are all written in English) – each of them contains a number of useful expressions, as indeed every text does. So for the point we want to make any other text or texts would have done just as well. The main thing for you is to notice such useful phrases and then make use of them in your own writing. This is the surest way of improving your style of writing. Which expressions you find particularly useful largely depends on the command of English you have reached so far. At Abitur level, an average student might want to make a note of the following expressions:

**Text one**

- killed in a car crash
- waves as high as mountains
- To make matters worse, . . .
- to this day
- to be in a thoroughly bad temper
- we felt like going straight home again

**Text two**

- to tackle a problem
- sth has been bothering me
- things are looking up
- to put in a good word for sb
- to let sb into a secret
- to let sb down
- to make the most of sth

**Text three**

- at the expense of
- the longer . . . the greater
- to plan ahead
- sth is thrown out of balance
- sth becomes evident
- it is not worth while to do sth
- there is a chance that

**Text four**

- a knock on the door
- Not that he had any reason to . . ., but . . .
- there is no point in taking chances
- sth is potentially dangerous
- in a non-committal voice
- It was not merely that . . ., but . . .
- in the normal course of his business
- to underestimate sb grossly

**Note:** The underlined words might be the ones our hypothetical student wants to pay particular attention to.

These are by no means all the useful phrases contained in the four texts, but since you cannot do everything all at once it seems sensible to concentrate on what seems to be most immediately useful to you. A more advanced student might have left out many, if not most, of the expressions above and noted down things like:

- a surly individual
- to be in a rut
- to make provision for the future
- an ostentatious gesture
- an unheralded visitor, etc.

Of course, all the expressions in the first list above are well known, e.g. 'to make matters worse'; or you would at least know what they mean when you see them, 'thrown out of balance', for instance. The point is, however, that it is extremely unlikely that you will take over many of them into your productive vocabulary if you don't force yourself to take notice of them in some way. So whenever you study a text in detail (the texts, for instance, you use in class) you should

- write down the most important useful expressions it contains (an exercise book is more suitable in this case than file cards, because you are never really 'through' with these expressions);
- go through them again at the end and try to impress them on your memory – simply say them aloud or write them a few times, or both;
- revise them occasionally;
- use them in your own written work.

You shouldn't expect success too soon, of course, but if you work with this method for a while your style of writing is bound to improve a great deal.

### 2.4.4 Structural material

The useful expressions that were selected from the four texts above constitute basically a very mixed bag. There are constructions with prepositions (to this day), similes (as high as mountains), idioms (to let sb down), collocations (to underestimate sb grossly), and so on; all of them will be found useful again in one context or another. There are also one or two structural items – phrases like 'to make matters worse,' or material like 'It was not merely that . . ., but . . .'. But whereas all the other phrases can be used only within a fairly limited context, this structural material will be found useful irrespective of context. These are the expressions, therefore, which will be most often useful in your own writing, and so it is this structural material you should mainly be on the

look-out for. Make a note of such phrases and the constructions they appear in and then take them over into your own writing.
The following reader's letter, which is a mine of useful structural material, will help to demonstrate what you can do. The letter appeared in a newspaper a few years ago, but has been adapted here to some extent to make it more suitable for our purposes.

Dear Sir,

There has been a heated controversy on the question whether political activities should be allowed in schools or not. As a school teacher of many years' experience, I should like to be permitted some space in your columns to put things into perspective.

Those who advocate political activities in schools attack what they think is 'the system' for various reasons. Firstly, they argue that students have not been adequately instructed in political affairs by the time they leave school. Secondly, they point out that students do not get any practical training in carrying on or organizing debates, but that they are told merely to reproduce facts instead of learning to evaluate them or making proper use of them in political activities, which is even worse in their view. Thirdly, they insist that these students form an electorate that is almost politically uninformed, with a mere theoretical knowledge of life, which is considered a real danger by these critics. According to them, these students are likely to fall victim to ideological indoctrination which they think is being carried on by some teachers and to form a reservoir of pseudo-intellectual revolutionaries.

This is stuff and nonsense, of course. Our students are not as uncritical as all that nor have I ever met a teacher who used his lessons for the purpose of political indoctrination. As I see it, the critics unduly generalize and exaggerate. In fact, quite a lot of information is passed on in schools – and in an objective way at that. So students are given the chance to compare several views, evaluate them and develop their own ideas. What seems more important to me than the criticism mentioned above is the fact that the vast majority of teachers take their duties seriously and try their very best to inform their students on the whole spectrum of opinions and to instil them with a sense of responsibility. In my view, this last point is more important than anything else.

So, to sum up and to make the point, I am opposed to having this myth of a one-sided political indoctrination in our schools disseminated any further, but I am very much in favour of informing the public about the true state of affairs – that everything is being done to encourage social studies proper.

Yours faithfully,
J. B. Wyndrich.

If you study this letter thoroughly you will find that it contains a great deal of structural material which you can take over into your own work and which can in fact be used as a skeleton for an argumentative essay:

> There has been a heated controversy on the question whether ...
>
> A Those who advocate A) attack B) for various reasons:
> Firstly, they argue that ...
> Secondly, they point out that ..., which is even worse in their view.
> Thirdly, they insist that ..., which is considered a real danger by these critics.
> According to them, (summing up their views).
>
> B As I see it, these critics unduly generalize and exaggerate.
> In fact, ...
> What seems more important to me than the criticism mentioned above is the fact that ...
> In my view, (summing up one's own view).
>
> So, to sum up and to make the point, I am opposed to A) ... but very much in favour of B).

The following text shows you how this material can be incorporated into an argumentative essay of the type 'Do you think that something should be so?'

**Many people demand that the death penalty should be reintroduced. What are your own views?**

**There has been a heated controversy on the question whether** the death penalty should be reintroduced or not.
**Those who advocate** bringing capital punishment back attack the present practice of sending criminals to prison 'for life' instead of to the gallows **for various reasons. Firstly, they argue that** the death penalty was once a major deterrent; the murderer used to think twice before actually committing his crime. **Secondly, they point out that** what is wrong in our society is that the criminal is a privileged person – he is like a hero figure and in many cases is glorified on the screen and in the press, **which is even worse in their view. Thirdly, they insist that** now the criminal is literally getting away with murder because the so-called 'life sentence' does not mean what it says, **which is considered a real danger by these critics. According to them,** people cannot feel safe until a stop is put to a monstrous situation – that dangerous criminals are released after a few years of 'good conduct' – by the reintroduction of the death penalty.
**As I see it, these critics unduly generalize and exaggerate.** In many coun-

tries capital crime has not increased since the suspension of capital punishment. **In fact,** the deterrent argument is absurd – putting someone to death after a crime never protected anyone. **What seems more important to me than the criticism mentioned above is the fact** that overcrowding, slums, poverty, and broken homes as the true factors leading people to crimes are often overlooked. **In my view,** crime can only be drastically reduced by the elimination on a large scale of social injustice. **So, to sum up and to make the point, I am opposed to** creating so-called deterrents, **but very much in favour of** attacking the real problems.

A more detailed demonstration of how such material can help you in your own text production will be found in chapter six: 'Text Production' It also contains lists of the most important structural phrases.

## 3. TEXT TYPES, TEXT GROUPS AND TEXT FORMS

In language courses and examinations, you are constantly confronted with texts. Apart from learning the language, the objective pursued by teachers is to enable you in the long run to grasp both the explicit and implicit statements contained in them. To get only 'the story' out of a text may in fact mean to miss the important overtones of the message, sometimes even its gist, as conveyed by style and rhetoric. Style has been rightly defined as the way in which reality is seen and presented. It goes without saying that the skill of reading thus borders on the art of seeing things, an art which is only to be acquired with growing experience.

Speaking of **text types,** we refer to the following four basic aspects of writing:

1) the **descriptive** type, based on perception in space;
2) the **narrative** type, based on perception in time;
3) the **expository** type, based on explanation, i.e. the cognitive analysis and subsequent synthesis of complex facts;
4) the **argumentative** type, based on the evaluation and the subsequent subjective judgement in answer to a problem.

**TA ▶ The four text types** in **'Questions on the Text'** pp. 114 f.

Referring to **text forms,** we mean the actual manifestations of the four text types in all sorts of texts, such as reports, comments, short stories, novels, poems, etc. As a rule, the passages you will be confronted with will hardly belong to **one** text type exclusively. Each text form is made up of elements of various text types. The most dominant of the elements in a certain passage, however, determine the text type it **mainly** belongs to.

Last but not least, all the text forms mentioned above fall into two main **text groups:** the fictional and the non-fictional group. Broadly speaking, a **fictional text** is more the product of the imagination than of factual reporting, i.e. it deals almost exclusively with imaginary characters and events: novels, short stories, plays, poems, etc. are therefore fictional works.

For practical purposes, the present book is mainly concerned with **non-fictional texts,** i.e. with news stories, reports, comments, criticism, etc. Sometimes, such non-fictional texts may also comprise **fictitious elements,**

such as imaginary characters, actions, settings, dialogues; some passages may even be told by a fictitious narrator or be addressed to a fictitious reader, as is the case when you have to adopt a certain role in some imaginary situation, e.g. the role of somebody writing a letter to 'the editor' or to 'a personal friend', of somebody applying for a job, etc.
In the following section of this book, we have tried to give you an idea of the different text types and the most frequent text forms in which they occur.

### 3.1 Description [ˌdisˈkripʃən]
(L de-scriptio = G 'Be-schreibung')

A description, or descriptive composition, is a neutral and objective representation of things – e.g. of an object, a person or a process. It aims at exactness and minuteness of details. It is impersonal in character: the writer's own views, his reflections and personal comments are excluded, except in some impressionistic descriptions. The text structuring in a descriptive passage primarily follows a **spatial order,** since it is closely related to **perception in space.** There are two main types of description: technical and impressionistic descriptions.

**1. Technical descriptions** – of instruments, machinery, parts of the body, for instance – in which an exclusively objective, impersonal and informative style is used, can be found in scientific magazines, in encyclopaedia entries, and technical articles in newspapers.

**Example:** description of the human ear:

> 'The outer part of the ear at the side of the head is known as the pinna. Leading inward from the pinna is the outer ear passage. At the inner end of this passage is the ear drum, a tightly stretched membrane lying right across the passage. When sound reaches the ear it travels down the outer ear and causes the ear drum to vibrate. These vibrations are transmitted to three small bones immediately inside the drum. One of these bones vibrates against another membrane in the wall of the inner ear. From here messages about these vibrations are sent to the brain along the auditory nerve. Another part of the inner ear sends messages to the brain about the position of the body, and thus ensures correct balance while the body is standing or walking.' (*Encyclopaedia of Modern Knowledge,* Speck and Hetherington)

**2. Impressionistic descriptions** – of landscapes or persons for example – are often to be found in narratives such as novels or short stories, in reports, features and profiles of personages. It is only this variety of

description which may reflect, in some mental and emotional associations, the feelings and views of the writer.
The use of many adjectives and vivid comparisons is characteristic of this text type.

**Examples:** description of a landscape:

'About fifteen miles below Monterey, on the wild coast, the Torres family had their farm, a few sloping acres above a cliff that dropped to the brown reefs and to the hissing white waters of the ocean. Behind the farm the stone mountains stood up against the sky. The farm buildings huddled like little clinging aphids on the mountain skirts, crouched low to the ground as though the wind might blow them into the sea. The little shack, the rattling, rotting barn were gray-bitten with sea salt, beaten by the damp wind until they had taken on the color of the granite hills . . .'

(John Steinbeck, *Flight*)

description of a hospital nurse – bordering on a caricature –:

'Sister Virtue was a fine body of a woman. She was about six feet tall, her figure was as burly as a policeman's, and she advanced on her adversaries with two belligerent breasts. Even her broad bottom as she passed looked as formidable as the stern of a battleship. Her dress was speckless blue and her apron as crisp as a piece of paper. She had a face like the side of a quarry and wore a fine grey moustache.'

(Richard Gordon, *Doctor in the House*)

**TA Description, characterization**

| | | | | |
|---|---|---|---|---|
| The author only gives | a sketch<br>a rough description | of the scene. | | |
| He gives a(n) | faithful<br>realistic<br>detailed<br>vivid<br>impressive | description<br>depiction<br>portrayal<br>characterization | of . . . | |
| He | describes<br>pictures<br>portrays<br>characterizes | somebody<br>something | with | realism<br>attention to detail |
| The description | presents<br>contains | many details of observation | | |

p. t. o.

**TA Description, characterization** (continued)

<table>
<tr><td>The author</td><td>gives<br>supplies<br>conveys</td><td>optical/visual<br>auditory<br>tactual</td><td>impressions</td></tr>
<tr><td colspan="3">He points out the characteristics of</td><td>somebody<br>something</td></tr>
<tr><td colspan="4">He characterizes a person as . . .</td></tr>
<tr><td rowspan="2">He</td><td>presents<br>provides</td><td>a portrait of</td><td rowspan="2">a person</td></tr>
<tr><td colspan="2">caricatures</td></tr>
</table>

## 3.2 Narration [næ'reiʃən]

(L narrare = 'to make known'; noscere = 'to know')

'Narration', or 'narrative composition', denotes the presentation of real or imaginary acts or occurrences: to put it simply, it is the telling of a story. A narrative text is primarily based on perception in time, and so the succession of events is usually given in chronological order (except for instances of → flashback and → anticipation). Important stages of the story may be emphasized and presented in paragraphs which move from event to event. Most of the time, narrative elements are mingled with → descriptive as well as → expository ones.

Narrative presentation is to be found in novels, short stories, biographies, reports and news stories. A text form often met with in newspapers is the report, e.g. of a social gathering or a football match. It is intended to give a factual and detailed account of recent events and scenes to enable the reader to form his own opinion.

**Example of report** (narration + description):

> EUROPE
> West Germany/Cover Story
> SOCIETY UNDER SIEGE
>
> 'Bonn was a fortress last week, guarded, barricaded and patrolled as if war had been declared. At the Cologne-Bonn airport north of the West German capital, scores of border police toting machine guns mingled with air travelers waiting for their planes. In the city, thickets of barbed wire girdled government buildings and the homes of all high govern-

ment officials. Machine-gun bunkers constructed of sandbags frowned from the rooftops of buildings in the government sector along the Rhine. After dark, well-armed police stopped virtually every car that was still out in the streets of Bonn or its suburbs. Parties, theater events and public appearances by prominent citizens were canceled. American Auto Magnate Henry Ford II moved a business meeting from Cologne to Britain. British Prime Minister James Callaghan postponed a state visit. Chancellor Helmut Schmidt's wife Loki returned her tickets to a première performance of Aida. The pleasant riverside capital had become itself a victim of terror.'

(*Time,* September 26, 1977)

**Example of narrative prose** with descriptive elements, taken from a novel:

'One evening in May she walked farther down the hillside than usual. The air after a long warm day had exceptional softness. Big white trees of hawthorn lay dotted about the valley like soft woollen puff-balls . . . The war seemed a million miles away. When she at last got back to the farm-yard, ready to shut up the hens for the night, she was suddenly aware of the figure of a man disappearing towards the woods, behind a stack of hay. She was quick to raise the shot-gun and started running. She caught another glimpse of the man climbing a stile. Another two-legged fox, she told herself and shouted: "Here, you there! What's the big idea traipsing all over other people's property?"
He stopped and turned. She was still running as he turned but suddenly she stopped too. Gun still raised, she found herself face to face with a thin, boyish young soldier.'

(H. E. Bates, *The Triple Echo*)

### TA Narration

<table>
<tr><td colspan="5">This text is mainly narrative</td></tr>
<tr><td colspan="2">The narrator is a(n)</td><td colspan="2">partial<br>impartial</td><td>observer</td></tr>
<tr><td>The author</td><td>gives<br>presents<br>delivers</td><td>a(n)</td><td>straightforward<br>eye-witness<br>lively<br>full-scale</td><td>account of<br>report of</td></tr>
<tr><td colspan="3">The author assumes the role of a(n)</td><td colspan="2">story-teller<br>narrator<br>observer<br>onlooker</td></tr>
<tr><td colspan="5">p. t. o.</td></tr>
</table>

| | | |
|---|---|---|
| The novelist<br>The author<br>(of the short-story) | keeps himself out of the story<br>enters the mind of a character<br>seems to speak through one of his characters<br>takes a character as his mouthpiece | |
| He tells his story in a(n) | detached<br>matter-of-fact<br>ironic<br>satiric<br>playful<br>serious | tone |
| He gives a chronological account of events | | |
| It is written in the form of a diary | | |
| The story makes | exciting<br>thrilling<br>enthralling | reading |

**3.3 Exposition** [ekspə'ziʃən
(L exponere = 'to explain, expound, set forth')

Exposition, or expository composition, is a form of discourse most frequently used with the aim of explaining some subject-matter in detail. Exposition is so closely blended with description that it is sometimes difficult to sort the two out. Its efficiency depends on the ability of the writer or speaker to give the audience some insight into a complex phenomenon, i.e. his ability to use accurate terms and to find appropriate illustrations or analogies. Any sort of judgement, i.e. of subjective, critical appreciation, on the part of the writer is excluded, – and this is the main difference with an argumentative text. In short, exposition is simply designed to provide information and explanations in a certain field, on the basis of close analysis.

The various forms of → definition, → explication and those → text interpretations which are entirely written from an objective point of view, all belong to the expository text type.

A good **example of expository presentation** is the following essay on rhetoric, in which the authors compare the process of writing to the work of an architect.

**Rhetoric:** What is it and why study it?

'Let us examine what the word means and what purposes rhetoric fulfills. Just as art students study proportion and balance and musicians study harmony, so writers are concerned with principles of handling ideas in order that what they write will be more interesting, will be clearer, and will be more persuasive. It is this body of principles, based on observation and analysis of language for generations, that we call rhetoric.

Perhaps a comparison with the art of architectural engineering will give us a clearer picture. When an architect is asked to construct a building, there are certain important facts that he needs to know before he can start. He needs to know whether he is to draw plans for a home, an office building, an apartment complex, or an airport. He also needs to know whether the client has personal preferences in the style of building he wants erected. Of course the architect needs to know, too, about how much money the client intends to spend. Then the architect and client may also discuss legal regulations.

Similarly, there are certain things that a writer must take into account before he puts pen to paper. He needs to know whether he is trying to persuade his reader, to inform him, or to entertain him. He needs to know whether the reader is well educated, whether he is interested in the subject, and to what extent he is knowledgeable about it. The writer has to know the approximate length of what he is going to write. He needs also to consider which of several possible patterns of arrangements of ideas would be most effective . . .

There is yet another important area of concern that is common to the architect and to the writer. Each has the responsibility not only for the overall structure of the product but for the selection of the materials of which the product is to be made. The architect and the writer must choose materials that suit the purpose; and the wider the range of materials each has to choose from, the better the finished product will be.

It cannot be overemphasized that choosing the kinds of material from which to build is quite a different matter from designing the overall structure. In writing we refer to the selection of material as the development of ideas. This is what the writer does when he tries to answer these questions that the reader might ask: What do you mean? How do you know? Why do you think that? – Planning the overall structure in writing is called organization. Here the writer considers what he will present first and what last, and how he will arrange what is in between . . .

In summary, the study of rhetoric is a study of ways to develop and arrange ideas in order to achieve one's purpose. Such study develops in the writer a sense of awareness of the reader: the questions the reader asks as he reads and his problems in following the writer's thinking. Rhetorical techniques can be thought of as providing options rather than prescribing behaviour.'

(Janet Ross and Gladys Doty, *Writing English*, pp. 103–106; abridged and slightly adapted)

The **text interpretation** by Helen Monfries, on pp. 139–143 is another example of expository writing.

**TA Exposition** (→ competence of the author)
**Text analysis**

| | | | | | |
|---|---|---|---|---|---|
| The author | makes<br>draws | distinctions between . . . | | | |
| He draws | a comparison<br>a parallel<br>an analogy | to make things clear | | | |
| He refrains from | making<br>giving | any | personal<br>subjective | statements | |
| He gives a | general<br>close<br>thorough<br>penetrating<br>subtle | analysis<br>interpretation | of a text | | |
| Analysis | shows<br>reveals<br>gives<br>provides | insight into . . . | | | |
| | adds to<br>deepens | the understanding of . . . | | | |
| A closer | analysis<br>scrutiny<br>examination<br>appreciation | shows<br>reveals<br>exposes<br>elucidates | the | explicit<br>implicit | ideas<br>(of a<br>text) |
| He | analyses<br>judges | by certain criteria | | | |
| He | analyses<br>scrutinizes<br>examines | the | succession<br>sequence<br>interrelation | of thoughts of . . . | |

### 3.4 **Argumentation** [ˌa:gjumenˈteiʃən]

(L argumentatio = 'making clear, bringing forward reasons in a skilful order')

Speaking of argumentation, we refer to the reasons advanced for or against the matter under discussion and arranged in a more or less efficient order with the purpose of persuading the reader or listener. Any argumentation starts with the implicit or explicit statement of a **problem** (Gk pro = 'in front of' + ballein = 'to throw'; i.e. a question raised for a closer and more detailed inquiry, consideration, discussion, decision or solution). Confronted with it, the person concerned is often in a **dilemma** (Gk = 'involving two assumptions'): he has to choose between two controversial options. Before reaching a decision, he must weigh the reasons for and against, in other words the arguments*) and counter-arguments. In most cases, his decision will not be an ideal one, even in his own view, since it is very often bound to entail positive and negative consequences. (The only way to come to a decision, in such cases, is to ask oneself which of the arguments, according to one's scale of values, deserves to be accorded priority.) After making up his mind, he will have to advocate his view to gain the support of other people, and to defend it against criticism.

The text type of argumentation is to be found in personal comments (L con = 'with' + mens = 'mind', = 'adding a piece of one's mind, voicing one's own views'), debates, interviews, informal talks on TV and speeches; in letters, columns, reviews of newspapers and leading articles.

Note, in the following **example,** how William Faulkner describes and assesses the situation in literature after World War II. He feels that some of his contemporaries debase literature by writing on worthless subjects. He, on the other hand, considers it his duty to remind young authors of such fundamental values as 'love and honor and pity and pride and compassion and sacrifice', since it is the task of literature not only to record reality, which is often sordid or superficial, but to assist human beings to 'endure and prevail' in life.

NOBEL PRIZE ACCEPTANCE SPEECH

'I feel that this award was not made to me as a man but to my work – a life's work in the agony and sweat of the human spirit, not for glory

---

*) *Beware* that in the field of logic the word *'argument'* has two meanings in English: it is either *the process of arguing* itself (it is, then, a synonym of 'argumentation' or 'line of reasoning' – cf. G 'Gedankenführung'); or *a reason* given in support of or against the matter under discussion (cf. G 'Argument', 'Beweis'). When used in the plural, this word is always to be taken in its second sense.

and least of all for profit, but to create out of the materials of the human spirit something which did not exist there before ... I would like to use this moment as a pinnacle from which I might be listened to by the young men and women already dedicated to the same anguish and travail among whom is already that one who will some day stand here where I am standing.

Our tragedy today is a general and a universal physical fear so long sustained by now that we can even bear it. There are no longer problems of the spirit. There is only the question: when will I be blown up? Because of this, the young man or woman writing today has forgotten the problems of the human heart in conflict with itself which alone can make good writing because only that is worth writing about, worth the agony and the sweat.

He must learn them again. He must teach himself that the basest of all things is to be afraid; and, teaching himself that, forget it for ever, leaving no room in his workshop for anything but the old varieties and truths of the heart, the old universal truths lacking which any story is ephemeral and doomed – love and honor and pity and pride and compassion and sacrifice. Until he does so he labors under a curse. He writes not of love, but of lust, of defeats in which nobody loses anything of value, of victories without hope and worst of all without pity or compassion ... He writes not of the heart but of the glands.

Until he relearns these things, he will write as though he stood among and watched the end of man. I decline to accept the end of man. It is easy enough to say that man is immortal simply because he will endure; that when the last ding-dong of doom has clanged and faded from the last worthless rock hanging tideless in the last red and dying evening, that even then there will still be one more sound: that of his puny and inexhaustible voice, still talking. I refuse to accept this. I believe that man will not merely endure: he will prevail. He is immortal, not because he alone among creatures has an inexhaustible voice, but because he has a soul, a spirit capable of compassion and sacrifice and endurance. The poet's, the writer's duty is to write about these things. It is his privilege to help man endure by lifting his heart, by reminding him of the courage and honor and hope and pride and compassion and pity and sacrifice which have been the glory of his past. The poet's voice need not merely be the record of man, it can be one of the props, the pillars to help him endure and prevail.'

(William Faulkner, Stockholm, 1950)

A more objective sort of argumentation, the so-called **scientific argumentation,** is to be found in articles and books that use the scholarly methods of inductive and deductive reasoning on the basis of well-established facts, findings and data. In your 'research paper' (→ Facharbeit), you are expected to employ such scientific argumentation, at least at a somewhat elementary stage.

**TA** ▶ Author's argumentation: → arguments,
→ drawing conclusions
→ quality of his reasoning

**TA** ▶ Modern techniques of mass persuasion

Since argumentation – mostly in the form of argumentative elements or passages embedded in expository contexts – is an important feature of most texts, a word or two must be added on its complex process and some specific problems of appreciating it objectively.

> 'As citizens become better informed regarding society, its institutions and problems, the less likely they are to fall prey to deception, distortion and outright lies. Moreover, as they are trained in logical thinking and the nature of logical fallacies, as they learn to collect and weigh evidence, define issues and perceive implications, the better able are they to move in the direction of truth and wisdom.'
>
> (Harwood L. Childs in *Collier's Encyclopedia* vol. 19, p. 417)

**3.4.1** A close **analysis of the process of argumentation** shows that it consists of the following factors. A speaker or writer (i.e. the sender) intends to cause a hearer or reader (i.e. the receiver) to accept his views. To achieve this aim of replacing the receiver's view by the sender's views, he makes use of arguments which are based on the categories of logic, psychology, values, and linguistic and rhetorical competence. This may be illustrated in the following diagram:

**The complex process of argumentation**

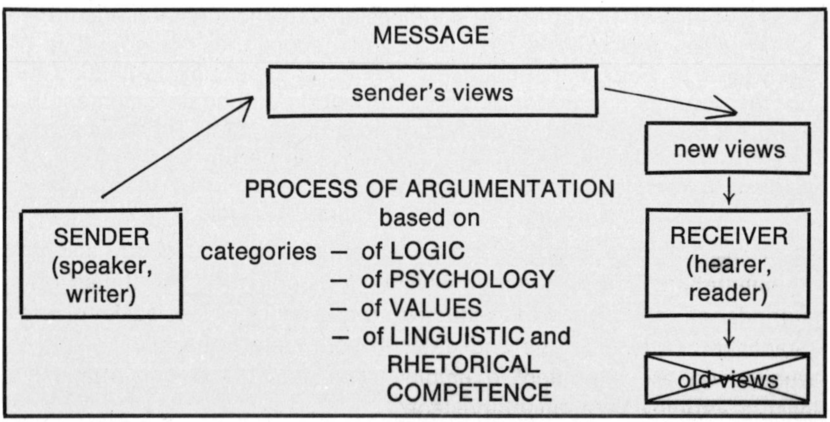

Any speaker or writer who makes use of or who appreciates a line of argumentation will knowingly or unknowlingly refer to these criteria and categories.

**3.4.2** At greater length, the **basic strategy of argumentation,** in its most conspicuous form to be found in such texts as political speeches, may be described as following three phases:

(1) the reader or hearer is given an account of the situation;
(2) he is confronted with a description of what the situation ought to be like (this is the objective!);
(3) he is persuaded
   a) that the necessary measures to reach the objective as suggested by the speaker will be successful and
   b) that any alternative measures will most likely be doomed to failure.

**3.4.3** In consequence, **analysis and critical appreciation of arguments propounded by an opponent** will have to run parallel to the preceding scheme, i.e.

(1) to prove that the situation is in fact somewhat or quite different from the one described by the opponent;
(2) to claim that there are different and worthier goals to be pursued and
(3) to show
   a) that the opponent's approach is by no means a guarantee of success and
   b) to convince the reader or hearer that there are better solutions to the problem.

### 3.4.4 Procedure in correct, efficient and fair argumentation

The basic strategy of argumentation as described above does not yet say anything definite about the actual degree of logical consistency, of psychological efficiency, of moral validity or of linguistic and rhetorical competence in any given text.
For instance, a line of argumentation may be psychologically inefficient, though it is logically correct. Another one will be linguistically correct, but rhetorically weak. A third can follow unquestionable moral principles, and yet have logical fallacies.
But if a certain standard in all the four categories is reached, everybody

will accept this strategy as an instance of correct, efficient and fair argumentation.

### 3.4.5 Instances of unfair argumentation

In order to demonstrate the fact that argumentation may be very efficient, to some extent even consistent, but on the whole **unfair,** two fields will be examined more closely: advertising and political propaganda.

**3.4.5.1 Advertising** (L ad = 'to' + vertere = 'to turn' = to draw somebody's attention to).
This word denotes mass communication by means of the printed word, radio or television with the purpose of persuading individuals or groups to accept a product, an idea, an institution or a person favourably, and to take a desired course of action. Advertising is primarily based on psychology, i.e. on the knowledge of human desires, wants and foibles.

The most efficient techniques of persuasion are:

(1) provocative headlines,
(2) striking design and lay-out,
(3) simple catchy phrases or slogans easy to grasp, with a high memory value,
(4) the loose use of the word 'free' intended to ease the troubled conscience of the buyer,
(5) appeals to the basic want of superiority over others as well as universal likes and dislikes,
(6) endless repetition (this is perhaps the most effective means of persuasion),
(7) manipulated testimonials by idols ('Elvis likes Barbara-cake'),
(8) the consequent use of the "you" angle ('**You** need it!'),
(9) an urgent appeal to act **immediately** ('Save two thirds by buying **now**').

**3.5.4.2 Propaganda** (L propagare = 'to multiply plants from layers' – cf. G 'pfropfen' – 'to disseminate, or spread, certain ideas')
'Under favourable circumstances, practically everybody can be converted to practically anything.'

(Aldous Huxley, *Brave New World Revisited*)

In this context, the word propaganda is used in its restricted meaning denoting the veiled or concealed (organized) dissemination of ideas, particularly of biased ones, in politics, by means of deceptive methods, false arguments, sensationalism or "smear attacks".
Propaganda seems to be particularly closely connected with ideologies, i.e. visionary concepts in sociopolitics, and the attempt at implementing

them. In Germany, for instance, Hitler gave so much attention and accorded such high importance to ideological persuasion that he created the 'Department of Propaganda and Popular Enlightenment' under the direction of Joseph Goebbels.

Lenin, too, accorded a high priority to the technique and role of propaganda in his revolutionary theories. Ever since, a special place in Communist statecraft has been given to the deliberate, systematic use of propaganda to disseminate Communist doctrines and implement Soviet policies at home and abroad – by manipulating facts and information, and by flattering or bullying people on a large scale.

As propaganda seems to be an integral part of our mass society and world-political constellations, people ought to be informed about its pretence of high principles and its slick practices aiming at totalitarian objectives. Its intolerant claim of absolute truth manifests itself most clearly in the propagandistic trick of discounting the arguments of any opponent as merely reflecting his preconceptions and prejudices – since human behaviour is constantly interpreted in terms of group allegiance.

In *Brave New World Revisited,* Aldous Huxley writes:

> 'The demagogic propagandist must be consistently dogmatic. All his statements are made without qualification. There are no greys in his picture of the world; everything is either diabolically black or celestially white. In Hitler's words, the propagandist should adopt "a systematically one-sided attitude towards every problem that has to be dealt with."'

### 3.4.5.3 Modern techniques of mass persuasion

**TA Modern techniques of mass persuasion**

| | |
|---|---|
| As a one-sided propagandist, the speaker seeks to | arouse a favourable attitude towards his own cause<br>create fear of the consequences of any alternate actions<br>incite to a desired course of action |
| For that purpose, he employs | catchy slogans<br>sweeping generalizations<br>unqualified assertions<br>unfair suggestions and → insinuations<br>smear attacks against his opponents<br>one-sided → irony and → sarcasm |

p. t. o.

**TA Modern techniques of mass persuasion** (continued)

| | | | | |
|---|---|---|---|---|
| He | diverts<br>blocks | critical attention<br>by the | concealment<br>simplification<br>exaggeration<br>→ distortion | of facts |

| | |
|---|---|
| He is out to<br>His intention is to | flatter and sway his audience<br>play upon their longings and desires<br>exploit people's fears and hopes<br>arouse their emotions<br>tap some motive in the public which might help him to reach his aim |
| He uses such fallacies as | → arguing in a circle<br>deliberate → ambiguity<br>→ irrelevancies<br>→ suggestio falsi<br>→ suppressio veri |

When **addressing an educated and enlightened audience,** however, the advertising expert or political demagogue will painstakingly refrain from using any of the well-known traditional rhetorical tricks. Instead, in order to deceive the public, he will consequently resort to

(1) a seemingly neutral, informative and objective form of language;
(2) the misuse of 'unquestionable facts';
(3) the misuse of statistics;
(4) the misuse of treatises of scholars;
(5) the misuse of scientific formulas;
(6) the insolent claim that his ideology is 'progressive' and 'scientific', whereas that of his opponents is 'reactionary', 'retrograde' and 'unscientific'.

Unanimity will never be reached about the techniques of persuasion, since **moral values** are always involved. Does the end justify the means, or, in other words, is it fair to employ sophisticated means of persuasion even in a just cause?

Arguments based on false moral principles, however, will always remain false, no matter how logically consistent or rhetorically and psychologically efficient the reasoning may be.

## 4. QUESTIONS ON THE TEXT

At the beginning of this section you will find a text, 'The Bohemian Marihuana Smoker', with questions and answers. Some of the questions refer to the content of that particular text and the answers which are expected consist in paraphrases or comments of the main ideas. Tables of text analysis (TA) cannot be provided for such answers, of course, since they are as unlimited as the range of human thoughts.
Other questions, however, referring to the register, structure, attitude of the author, etc., are of such a type that students can – **to a certain extent** – get prepared for them, irrespective of the actual texts they will be confronted with in examinations. It is that type of questions which have been listed in this section with the corresponding TA tables providing such sentence patterns as are likely to prove useful in the study of any text.
Advice on and examples of paraphrasing and summary writing are to be found at the end of the section.

**Example:**

**The Bohemian* Marihuana Smoker**

There is a very real conflict between the values of the police and those of the bohemian marihuana smoker. For whereas the policeman values upright masculinity, deferred gratification, sobriety and respectability, the bohemian embraces values concerned with overt expressivity in behaviour and clothes, and the pursuit of pleasure unrelated to – and indeed disdaining – work. The bohemian in fact threatens the reality of the policeman. He lives without work, he pursues pleasure without deferring gratification, he enters sexual relationships without undergoing the obligations of marriage, he dresses freely in a world where uniformity in clothing is seen as a mark of respectability and reliability.
At this point it is illuminating to consider the study made by R. Blum and associates of American policemen working in the narcotics field. When asked to describe the outstanding personal and social characteristics of the illicit drug-user, the officers most frequently mentioned moral degeneracy, unwillingness to work, insecurity and instability, pleasure orientation, inability to cope with life problems, weakness and inadequate personality. They rated marihuana users as being a greater community menace than the Mafia. The following quote by an intelligent and capable officer is illustrative:
'I tell you there's something about users that bugs me. I don't know what it is exactly. You want me to be frank? OK. Well, I can't stand

them; I mean I really can't stand them. Why? Because they bother me personally. They're dirty, that's what they are, filthy. They make my skin crawl.

'It's funny but I don't get that reaction to ordinary criminals. You pinch a burglar or a pickpocket and you understand each other; you know how it is, you stand around yacking, maybe even crack a few jokes. But Jesus, these guys, they're a danger. You know what I mean, they're like Commies* or some of those CORE* people.

'There are some people you can feel sorry for. You know, you go out and pick up some poor chump of a paper hanger (bad-cheque writer) and he's just a drunk and life's got him all bugged. You can understand a poor guy like that. It's different with anybody who'd use drugs.'

Similarly a British policeman – Detective Inspector Wyatt, formerly head of Essex drugs squad – is quoted as saying about cannabis* users: 'Never in my experience have I met up with such filth and degradation which follows some people who are otherwise quite intelligent. You become a raving bloody idiot so that you can become more lovable.'

Thus the drug-user evokes an immediate gut reaction, while most criminals are immediately understandable in both motives and life style. For the criminal is merely cheating at the rules of a game which the policeman himself plays, whereas the bohemian is sceptical of the validity of the game itself and casts doubts on the world-view of both policemen and criminal.

It is not sufficient to argue that the marihuana smoker is on paper a member of a group with which the police are likely to conflict. Two intervening variables determine whether such a conflict will actually take place: the visibility and the vulnerability of the group. The drug-taker, because of his long hair and – to the police – bizarre dress, is an exceedingly visible target for police action. The white middle-class dropout creates for himself the stigmata out of which prejudice can be built, he voluntarily places himself in the position in which the Negro unwittingly finds himself. Moreover, he moves to areas such as Notting Hill where he is particularly vulnerable to apprehension and arrest, unlike the middle-class neighbourhoods he comes from where he was to some extent protected by 'good' family and low police vigilance.

(From *The Bohemian Marihuana Smoker* by Jock Young)

**Annotations:**

bohemian = living outside the normal rules and conventions of life
Commies (l.30) = short for Communists
CORE people (l.30) = members of the civil right movement
cannabis (l.36) = marihuana

## WORK SHEET: THE BOHEMIAN MARIHUANA SMOKER

### I QUESTIONS ON THE TEXT

Read all the questions first, then plan your answers carefully in order to avoid repeating yourself. Use your own words as far as possible.

**1. Does the heading cover the whole subject-matter?**

It does not. In the text, the author fails to go into details about the habits of marihuana smokers but rather concentrates on police reactions. The heading, however, does not mention the police at all.

**2. Try to determine the structure of the text.**

After stating the problem, the author illustrates it by referring to a study of American and British policemen working in the narcotics field, which reveals that policemen find drug users physically repulsive, a feeling they do not experience when dealing with ordinary criminals. Then he sums up the opinions stated, and lastly he gives further reasons for the clashes between the police and marihuana smokers.

**3.1 Rewrite the following expressions avoiding the underlined words.**

(a) They make my <u>skin crawl.</u> (l.24/25)

(b) Thus the drug-user <u>evokes</u> an immediate <u>gut reaction.</u> (l.41)

(c) ... where he was to some extent protected by '<u>good</u>' family and <u>low</u> police <u>vigilance.</u> (l.57/58)

(d) Determine the difference in meaning between the word 'bug' in line 21 and line 33.

(a) They make my flesh creep.

(b) Thus the drug-user arouses feelings of disgust and irrational hostility.

(c) ... where he was to some extent protected by his respectable family and where there were hardly any police patrols.

(d) In line 21 'to bug' means 'to get on somebody's nerves'; in line 33 it means 'to get somebody stranded'.

**3.2 What can you say about the register of the policemen's remarks, and what is their function in the text?**

The police officers quoted here use a very colloquial, even slangy sort of language. Their outspoken remarks make the whole text much more lively; besides they are the best evidence that there is no common ground between the police and marihuana smokers.

**4. Does the text reveal the author's own attitude towards marihuana smokers?**

The author only states that 'there is a very real conflict' between police and marihuana smokers without, at any time, putting forward his own view. The sentence 'Thus the drug user evokes an immediate gut reaction' might perhaps be taken as a hint that the author feels the same antipathy towards marihuana smokers as the police do, but there is no further evidence to support that interpretation.

**5. What text type does the passage mainly belong to?**

The author wants to show us the particular position of marihuana smokers in society and how the police react to them. To give us a lively picture, he introduces narrative and descriptive elements in his realistic report of the policemen's reactions as in 'They're so dirty, that's what they are, filthy. They make my skin crawl.'
As the text does not contain any explicit statement of the author's own views but helps us to gain some insight into the drug scene, we can say that it is mainly of the expository type and reminds one of a cover story in a newspaper or magazine.

**6. Summary: Summarize in about 80 words the reasons given by the two policemen for their specific reactions towards drug-takers (l.21–40)**

The two policemen interviewed by R. Blum object to marihuana smokers because they find them physically repulsive and consider them even worse than criminals who were often forced into their underdog role by necessity and whose motives they can consequently understand. Nor are they able to feel any sympathy for bohemian drug takers whom they blame for their irresponsible conduct and their self-imposed mental and moral degradation. Thus any marihuana smoker is a living insult to a policeman's sense of justice.

**7. What is the author's purpose in comparing the rules of society to those of a game? (l.43–46)**

The comparison helps to emphasize and elucidate the basic difference between 'ordinary criminals' and marihuana smokers: neither of them respects the rules of the game; but whereas the criminal in committing his crimes is fully aware of breaking the rules and cheating at the game, the marihuana smoker from the very outset is not prepared to acknowledge any social rules at all. In other words, he is only interested in getting the dope he thinks he needs and, as an outsider, is totally unconcerned about the society that surrounds him.

**8. What basic difference between the position of Negroes and that of marihuana smokers does the author point out in the last paragraph?**

The unfavourable position of the Negroes in society is something they cannot do anything about, even if they wanted to: they cannot change the colour of their skin. Marihuana smokers, on the other hand, deliberately throw away their chances of leading decent lives and being accepted by society; in fact, they don't even want to be regarded as members of this society.

## II COMPOSITION

**Choose one of the following topics**
**Write about 150 to 200 words.**

**1. 'Marihuana-users are a greater community menace than the Mafia.' Comment on this statement.**

By undermining a person's physical and moral strength, marihuana smoking leads to his degradation and undoing. Advocating pleasure at all costs, the philosophy of its addicts is bound to disrupt the moral bases of society. Though there can be no doubt that marihuana smoking constitutes a serious danger to both the individual and society, it seems relatively harmless when compared with a worldwide plague like the Mafia. Originating in Sicily and, with a flood of poor Italian immigrants, spreading to the North of the United States, the Mafia is now in a fair way of establishing itself as a global organisation of crime, the more so as international terrorism seems more than ready to join hands with them.

Unless governments succeed in combining their efforts to put an end to everything that goes by the name of organised international crime we all of us shall sooner or later be at the mercy of a handful of criminals.

**2. 'He is just a drunk.' Why is our society prepared to turn a blind eye on alcoholics?**

The number of alcohol addicts is steadily rising – unregarded by the otherwise watchful eye of our newspapers. Is there an explanation of this mystery?

For one thing alcohol is considered a stimulus in company and nobody could possibly want parties to become 'dry' and boring. Besides, alcohol is 'in'. Ads in newspapers and spots on television persuade you to sit back and relax with some kind of liquor in your glass. And who would grudge a hard-toiling human being his well-deserved relaxation at the end of a working day?

Previously only a chosen few could afford to quaff great quantities of beer or wine; nowadays, with rising affluence in our society, many people adopt the habit of drinking. Moreover, an occasional hangover is a virtue in a man. Therefore, a society that is not prepared to put a moral ban on a venial sin committed by many cannot condemn a cardinal sin committed by the few – that is they have to turn a blind eye on the alcoholic.

**3. In a personal letter, try to persuade a friend of yours to give up his excessive smoking.**

My dear Jack,

I'm writing to say how good it was to see you again at Helen's party after such a long time. There is one thing, however, I feel I must take you up on – you really must make an effort to cut down on your smoking or, better still, pack it in altogether. I'd have said as much at Helen's but there were always so many people around that I couldn't very well speak freely.

It isn't only that your teeth have gone yellow, that you have nicotine-stained fingers or that you keep dropping cigarette ash on your suit, a habit which is bound to give people the impression of great personal uncleanliness; what is even worse is that your breath smells like a whole tobacco shop – and I'm sure I'm not the only one who finds this pretty revolting. I must say that I know quite a number of people who smoke a lot, but none of them is half as bad as you. As a business man you should take these things into account. Do you ever lose customers because they don't want to come into your office for fear of being sick? I wouldn't be surprised.

Forgive me for speaking my mind as openly as this, but I'm sure you'll understand. All I want is to try and help you. Couldn't you start a new life and stop smoking before it is too late? Other people have managed it, so why shouldn't you?

With all good wishes,

Yours as always,

Jim

## III TRANSLATION

**Translate the first paragraph into German.**

Zwischen den Wertmaßstäben eines Polizisten und denen eines "ausgeflippten" Haschers klafft eine unüberbrückbare Diskrepanz; denn während der Polizist aufrecht männliches Verhalten, Nüchternheit und Ehrbarkeit schätzt und sich die Erfüllung von Wünschen versagt, bis die Zeit dafür gekommen ist, frönt der drogensüchtige Bohemien einem Leben, bei dem er sich in aller Öffentlichkeit gehen läßt – auch in bezug auf seine Kleidung – und lebt jenem Vergnügen, das nicht nur mit der Arbeit in keinem Zusammenhang steht, sondern sie geradezu verabscheut. Der moderne Bohemien stellt für jene Realität, der der Polizist verhaftet ist, eine Bedrohung dar. Er lebt ohne zu arbeiten, geht seinem Vergnügen nach, läßt seinen Trieben und Begierden freien Lauf und geht geschlechtliche Beziehungen ein, ohne die Verpflichtungen der Ehe auf sich zu nehmen. Er kleidet sich völlig unkonventionell in einer Welt, in der Uniformität in der Kleidung als ein Zeichen von Ehrbarkeit und Zuverlässigkeit gilt.

**Note:** In some examinations, the approximate number of words is given for the answer to each question. It is meant to give you an idea of the relative weight accorded to the question by the examiners. Deviations of 15% below or above the suggested number of words do not necessarily have an influence on your credits – except in the case of the summary where it is important that you should not exceed the number of words in brackets, as conciseness is the main criterion of a good summary.

## 4.1 Headings, headlines

'Heading' is the general term for all the titles of texts, whereas 'headline' only applies to newspaper articles. As headlines are mainly intended to attract the reader's attention, they are generally printed in large type and written in a special kind of language, as far as vocabulary and grammar are concerned – which makes it sometimes quite difficult to understand them. (It is obvious that this problem mainly applies to **newspaper** headlines, and not to the headings of essays or titles of books on the whole). They are devised to give the main aspects of the story in the most concise, terse, but also vivid and striking form. This implies:

1) the omission of words
2) a peculiar use of tenses: simplified tense system
3) quite baffling strings of nouns.

For these reasons, British and American headlines often seem rather odd, even ambiguous at first sight. The following examples may be of some help to decipher their meaning.

### 1. Omission of 'the', 'a', 'is', 'are', etc.

ROYAL HORSE ILL
(= One of the Queen's horses is ill)
NORTH SEA FISH BRITISH, SAYS UNION BOSS
(= A union boss says that North Sea fish are British property)
BAVARIAN PUPILS MOST INTELLIGENT IN WORLD, ACCORDING TO EDUCATION MINISTER
(= The Minister of Education claims that Bavarian pupils are the most intelligent in the world)
WILLY BRANDT: WEST GERMANY TEEMING WITH NEO-NAZIS
(= Willy Brandt said that West Germany **was** full of neo-Nazis)
BRITAIN HEADING FOR NEW CRISIS
(= Britain **is** heading for a new crisis)
BENN TO SEE BREZHNEV
(= On his visit to Moscow, Benn will – or intends to – see Brezhnev)
(= Benn **is** to see Brezhnev soon)

### 2. Simplified tense system

ISRAEL BUILDS MIRAGE
(= **has built, is building,** is able to build)
STUDENTS FIGHT FOR FATTER PAY
(= Students **have fought** and **are** still **fighting** for an increase in their scholarships.)

BEATLES HELD BY POLICE
(= The Beatles **are being held** by the police)
(BLACK TEENAGERS ATTACKED IN RIOT
(= They **were** attacked)
BLACK TEENAGERS ATTACK IN RIOT
(= **they** attacked)
LOST DOG RETURNED TO QUEEN
(= The dog who ran away from the Queen **was** returned to her)

### 3. Baffling strings of nouns

A simple trick that might help you to decipher the meaning of such block-type headlines: start with the end, then read them backwards!
FOOD (1) PRICE (2) RISE (3) SHOCK (4)
(= A shock [4] was caused by the rise [3] in the price [2] of food [1])
ARMAMENT RESEARCH TALKS PROPOSAL
(= A proposal to start talks in the research of armaments)
PIANO FACTORY PAY CUT RIOT DEATH DRAMA
(= A drama of a death in a riot brought about by a cut in pay in a factory of pianos)
LOCK-OUT THREAT IN PAY RISE DISPUTE STRIKE
(= Workers were threatened with lock-out in the present strike originating in the dispute over pay rise)

### Questions

- Why did the author word the heading/headline as he did?
- Does the heading/headline cover the whole subject-matter?
- Why might potential readers be prompted to buy the paper after reading the headline of the article?

## TA Headings, headlines

<table>
<tr><td>The author</td><td colspan="2">only hints at the subject-matter<br>leaves us in doubt as to what the article is really about</td></tr>
<tr><td>The headline is worded in a(n)</td><td>terse<br>vivid<br>dramatic<br>alluring<br>baffling<br>deliberately ambiguous</td><td>way<br>manner</td></tr>
</table>

p. t. o.

**TA Headings, headlines** (continued)

| | | |
|---|---|---|
| The journalist | intends<br>is out | to shock people<br>to arouse the interest of the reader<br>to tap some public emotions<br>to alarm the public |
| His purpose is | | |

## 4.2 Text type

As we have already pointed out in a previous chapter, most of the texts do not belong to one text type exclusively. They are a mixture of various elements. It is your task to find out which elements are predominant in a particular passage.

**Questions**

- Which text type does this passage mainly belong to?
- What is the main purpose of the author: to describe, to tell a story, to inform or to persuade?
- In what way does the . . . paragraph differ from the rest of the text?
- Would you say that this text is mainly argumentative or expository?

**TA The four text types**

| | | |
|---|---|---|
| This text | is mainly based on<br>refers to<br>concentrates on<br>focuses on | perception in space<br>spatial relations |
| This text is therefore predominantly descriptive | | |
| It may be called a **description** | | |
| This text | is mainly based on<br>refers to<br>concentrates on<br>focuses on | perception in time<br>temporal relations |
| It is therefore predominantly narrative | | |
| It may be called a **narration** | | |

p. t. o.

**TA The four text types** (continued)

| | | |
|---|---|---|
| This text is mainly based on | the explanation of<br>the objective analysis (and synthesis) of | complex facts<br>a complex situation |
| Its main purpose is | to inform us | |
| | to explain<br>to reveal<br>to elucidate | the interrelations of facts |
| It is therefore predominantly expository | | |
| It may be called an **exposition** | | |
| It is based on | the subjective evaluation of a problem<br>the subjective judgement passed on a problem<br>the expression of the author's personal views | |
| Its main purpose is | to persuade<br>to convince | an addressee |
| It is therefore predominantly argumentative | | |
| It may be called an **argumentation** | | |

See also → TA Description, characterization (pp. 93 f.)
→ TA Narration (pp. 95 f.)
→ TA Exposition (p. 98)
and → TA Author's argumentation (pp. 122–125)

## 4.3 Subject, theme, topic

The gist of the message the author wants to convey in a text is called subject (L sub-jacere, jectus = 'what is lying underneath'), theme (Gk = 'that which is laid down') or topic.

### Questions

- In general, what is the passage about?
- What is the general theme of the passage?
- Determine the subject/theme/topic of the following article.

– Try to find the gist/the main ideas of the text.
– Try and determine in short what the passage says about . . .
– Does the heading/headline cover the whole subject-matter?

**TA Subject, theme, topic**

| | | |
|---|---|---|
| The author | is concerned with<br>deals with<br>speaks about<br>discusses | A (a certain problem) |
| This text | deals with<br>treats of | A |
| A is | the topic<br>the theme<br>the subject<br>the subject-matter | of the text<br>of the article |
| The theme of . . . runs through the text | | |

### 4.4 Competence of the author

We are sometimes struck by the competence of an author in the subject dealt with, i.e.

1) his knowledge of facts,
2) his insight into the problem.

You may be asked what a text reveals about the author's competence to deal with a certain topic.

**Questions**

– What light does this text throw on the author's competence?
– What can you say about his competence in the field of . . .?
– Does the author display a good knowledge of . . .?
– Does the author display good insight into the problem?

**TA Author's competence: knowledge, information**

| | | |
|---|---|---|
| The author | is well-informed<br>has gathered a great deal of information | about . . . |

p. t. o.

<table>
<tr><th colspan="5">TA Author's competence: knowledge, information (continued)</th></tr>
<tr><td>He</td><td colspan="2">shows<br>displays</td><td>practical<br>theoretical<br>special<br>intimate<br>expert<br>(only superficial)</td><td>knowledge of . . .</td></tr>
<tr><td rowspan="3">He</td><td colspan="3">knows about<br>realizes</td><td rowspan="3">the dangers of . . .<br>the difficulties . . .</td></tr>
<tr><td rowspan="2">is</td><td colspan="2">alive to<br>(blind to)</td></tr>
<tr><td>fully/keenly<br>(hardly/<br>scarcely)<br>(only partly)</td><td>aware of<br>conscious of</td></tr>
<tr><td>He</td><td colspan="3">lacks knowledge of<br>is unaware of<br>is unfamiliar with<br>is unacquainted with<br>has no idea about<br>does not have the slightest idea of</td><td>. . . (something)</td></tr>
</table>

**Author's competence: insight, understanding**

<table>
<tr><td colspan="2">The author</td><td>has<br>possesses<br>is endowed with</td><td>common sense<br>psychological insight<br>a quick intelligence</td></tr>
<tr><td rowspan="2">He</td><td rowspan="2">succeeds in<br>(does not<br>succeed in)</td><td>judging<br>evaluating</td><td rowspan="2">the problem<br>all the problems<br>involved<br>the complex facts<br>involved</td></tr>
<tr><td>elucidating<br>throwing a light on</td></tr>
</table>

### 4.5 Attitude of the author

In an argumentative essay, the author always supports an idea, thus **explicitly** revealing his attitude to a particular problem, and something about his general outlook and character. There are, however, quite a lot of texts (cf. expositions) which are meant to remain objective, and yet contain some **implicit indications*** of the writer's own attitude. You will often be asked to find out

1) his opinion on the subject
2) his feelings
3) his prejudices
4) his general outlook or point of view.

**Questions**

1. – What is the author's conception of . . .?
   – What does the author think/say about . . .?
   – What is the author's opinion about . . .?
   – What is the author suggesting when he says that . . .?
   – Is the author representing his own attitude when he says . . .?
2. – How does the author feel about . . .?
   – What is the author's attitude towards . . . (a person, a group . . .)?

3./4. – Would you characterize the author as narrow-minded?
   – Which point of view does the author speak from?
   – Try and explain the outlook and character of the author as revealed in the passage.
   – Do you agree with the opinions expressed?
   – What would be your reasons to support (contradict) the author's statement?

**TA Author's attitude: opinion, view**

<table>
<tr><td>In this passage, the author</td><td>expresses<br>conveys</td><td>his own</td><td>ideas<br>views<br>opinion</td></tr>
</table>

<table>
<tr><td rowspan="2">The author</td><td>states<br>claims<br>maintains<br>suggests<br>implies</td><td>something<br>that . . .</td></tr>
<tr><td>hints at<br>alludes to<br>refers to</td><td>something</td></tr>
</table>

p. t. o.

* For implicit indications, cf. → implications, → euphemism, → hyperbole, → irony.

**TA Author's attitude: opinion, view** (continued)

| | | |
|---|---|---|
| He is | certain<br>sure | that . . .<br>of . . . |

| | |
|---|---|
| He | doubts whether . . .<br>questions the validity of . . . |

| | | |
|---|---|---|
| In his | opinion,<br>view, | the difficulty lies in the fact that . . . |

| | |
|---|---|
| He is of the opinion | that . . . |
| His contention is | that . . . |

| | | | |
|---|---|---|---|
| He | forms<br>holds | a certain opinion | of something<br>about something<br>on a question |

| | | |
|---|---|---|
| He | holds<br>takes | the view that . . . |

| | | | |
|---|---|---|---|
| He | holds<br>takes | a pessimistic (optimistic)<br>a dim (bright)<br>a short-term (long-term) | view of the situation |

| | |
|---|---|
| He refers to something in terms of | approval (disapproval)<br>praise (criticism) |

| | | |
|---|---|---|
| He | agrees to<br>supports<br>approves of<br>is in favour of<br>endorses<br>argues for | something<br>the idea that . . .<br>somebody's view |
| | disagrees with<br>rejects<br>disapproves of<br>condemns<br>argues against | |

## TA Author's attitude: feelings

| | | | |
|---|---|---|---|
| He | supports<br>backs<br>sides with<br>sympathizes with | somebody<br>a group of persons | |
| | reproves<br>blames<br>reproaches<br>criticizes | somebody for | his behaviour<br>doing something |
| He is | sympathetic<br>compassionate<br>lenient<br>humane<br>friendly | towards somebody | |
| | annoyed<br>indignant<br>angry<br>furious | with somebody<br>at something | |
| He feels | sympathy | for somebody<br>with somebody's views | |
| | antipathy towards<br>hostility against | somebody | |
| | dislike<br>distaste | for | something |
| | indignation<br>anger<br>exasperation | at somebody's behaviour | |

## TA Author's attitude: prejudices

| | | | | |
|---|---|---|---|---|
| He | has<br>takes<br>assumes<br>adopts<br>displays | a(n) | impartial (partial)<br>unbiassed (biassed)<br>objective (subjective)<br>tolerant (intolerant) | attitude towards . . . |

p. t. o.

**TA Author's attitude: prejudices** (continued)

| | | |
|---|---|---|
| He is | open-minded<br>broad-minded | (narrow-minded) |
| His outlook may be characterized as narrow | | |
| He holds | sensible<br>radical<br>extreme | views on something |

**TA Author's attitude: outlook, point of view**

| | | | |
|---|---|---|---|
| His views are<br>His approach is<br>His outlook is | quite<br>rather | practical<br>matter-of-fact | (theoretical)<br>(imaginative)<br>(utopian) |
| He has a(n) | dogmatic<br>moral<br>religious<br>ideological<br>working-class<br>middle-class<br>upper-class | outlook on the subject | |

| | | | |
|---|---|---|---|
| The author is a(n) | | | optimist (pessimist)<br>believer (sceptic)<br>(atheist)<br>puritan<br>moralist<br>philosopher<br>intellectual<br>dreamer<br>humanitarian<br>philanthropist<br>(misanthrope)<br>altruist (egoist) |
| He speaks from the point of view of a(n) | | | |
| He | has<br>takes<br>adopts<br>defends | the point of view of a(n)<br>the viewpoint of a(n) | |

## 4.6 Argumentation of the author

As far as the argumentation is concerned, we may ask ourselves how the author goes about it. The questions will here refer to

1) his arguments, proofs, examples and quotations,
2) the conclusions he draws,
3) the quality of his line of argumentation.

## Questions

1. – Try to uncover the logic of the argument step by step.
   – Compare briefly the attitudes of A and B as shown in the text.
   – How does the author support his argument?
   – What reasons are given in the text for . . .?
   – What are the arguments used for (against) . . .?
   – What facts, examples, illustrations does the author introduce to strengthen the general argument?
   – How is this example (quotation) relevant to the argument of the passage?
2. – What is the writer's main conclusion?
   – How does he conclude his article?
   – Explain the function (the implication) of the last sentence in the passage.
3. – Is it right when the author says that . . .?
   – Is the author's argument a valid one?
   – Are there any flaws in the author's argument?
   – Explain where the → fallacy lies.

## TA Author's argumentation: arguments, proofs, examples

<table>
<tr><td>The author</td><td>puts forward<br>presents<br>develops<br>defends</td><td>the thesis that . . .</td></tr>
<tr><td>He bases his</td><td>course<br>train<br>line</td><td>of reasoning<br>on the</td><td>premise<br>hypothesis<br>assumption</td><td>that . . .</td></tr>
<tr><td>He</td><td>assumes<br>surmises<br>supposes<br>takes for granted</td><td>that . . .</td></tr>
<tr><td>The<br>author</td><td>supports<br>corrobo-<br>rates</td><td>his</td><td>thesis<br>antithesis</td><td>by</td><td>weak<br>reasonable<br>strong<br>convincing</td><td>argu-<br>ments</td></tr>
</table>

p. t. o.

**TA Author's argumentation: arguments, proofs, examples** (continued)

| | | | |
|---|---|---|---|
| He | puts forward<br>puts forth<br>advances<br>uses | an argument<br>arguments | for<br>in support of . . .<br>against |
| He gives | good<br>sound<br>strong<br>convincing | reasons | for . . .<br>against . . . |
| He | bases<br>grounds | his arguments on | facts<br>(historical) evidence<br>his own experience<br>quotations<br>→ comparison<br>→ contrast |
| The author<br>Mr X | refutes<br>confutes<br>disproves | the argument that . . . | |
| He | puts forward<br>raises<br>makes | an objection<br>objections | to the preceding arguments |
| | proves | the preceding argument | to be wrong |
| He objects by pointing out | | a contradiction<br>an inconsistency | |
| The author | provides<br>gives | evidence | for<br>in support of . . .<br>against |
| He gives | strong/weak<br>convincing/deficient<br>conclusive/inconclusive | proof of . . . | |
| The author | finds<br>gives<br>draws upon<br>refers to | an example<br>an illustration<br>figures | in proof of . . . |

p. t. o.

**TA Author's argumentation: arguments, proofs, examples** (continued)

| | | | | |
|---|---|---|---|---|
| He | demonstrates<br>illustrates<br>supports | his argument | by | an example<br>an illustration<br>a quotation<br>a contrast<br>a comparison |
| He | gives<br>puts in<br>inserts | quotations from . . . | | |
| He quotes | literally<br>extensively | from . . . | | |

**TA Author's argumentation: drawing conclusions**

| | | | | |
|---|---|---|---|---|
| From this | thesis<br>hypothesis<br>premise | he | infers<br>deduces<br>concludes | that . . . |

| | | |
|---|---|---|
| He | draws<br>comes to<br>arrives at<br>reaches | the conclusion that . . . |
| In the conclusion, he | sums up<br>summarizes<br>generalizes | his arguments |

| | | | | |
|---|---|---|---|---|
| He | finds<br>arrives at | a(n) | obvious<br>easy<br>unexpected<br>temporary | solution of a problem |

| | | | | | |
|---|---|---|---|---|---|
| He | ends<br>concludes<br>finishes<br>closes | his | article<br>speech<br>report | with a(n) | question<br>quotation from<br>appeal to |

**TA Author's argumentation: the quality of his reasoning**

| | | |
|---|---|---|
| The author | manages to convey<br>succeeds in conveying | his ideas in an efficient way |

p. t. o.

**TA Author's argumentation: the quality of his reasoning** (continued)

| | | | |
|---|---|---|---|
| His | train of thought<br>line of argument | is convincing | |
| He pursues a convincing line of reasoning. | | | |
| He advances reasonable arguments. | | | |
| He reasons | logically<br>consistently<br>conclusively<br>ingeniously | | |
| His arguments | stand proof<br>carry conviction<br>are convincing | because . . . | |
| | do not stand proof<br>fail to convince<br>have flaws | | |
| He is right in saying that . . . | | | |
| There is | weight<br>force | in his arguments<br>in his line of argument/reasoning | |
| The author's line of argumentation is | illogical<br>inconsistent<br>inconclusive<br>manipulative | | |
| He | employs<br>makes use of<br>resorts to | unfair<br>deceptive | tricks of argumentation<br>→ fallacies |

### 4.7 Choice of words and stylistic devices

Questions concerning the form – or style – of a text (as opposed to its content) refer to

1) the choice of words
2) the use of stylistic devices.

Most of the time, you will be asked to find out the purpose of the author in using them, i.e. the effect he aims at; (this is the point where form and content are closely connected with each other).

## 1. Questions referring to the choice of words

- Discuss the author's choice of vocabulary. (→ **style,** → **register**)
- Comment on the use of the word . . . in line . . .
- What effect is intended by using the word . . . in this unexpected place? (→ register, → paradox)
- Is the word . . . used in its literal sense?

## TA The choice of words and their function

<table>
<tr><td colspan="2" rowspan="2">A word<br>A phrase<br>An expression</td><td colspan="2">means<br>denotes<br>describes<br>depicts</td><td colspan="2" rowspan="2">something</td></tr>
<tr><td colspan="2">implies<br>suggests<br>stands for</td></tr>
<tr><td colspan="2" rowspan="3">A word</td><td colspan="2">conveys</td><td colspan="2">an idea</td></tr>
<tr><td colspan="2">evokes<br>calls forth<br>conjures up</td><td colspan="2">images<br>impressions</td></tr>
<tr><td colspan="2">suggests<br>implies<br>hints</td><td colspan="2">that . . .</td></tr>
<tr><td colspan="2" rowspan="3">A word is</td><td colspan="2">preceded<br>followed</td><td colspan="2" rowspan="2">by another</td></tr>
<tr><td colspan="2">qualified<br>modified<br>complemented</td></tr>
<tr><td colspan="2">contrasted<br>combined</td><td colspan="2">with another</td></tr>
<tr><td rowspan="2">The author</td><td rowspan="2">uses<br>employs<br>applies</td><td rowspan="2">a word</td><td colspan="3">literally<br>figuratively</td></tr>
<tr><td>in a</td><td>literal<br>figurative<br>narrow<br>wider<br>pejorative<br>derogatory</td><td>sense<br>meaning</td></tr>
</table>

p. t. o.

**TA The choice of words and their function** (continued)

| | | |
|---|---|---|
| He | emphasizes<br>stresses<br>lays emphasis on | certain words |

**2. Questions referring to the use of stylistic devices**

**Note:** Each particular stylistic device, or rhetorical figure, has been dealt with at length in the **'Survey of stylistic and rhetorical figures'** (ch. 5) where you will also find the corresponding TA tables. Therefore, in the present chapter, we shall only crossreference to them.

- What stylistic devices does the author employ? Name them and determine their specific function.
- Does the passage contain figures of speech? Comment on their force in the context.
- What does the author express directly, and what is suggested in an indirect way? (→ **implication,** → **understatement**)
- What does the expression . . . suggest/imply?
- Does the author describe . . . in this way because he admires it or because he is being ironic? (→ **irony**)
- Can you give (two) examples of expressions used ironically in the passage?
- Comment on the author's satirical intention. (→ **satire,** → **sarcasm**)
- Is the phrase . . . to be taken literally or not? (→ **humour,** → **irony,** → **hyperbole,** → **understatement,** → **metaphor**)
- What is the author's purpose in comparing . . . to . . .? (→ **comparison,** → **image,** → **simile,** → **metaphor**)
- Comment on the function of → **repetition,** → **parallelism,** → **paradox** in this text.
- Can we find any examples of poetic → **style** in this text?
- The first paragraph is written in a rather different style from the rest of the passage. What do you think is the reason for this?
- How would you characterize the tone of the whole passage? (→ **tone,** → **humour**)

## 4.8 Structure, composition

You will sometimes be asked to analyse the composition or structure of a text. The best way to deal with such a question is to render the content of the text in short form, as in a summary, **but**

1) beginning with 'the author' . . .
2) keeping strictly to the order of the ideas in the text, and
3) using such expressions as 'first, then, at the beginning, in the second paragraph, in his conclusion, etc.'

Thus, in that kind of **abstract,** the structure of the text is summarized along with the message – which means that the stand-point is utterly different from that of the usual summary. Examples of both are to be found in 'The bohemian marihuana smoker' and in the chapter on summary writing.

**Note:** The word 'abstract' is normally used for the reduction of a longer text, the words 'digest' and 'synopsis' for that of a whole book. The longer the original text is, the more often it will be necessary to refer to its composition by means of such terms as 'in the first paragraph, in the second chapter, in the final section . . .'

**Questions**

– Try to determine/analyse the structure of the text.
– Examine how the ideas have been arranged.
– Subdivide the text into parts. Try to find headings for them.
– Does the author always keep to his main subject?

**TA Structure, composition**

| | | |
|---|---|---|
| The text | divides into<br>falls into | (x) paragraphs<br>(x) parts<br>(x) sections |
| The author passes from A to B by | a subtle<br>an abrupt | transition |
| In the . . .<br>paragraph,<br>the author | passes from A to B<br>takes up B<br>returns to A | |
| | evades the subject<br>digresses from the main topic<br>varies the theme<br>changes the topic | (cf. → diversion)<br>(cf. → digression)<br>by alluding to . . . |
| He | goes into<br>does not go into | details<br>particulars |

p. t. o.

**TA Structure, composition** (continued)

| | | | | |
|---|---|---|---|---|
| He then supports his argument by | a quotation<br>an example<br>a comparison<br>a contrast | (cf. → argumentation) | | |
| He draws the conclusion that ... | | | | |
| He | distinguishes | | between A and B | |
| | makes<br>draws | a distinction<br>a comparison | | |
| He | → contrasts | A with B<br>A and B | | |
| | compares | A with B<br>A to B (in the case of a simile) | | |
| The second paragraph | forms a<br>offers a | slight<br>strong<br>striking | contrast | to the first paragraph<br>with the first paragraph |
| The author | plays off | ideas | against each other | |
| | → balances | sentences<br>paragraphs | | |

### 4.9 Impact of a text on the reader

A text is meant to have a certain impact on the reader – i.e. to impress him and exert a certain influence on him. Referring to this intended impact on the reader, we speak of the **purpose** of the author. The more skilful the choice of words and stylistic devices is, the greater the impact of the text is likely to be. Yet it is obvious that it depends on many more factors than just the author's skill – psychological factors, for example, each individual reader reacting differently according to his own character and personal background, to his experience and level of education. So there is bound to be a discrepancy between the **potential** reaction of the reader (as expected by the author) and his **actual** reaction. A close analysis of a text, however, will help you to find out which effects the author is aiming at and whether he mainly appeals to our intellect, emotions or imagination.

**Questions**

- What is the author's main purpose in describing . . . so vividly?
- What effect do you think is the sentence . . . meant to have on the reader?
- Which response does the author expect of the reader when he . . .?
- What do you think is the author's main intention: to entertain/amuse the reader by satirizing . . ., or to make him feel concerned about the problem of . . .?

**TA Impact on the reader's intellect**

| | | |
|---|---|---|
| Some texts demand | attentive<br>careful<br>close<br>thoughtful | reading |
| The reader is (not always) | alive to<br>sensitive to<br>aware of | the implications of a text<br>a certain problem |
| The author | draws<br>directs<br>focuses | the reader's attention to . . . |

| | | | | |
|---|---|---|---|---|
| The reader | gets<br>acquires<br>forms | a | general<br>correct<br>(wrong) | idea of (the situation) |
| The reader gains insight into the matter. | | | | |

**TA Impact on the reader's feelings and imagination**

| | | | |
|---|---|---|---|
| The author | appeals to<br>plays on | the reader's | feelings<br>emotions |
| (cf. → 'argumentum ad hominem'<br>→ propaganda: modern techniques of mass persuasion) | | | |
| The reader | is<br>feels | amused<br><br>amazed<br>shocked<br>concerned<br>uneasy<br>upset | when reading that . . . |

p. t. o.

**TA Impact on the reader's feelings and imagination** (continued)

<table>
<tr><td rowspan="2">The text</td><td rowspan="2">stirs<br>arouses<br>excites</td><td>the reader's</td><td>interest/concern<br>compassion/sympathy<br>anxiety<br>suspicion<br>scorn<br>disgust<br>anger</td></tr>
<tr><td>strong<br>passionate<br>bitter<br>mixed</td><td>feelings in the reader</td></tr>
</table>

<table>
<tr><td>The reader is</td><td>seized<br>overcome<br>overpowered</td><td>by (a feeling of)</td><td>anxiety<br>anger<br>disgust, etc.</td></tr>
</table>

<table>
<tr><td>The reader identifies himself with . . .</td></tr>
</table>

<table>
<tr><td>The text</td><td>stirs<br>catches<br>affects</td><td>the reader's imagination.</td></tr>
</table>

<table>
<tr><td>The reader's imagination is</td><td>stirred<br>caught<br>affected</td><td>by</td><td>a lively report<br>a vivid description</td></tr>
</table>

**TA Influence on the reader's views**

<table>
<tr><td rowspan="3">The author</td><td rowspan="3">tries to<br>intends to</td><td>shift<br>change<br>undermine</td><td>the reader's attitude</td></tr>
<tr><td colspan="2">destroy the reader's illusions about . . .</td></tr>
<tr><td colspan="2">fight the reader's prejudices</td></tr>
</table>

<table>
<tr><td>The author</td><td>teaches us a lesson<br>drives home a moral</td></tr>
</table>

<table>
<tr><td>We may draw a moral from the text: . . .</td></tr>
</table>

p. t. o.

**TA Influence on the reader's view** (continued)

| | | |
|---|---|---|
| A text<br>An argument | produces<br>evokes<br>calls forth | a certain response in the reader |

| | | | | |
|---|---|---|---|---|
| The reader feels | a<br>the | sting<br>prick<br>twinge | of conscience<br>of remorse | when reading that . . . |

| | | |
|---|---|---|
| The article | troubles<br>alarms | his conscience |

| |
|---|
| He has a guilty conscience when reading that . . . |

## 4.10 Paraphrasing

A paraphrase (Gk paraphrazein = 'to point out, tell, show, paraphrase') is the rewording of a phrase or passage in another, usually **simpler** and **clearer** form. It follows the original exactly without omitting any of the thoughts.

Paraphrases, in examinations, are meant to test your comprehension of ideas and your competence to express them clearly and accurately in your own words.

Since the use of dictionaries is permitted in the Kollegstufe, Abitur and in some language tests for undergraduates, you will hardly ever be asked to explain words by means of definitions, synonyms, antonyms, enumerations or illustrations – for the obvious reason that you could look them up. But more often than not you will be asked to 'give paraphrases' or 'rewrite the indicated passages in another form'. These expressions or passages will always be linguistically complex phrases. Four types seem to be recurring:

1) phrases belonging to a special register
2) metaphorical or figurative expressions
3) proverbs, pithy sayings or witty remarks
4) idioms

It will be your task, in any case,

a. to show that you have understood the passage;
b. to rewrite it in a simple, straightforward way: this means that you have to replace obsolete or technical terms, metaphorical or figurative statements and idiomatic expressions by **plain** English.

## 1. Phrases belonging to a special register

Here are two examples expressing the same idea but taken from different → registers:

**Journalese** (i.e. the jargon of some journalists who try to impress their readers by using bombastic terms, far-fetched periphrases and intricate sentence patterns):

> 'To be, or the contrary? Whether the former or the latter be preferable would seem to admit of some difference of opinion; the answer in the present case being of an affirmative or a negative character according as to whether one elects on the one hand to mentally suffer the disfavour of fortune, albeit in an extreme degree, or on the other hand to boldly envisage adverse conditions in the prospect of eventually bringing them to a conclusion.' (Sir Arthur Quiller-Couch)

If you happen to feel somewhat baffled, look at our second example, Hamlet's famous soliloquy; you may find it rather illuminating though it is, of course, poetic diction.

**Poetic register:**

> 'To be or not to be: that is the question:
> Whether 'tis nobler in the mind to suffer
> The slings and arrows of outrageous fortune,
> Or to take arms against a sea of troubles,
> And by opposing end them.' (Shakespeare)

You should now proceed to render it in plain English. This might be a way of doing it: 'We are sometimes urged to ask ourselves whether it is worthier to endure all the hardships of life or to put an end to it all by committing suicide.'
A good example of **officialese** (an equally obscure jargon often met with in official statements issued by the Government, corporations, trade-unions, etc.) is to be found in the text 'Please do not spit' on pp. 136 f.

## 2. Expressions used in a figurative or metaphorical sense

Words have sometimes accepted new meanings because – as a consequence of some perceptible likeness – they have been 'transferred' from their original field ('literal meaning') to a new one ('figurative meaning'). This may happen in the following way:

a.

| concrete object A (literal use) | ⟶ (transferred to) | concrete object B (figurative/metaphorical use) |
|---|---|---|

e.g. – the foot (of the body) ⟶ the foot of a mountain
– the eye (of the body) ⟶ the eye of a needle

b.

| concrete object (literal use) | ⟶ (transferred to) | abstract phenomenon (figurative/metaphorical use) |
|---|---|---|

e.g. – the key to a door ⟶ the key to a book, to a problem
– the water was boiling ⟶ Mr X was boiling with indignation
– he is lame in the left leg → this is { a lame argument / a lame excuse }

**Examples** of paraphrases:

– Jane is a beautiful flower.
(= she is a pretty girl)
– He is aflame with a thirst for knowledge.
(= he is very keen on learning)
– He flies high (= he is ambitious)
– The book was a mine of information.
(= the book was full of information)
– The torrent of his eloquence carried away the audience.
(= his power of speech roused the enthusiasm of the audience)

cf. → analogy, → simile, → metaphor.

**3. Proverbs, pithy sayings, witty remarks**

– A stitch in time saves nine.
(= a little trouble taken early will save a great deal of trouble later on)
– It takes two to make a quarrel.
(= when two persons or parties quarrel, you can never put the blame on one party alone; it is a common experience that both are at least partly to blame)
– Marry in haste, repent at leisure.
(= couples who marry without knowing each other properly will have ample opportunity to regret it later on)

- 'Some books are to be tasted, others to be swallowed, and some few to be chewed and digested.' (Bacon)
  (= some books deserve only to be run through, others may be read rapidly at a sitting, and a few want a close study so that the author's ideas may be thoroughly grasped)
- 'Gesticulation for the French is not a pointless accompaniment of speech; it is an organic part of it.' (George Mikes)
  (= the gestures a Frenchman makes while speaking are just as important as his actual words to convey his meaning)

**4. Idiomatic expressions**

- In their courses, the students 'had the time of their lives' (= they had great fun).
- Whenever they could, they 'pulled the teacher's leg' (= they teased him and made a fool of him), though he often 'bit their heads off' (= he scolded them angrily).
- When they looked at the examination paper, however, they 'had faces as long as a fiddle' (= they looked dismal).
- Barbara 'could not make head or tail of it' (= could not understand it at all).
- But Anne proved that she 'had a good head on her shoulders' (= that she had common sense, practical ability) by looking up the key-term of each idiom in the *Advanced Learner's Dictionary.*
- So, in examinations, don't be 'at sixes and sevens' (= confused), but try to keep 'as cool as a cucumber' (= self-possessed, unexcited)!

**Note** that the key-terms of the idioms listed above have been underlined. Of course, when rendering a passage full of metaphorical and idiomatic expressions into German, you should never try to translate it literally – the result might be absurd.

## 4.11 Summary-writing

(L summus = 'highest'; summa = 'sum; the gist, the essentials of something')

### A. What is a summary?

1) It is **a restatement in shortened form** of the theme and chief ideas of a text: it is rarely more than one third of the length of the original and may be only one fifth.

2) A summary gives only **the gist or 'heart' of a passage:** it leaves out repetitions and such details as examples, illustrations, comparisons, reported speech and adjectives.
3) It is written entirely in the words of the person writing it, i.e. **in your own words**, not in the words of the original text: avoid the temptation to use long phrases and sentences from the original.
4) It is written **from the point of view of the author** whose work is being summarized: do not begin with such expressions as 'the author says' or 'the paragraph means'. Begin as though you were summarizing your own writing.

**B. How to write a summary.**

1) Read carefully, twice if necessary, the text to be summarized.
2) Then put the text aside and ask yourself: what does the author want to say? Answer this question in **one** sentence so as to form a clear idea of the theme or subject.
3) Now try to remember – still without looking at the text – which points are closely linked with this theme (all the others are superfluous), and formulate them as simply as you can in your own words. If the text contains technical terms which are indispensable, you may retain them; if not, find synonymous expressions for the 'keywords' and try to include a few of them in one more general term (G 'Oberbegriff').
4) Arrange the main points in a skilful logical order.
5) Write the summary, which should not read like a mere list of points: combine sentences by
   a. using connectives such as 'but, yet, however, therefore, consequently', etc.,
   b. subordinating some of the ideas to others ('although, since, as, in order to', etc.)
6) Re-read your summary:
   – check if you have stuck to the maximum number of words; if not, condense;
   – improve the choice of words;
   – check and improve your links;
   – vary sentence structure.

**Example:** Write a summary of the following text in not more than 100 words.

**Please Do Not Spit**

1. Expectoration is forbidden.
2. Please do not spit.

These are two versions of a notice to the public that were displayed at one time in certain English buses. Number 2 is a good example of clean English. Number 1 is stilted, official English. It serves its purpose less efficiently than the simpler version. Some people may not know the meaning of the word 'expectoration', which is an unfamiliar Latinism. Although this notice contains only three words where the other has four, it is in fact longer; there are 24 letters instead of 15. In spite of this it is less inclusive, omitting the 'please'. It has a gloomy, negative tone. The other version is more polite and altogether more human.

If you adopt the style of 'please do not spit' and avoid the style of 'expectoration is forbidden', you will go a long way towards writing clean English. You may think that this is so easy as to be not worth mentioning. It might never have occurred to you to write in the style of the first notice. But language of that kind is still common enough in official letters and documents, and it is not always easy to escape from its influence without making a conscious effort.

Here for example is a passage from an official letter written by the director of a government department:

'In the absence of legislation designed to regulate the use of reference books now being issued to Native women, it would be premature at this stage to prescribe the endorsement of entries which may be made in such books and consequently it is felt that any explanations or clarifications to be made to Native women should be held in abeyance until the Department has finalized the regulations incidental hereto.'

In clean English this might be expressed as follows:

'Although we are now issuing reference books to Native women we have not yet finally decided upon the regulations governing the use of these books. We regret therefore that it is not yet possible to explain the books and to advise Native women how to use them.'

Perhaps this simpler version makes the indecision or inefficiency of the department more obvious. But if there is inefficiency it can easily be detected behind the pompous official jargon of the original. It would save everybody time if it were written in simple, direct language.

It is easy enough to write 'Please do not spit', but it is only by hard and clear thinking that we can make all our statements and directions as clean and simple and pointed as this one.

(From *A Short Guide to English Style,* by Alan Warner, Oxford University Press, London 1961)

**a. Subject:** We should use plain English and not officialese.

(After taking notes and arranging them in a skilful order, you may finally arrive at the following outline:)

**b. List and arrangement of main points**

1) Although **officialese** is widespread ('still common'), we should avoid it since it is
   - wordy ('pompous', 'stilted')
   - full of old-fashioned, unknown words ('unfamiliar')
   - unpleasant, impolite ('gloomy, negative tone'),

   and implies
   - lack of lucidity
   - incompetence ('inefficiency, indecision')
2) Instead we should use **plain English,** which is
   - clear } ('clean, simple, direct')
   - current }
   - concise ('saves people's time')

(Such an outline will be of great help to you when writing the final version which might look like this:)

**c. Summary**

As may be seen in the notice 'Expectoration is forbidden', there is still a widespread trend to use officialese – a wordy and 'pompous' jargon. It contains many old-fashioned or unknown words and often originates in a lack of intellectual lucidity or even honesty since it is sometimes used to cover up incompetence.
Instead, we should try hard, out of consideration for the others, to express our ideas in clear, concise and current English – even if this is not always as easy as in the notice 'Please do not spit' for 'Expectoration is forbidden'. (93w)

An → **'abstract',** or structural analysis, of the same text would read like this:

The author first quotes two equivalent public notices: 'Expectoration is forbidden' and 'Please do not spit' and then comments on the different sorts of language they make use of – officialese and plain English.
In the third and fourth paragraphs, we are given an example of a longer notice – again in officialese and plain English. The author goes on to point out how obscure officialese is, and concludes by saying that it is much preferable, yet not always so easy, to express oneself in straightforward, clear English.

**Note** that in that kind of 'abstract' the → structure of the text is summarized along with the message, as you can see in such terms as 'The author first quotes . . ., in the third paragraph . . .', etc.

## 4.12 The overall interpretation

(L 'inter' = 'in between' + 'pretis' = 'the act of explaining the meaning of something')
The overall interpretation of a text is the explanation of those aspects which are not immediately plain or explicit. Of course, only one example can be given. It is taken from Helen Monfries' excellent book: *An Introduction to Critical Appreciation for Foreign Learners* (MacMillan 1970). She succeeds in demonstrating how to work out an overall **interpretation of the following text** in three steps:

A. detailed examination of the text by means of relevant questions and answers,
B. skilful organization of the main ideas in an outline,
C. model version of a text interpretation.

'The trouble is that the English nature is not at all easy to understand. It has a great air of simplicity, it advertises itself as simple, but the more we consider it, the greater the problems we shall encounter. People talk of the mysterious East, but the West also is mysterious. It has depths that do not reveal themselves at the first gaze. We know what the sea looks like from a distance: it is of one colour, and level, and obviously cannot contain such creatures as fish. But if we look into the sea over the edge of a boat, we see a dozen colours, and depth below depth, and fish swimming in them. That sea is the English character – apparently imperturbable and even. The depths and the colours are the English romanticism and the English sensitiveness – we do not expect to find such things, but they exist. And – to continue my metaphor – the fish are the English emotions, which are always trying to get up to the surface, but don't quite know how. For the most part we see them moving far below, distorted and obscure. Now and then they succeed and we exclaim 'Why, the Englishman has emotions! He actually can feel!' And occasionally we see that beautiful creature the flying fish, which rises out of the water altogether into the air and the sunlight. English literature is a flying fish. It is a sample of the life that goes on day after day beneath the surface; it is a proof that beauty and emotion exist in the salt, inhospitable sea.'

(From: E. M. Forster, *Abinger Harvest*)

### A. Detailed examination of the passage by means of relevant questions and answers

**1) What is the subject of this passage?**

The English character.

**2) State as briefly as possible what Forster says about it.**

He says that the English nature is complex, despite its apparent simplicity. Beneath an impassive exterior there are depths of feeling which show themselves only very occasionally. He cites the beauties of English literature, as the best proof of this sensitivity.

**3) What is the author trying to do? – tell a story? describe? explain? persuade?**

He is trying to **explain** the English nature, to **persuade** his readers that it is not exactly as it may seem.

**4) What strikes us most obviously in the passage?**

The comparison with the sea.

**5) Why does it strike us?**

Because it occupies most of the passage. It is sustained from l.5 right to the end. Let us trace it:
(a) The sea is like the English character because it looks flat and even, as if there were nothing underneath.
(b) If we look more closely into the sea, we see various colours and depths: these are like English romanticism.
(c) We also see fish swimming below the surface of the sea. These are like English emotions; they are there but have difficulty in showing themselves.
(d) The beautiful flying fish which sometimes rises right up into the air is like English literature.
We can say then that this comparison is very carefully and thoroughly worked out, and it is apt. Notice (l.12/13) that Forster even points out that he is using a metaphor.

**6) What does Forster gain by using a metaphor rather than writing throughout in abstract terms?**

Liveliness, colour, concreteness, greater clarity.

**7) Can you say anything about Forster's manner and tone? Is he serious? humorous? forceful? dogmatic? indignant? good-humoured? gentle? friendly? proud? modest?**

**Friendly.** He places himself alongside his reader:

(a) 'The trouble is . . .' (l.1), as if the English nature were a great problem to him too.
(b) He uses the pronoun 'we', and seems to examine the problem **with** his reader.
(c) He mentions things which are generally familiar, e.g. 'the mysterious East'.

**Good-humoured.** He is English, but he is able to be quite frank about defects in the English character, and to laugh at them.

**Humorous.** He makes us smile at the picture of the English emotions, like fish, 'always trying to get up to the surface', but not knowing how to do it. The remark that the sea 'obviously cannot contain such creatures as fish' is ironical, and there is irony in his quotation of remarks such as 'Why, the Englishman has emotions! He actually can feel!'

**Serious?** Beneath his humorous teasing tone, we can feel that he is serious in his attempt to explain the character of his countrymen. The overall tone is modest but the end is proud and dignified.

8) **Can you comment on the language of the passage (i.e. identify the register)? (formal? conversational? colloquial? archaic? modern? difficult? simple? specialised? straightforward?)**

It is essentially modern, simple and straightforward. The vocabulary is not difficult. The sentences vary in length, but their structure is not complicated. It is the voice of polite conversation.

9) **Listen to the sentences and try to establish whether the rhythm matches the pattern of Forster's argument and helps to convey his feeling***).

First sentence: fairly short and abrupt. l.2 to l.7: broken up into fairly abrupt phrases.

l.7: 'But if we look into the sea . . .' begins with an 'if' clause, and this whole sentence is built up to be longer, to rise to a climax.

l.9: 'That sea is the English character – apparently imperturbable and even'. Smooth and sober rhythm, given by the substantial words and by the balance between the two halves of the sentence.

l.10: 'The depths and the colours . . .' The sonorous rhythm seems as if it is to be continued, but then Forster breaks off into a lighter, quicker phrase, 'we do not expect to find such things . . .' And in the sentences that follow, as far as the exclamations ('He actually can feel!), the rhythm is often changed and interrupted to convey excitement.

l.17: 'And occasionally we see that beautiful creature . . . the sunlight': a long complex sentence, rich in long vowels.

l.19: 'English literature is a flying fish.' A short and simple sentence but emphatic.

l.19/21: Note that the last sentence divides into two long and beautifully balanced periods.

---

*) This is rather a difficult question – more likely to be raised in the case of a poem. The answer implies a somewhat subjective, subtle approach to the text, and can hardly be expected from students of English at High School level. We have made a point, however, of reproducing Helen Monfries' interpretation in its entirety.

**B. Organization of the main ideas.**

This has been a fairly detailed analysis. The following is a short critical essay that might come out of the observations you have made. The order of your points may, but need not necessarily, follow that of the questions you have answered. The danger of following that order too strictly is that you may get a list of statements loosely strung together rather than a coherent and persuasive whole. It is certainly advisable to make a rough plan of the points that you think must be brought out. Here, for instance:

(a) The subject: the English character; the complexity that underlies its apparent simplicity.
(b) The attempt to persuade and the tone adopted – good-humoured, gentle, friendly – humour and irony.
(c) The sustained and detailed comparison with the sea, its colours and fish.
(d) Translation of the author's feeling by sound and rhythm.
(e) Conclusion: Forster's attitude towards his country.

**C. Model interpretation**

Forster's argument is that the English character is complex, despite its apparent simplicity. Beneath an impassive exterior there are depths of feeling which show themselves only occasionally. He cites the beauties of English literature as the best proof of this sensitivity.

With good humour, and in a tone that is gently firm, the author seeks to persuade us of the truth of his argument. By his first sentence, 'The trouble is that the English nature is not at all easy to understand', he lets us know plainly that he, an Englishman, fully sympathises with those who find the English character puzzling. Using the pronoun 'we', he seems to invite us amicably, even slyly, to examine this mystery with him. As he surmises, we have often heard people talk of the 'mysterious East', and his suggestion of a mysterious West engages our sympathy and interest. He then embarks upon the metaphor that is going to sustain him until the end of the argument: the English character is like the sea. From a distance it looks flat and even, and, he adds ironically, 'obviously cannot contain such creatures as fish'. The comparison is followed in detail: the colours that we perceive upon closer inspection are the unsuspected 'English romanticism and sensitiveness', and the fish that are there after all are the English emotions, which 'are always trying to get up to the surface, but don't quite know how'. This gentle and sympathetic humour gives place to the obvious irony with which Forster quotes exclamations that he imagines on the lips of surprised foreigners: 'Why, the Englishman has emotions! He actually can feel!' The author has warmed to his subject.

Now with dignified restraint he brings us to his final point of comparison: the beautiful flying fish that occasionally flashes out of the water is like English literature, a beauty that is always to be found under the less welcoming exterior. The comparison has been exploited with great thoroughness. Forster even points out that he is continuing in the same metaphor throughout, admitting, in fact, that he is using it to prove an argument.

The tone of the passage is restrained, the language that of polite conversation. But does not the feeling of the author make itself heard in the pattern of sound and rhythm? The first few sentences of preamble are deliberately made to sound flat and terse. As the author becomes more positive, his rhythms become more emphatic. The excitement at finding fish in the water and emotions in the Englishman is translated by quick rhythmic changes leading to the humorous climax of the exclamations. Then the passage again gains in emphasis to end in a sonorous and beautifully balanced conclusion.

Forster here shows himself critical of the English character, but it is the kind of criticism that people often level against something that they really love and are proud of. He wishes to show that he is aware of how the English must appear to the outside observer; but he also wishes to defend his fellow-countrymen and to reveal their greater depth to those who may have judged only the surface.

**NOTE:** Observe the use of quotations and how these have been incorporated, and notice that even only one or two important words borrowed from the text must be acknowledged by quotation marks.

## 5. SURVEY OF STYLISTIC AND RHETORICAL FIGURES

It is a common error to assume that non-fictional texts do not contain any stylistic or rhetorical figures. When reading the text 'A Woman's Tears', you will see that this is simply not true since it abounds in instances of metaphor, hyperbole, alliteration, pun, paradox, irony and humour. For that reason we have chosen to make this text precede the survey of stylistic and rhetorical figures in order to provide a vivid, concrete approach to this field. The questions and answers, of course, have been especially conceived to draw your attention to those stylistic devices contained in the text and their intended effect on the reader.

**Example:**

A WOMAN'S TEARS
The injustice of crying as
an exclusively female weapon
(Michael Farrell)

Many years ago, I stood with a group of off-season tourists, viewing the Eiffel Tower for the first time. As our French guide spoke, I became aware of loud convulsive sobbing behind me. I turned and asked the distraught young lady what was wrong. 'Oh,' she gurgled, 'it's too beautiful.'

Since that day of lunacy, the world has seen many revolutionary changes – including the onset of Women's Liberation. But even that hasn't affected the phenomenon of the Sobbing Women. Despite all demands for equality, the fair sex still reserve the exclusive right to cry at any time, anywhere and for any reason.

The injustice of all this is that men are not even allowed to join in. If I had cried at the beauty of Paris, I would have been instantly regarded as weak, childish or simply a sniffling sissy. The young lady, however, by turning on the waterworks, quickly became the pet of the package tour.

Men, of course, seldom wonder why they are not allowed to cry. And this is hardly surprising for, even before they reach the Use of Reason, they are victims of a universal, female conspiracy. As toddlers – irrespective of sex – we are all encouraged to cry. But once we become aware of The Difference, a strange maternal coercion goes into action. Little girls may now happily carry on crying – but little boys are quickly dehydrated. 'Boys Don't Cry' a world of mothers instinctively warn – and a world of little fellows make the obvious choice between drying their eyes or being branded as a third gender.

Of course, as they grow up, they soon find other ways of expressing their emotions. Not being allowed to cry, they curse when frustrated, break windows when angry and get drunk when happy. And meanwhile, the female cleverly assures them that such behaviour is the mark of masculinity – knowing that the Weeping Weapon is now her exclusive possession.

Using this weapon, sweethearts have, for centuries, melted the hardest heart with a single tear. And later, wives have subtly acquired hats, holidays and higher allowances by simply uttering a sob and running to a room. In time, the actual tear became unnecessary – the threat was effective enough.

Women's Liberation, of course, should have ended all that. For, if women were graciously allowed to curse, get drunk and break things, then, for crying out loud, men should have been liberated from their tearless imprisonment. Sadly, however, that wasn't allowed to happen.

So, in every cinema, our womenfolk are still crying their eyes out while their male escorts are not even allowed to weep at the box-office – where tears are surely more justified. At wakes, weddings, christenings and concerts, handkerchiefs are still shamelessly damming the downpour. And, in offices, every boss becomes a heartless rogue whenever a scolded typist decides to administer her watery coup de grace.

The old defence mechanism of the new liberated female is working as well as ever – she still has every male wrapped up as snugly as a packet of tissues.

The obvious solution – but one I would only cautiously recommend – is for men to forget their enforced abstinence, begin to cry and so assert their rights through their tear-ducts.

It is very unlikely, however, that **she** will be as impressed by tears as **you** have been trained to be. More likely, she will continue crying and beat you by a long sob. Not only has she got practice and experience on her side but, despite her loud protestations of equality, she is really just a little girl in search of constant consolation. And, apparently, if she can't find that consolation in you, she'll look for it elsewhere.

The image of liberation is still more important to every female than the reality of it. And that's why I, in now decrying the Crying Game, know that I'm really perpetuating it. For men, reading this, will shrug resignedly and await the floods. Women, of course, will say I'm cruel, cry self-pityingly and seek a shoulder to sob out.

The only consolation I can offer our male population is that I understand the situation – and, were I allowed, I'd willingly shed a tear for every one of us.

(From: *Herald Tribune,* 2nd Jan. 1976)

## WORK SHEET: A WOMAN'S TEARS

### I. QUESTIONS ON THE TEXT

Read all the questions first, then plan your answers carefully in order to avoid repeating yourself. Use your own words as far as possible.

**1) In what way does the first paragraph differ from the rest of the text? – Comment on its function.**

The first paragraph is narrative, whereas the rest is mainly argumentative, with the argumentation being carried out in a joking tone from the very beginning. The telling of an incident which took place in Paris some years ago provides a very lively introduction to this article on women's tears. The author then imagines how he would have been treated, if **he** had cried instead of the young lady. And this sets him thinking and joking about the unequal chances men and women get of expressing their feelings.

**2.1) Give a paraphrase for each of the following expressions.**

(a) . . . by turning on the waterworks (l.14)
(b) . . . men should have been liberated from their tearless imprisonment (l.38/39)
(c) . . . handkerchiefs are still shamelessly damming the downpour (l.43/44)

(a) . . . by shedding tears
(b) . . . men should have been given the right to cry.
(c) . . . women are not ashamed of crying their eyes out and wiping them ostentatiously with their handkerchiefs.

**2.2) Are the above expressions to be taken literally?**

They are not; all of them are used in a metaphorical sense, since the term 'waterworks', for instance, has been transferred from its original meaning 'fountains' to a new one 'tears'. The absurd analogy it implies forms the basis of the humorous tone of the whole text.

**3) 'Decrying the Crying Game' (l.59) – Determine the stylistic figure contained in this expressions. What are its implications?**

This is a pun. The author plays on the words 'crying' and 'decrying' which are almost homophones since they sound very much alike, but have got different meanings: 'to cry' means 'to weep', whereas 'to decry' means 'to criticize'. Thus this expression contains the key terms of the text, in other words, the gist of it; in fact, it might even serve as a sub-title, reminding us of the epigrammatic wording and joking tone of limericks.

4) **What is the tone of the whole passage and what effects does the author aim at?**

The tone of the passage is definitely humorous. The picture the author draws of women in general is pretty ridiculous: the whole text – in fact a long string of jokes! – is mainly intended to amuse the reader by satirizing women, particularly by exposing their inconsistency. It abounds in instances of irony, such as: 'she has got practice and experience on her side' (l.54/55). Even when, at the end, the author claims to feel sympathy for all men, he cannot help ending the sentence with one more joke, saying that he would readily cry over their miserable situation . . . if only he were allowed to!

5) **Exaggeration recurs throughout the text. Find instances of it and show how they contribute to the general tone.**

The text abounds in exaggerations. Right at the beginning, for instance, we are told about a woman 'sobbing convulsively' (l.3) – whereas she probably only got moist eyes at the sight of the Eiffel Tower! Then it seems that **all** women in the world (cf. 'a world of mothers' l.22), following their common instinct, have tacitly agreed to forbid their little boys to cry. As for women's tears, they are not just a few isolated drops: they are real 'floods' (l.61) or 'waterworks' (l.14) which, apparently, can be turned on and off at will and for definite purposes! All these hyperboles, which do contain a grain of truth, are intended to produce a humorous effect.

6) **Can you find a few examples of alliteration in the third paragraph and in lines 31 to 35? Comment on their intended effect on the reader.**

In line 13, the words 'simply', 'sniffling' and 'sissy' obviously alliterate, not for poetical purposes, of course, but to show how ridiculous a man would look who would weep at the sight of the Eiffel Tower: the alliteration of the 's'-sound conveys the auditory image of a little boy – possibly one with a lisp! – crying all the time. In lines 31 to 35, the accumulation of the alliterating 'h' produces a humorous effect by emphasizing the exaggeration of the whole paragraph; it just shows that women can obtain practically everything with their tears: '**h**ats, **h**olidays and **h**igher allowances'!

7) **There is an obvious contradiction in line 9, as well as in line 46. What do you call this stylistic device? Which trait in women's character does it hint at?**

The terms 'equality' and 'exclusive right' (l.9) constitute a paradox: as soon as one of the parties retains some exclusive rights, we can no longer speak of absolute equality. In the same way, the sentence 'The **old** defence mechanism of the **new** liberated woman is working as well as ever' (l.46) is paradoxical. Here, the contrast between the ideas is even emphasized by the use of parallelism: the words 'old' and 'new' are balanced against each other, and the expression 'defence mechanism' is opposed to 'liberated woman'. By thus pointing out the discrepancy between women's claims of emancipation on the one hand, and their childish behaviour on the other hand, the author seems to suggest that they are utterly inconsistent.

**8) How would you characterize the author's attitude towards women considering the style and tone of the whole article?**

The article reads like one long satire on woman's shortcomings: the author depicts her as hopelessly inconsistent – she insists on being the equal of man, yet regards crying as her particular privilege –, whimsical and wilful (l.32 to 33), unfair in the way she brings up her children (l.22: 'Boys Don't Cry'), and even capable of unfaithfulness (l.57). As the whole article, however, is full of gross exaggerations and obviously meant to entertain the reader, there is no telling what the actual attitude of the author is towards women. He is most certainly baffled at their demeanour, and yet there seems to be some sympathy in the sentence: '... she is really just a little girl in search of constant consolation' (l.55/56) – perhaps even the slightest hint that he, himself, is quite willing to offer the 'little girl' that comfort she is craving for!

## II. COMPOSITION

**'Boys Don't Cry.' – Would you make a difference in bringing up boys and girls?**

Now and again you can hear mothers blame their sons for crying over a broken toy or because they have hurt themselves: 'Boys don't cry', they will warn. But why shouldn't boys cry after all?

To begin with, there is no denying the fact that, generally speaking, there is a basic difference of temperament between boys and girls: in spite of numerous exceptions to this 'rule', we may assume that most boys are tougher and less sensitive than most girls are. Now here is the controversial point: some people argue that this very feature in a boy's character is a token of his masculinity – something very much to be wished for and encouraged; even at an early age, a little boy is expected to prove as hard as a man 'should' be, and tears, generally looked upon as a sign of weakness and effeminacy, are said to be unworthy of him.

In my view, however, those who encourage such callousness in boys fail to realize that hardness towards oneself often entails hardness towards the others: one who has not been allowed to cry as a child will dislike tears in the eyes of anybody else – whether man or woman – later on. He will make his way in life but will probably lack understanding and kindness. Now, kindness and compassion are most certainly qualities to be encouraged in children – irrespective of their sex. And the very fact that boys, on the whole, tend to be hard, even somewhat aggressive by nature, should set mothers thinking about the 'value' of tears. I, personally, would regard them as something very natural, a proof of sensitiveness rather than weakness, and in that respect I would make no difference whatsoever in bringing up boys and girls.

## III. TRANSLATION

Translate the last four paragraphs (l.49–65) into stylistically equivalent German.

Die Lösung, die auf der Hand liegt – die ich jedoch nur unter Vorbehalt empfehlen möchte! – hieße: daß auch die Männer ihrer aufgezwungenen Tränenabstinenz ein Ende setzen, ebenfalls zu heulen anfangen und so ihre Rechte mittels der Tränendrüsen durchsetzen sollten.

Es ist jedoch höchst unwahrscheinlich, daß *sie* sich von Tränen so beeindrucken läßt wie *Sie*, der Sie dazu erzogen worden sind. Wahrscheinlicher ist, daß sie einfach weiterheult und Sie um einen langen Schluchzer schlägt. Dabei kommen ihr nicht nur lange Übung und Erfahrung zustatten, sondern in Wirklichkeit ist sie – trotz ihrer kreischenden Forderungen nach Gleichberechtigung! – doch nichts weiter als eine kleine Suse auf der Suche nach ständigem Trost.

Und wenn sie diesen Trost schon nicht bei Ihnen finden kann, wird sie sich halt anderweitig danach umsehen müssen. Die Idee der Emanzipation ist jedem Weibsbild immer noch wichtiger als deren tatsächliche Verwirklichung. Und genau aus diesem Grunde bin ich mir dessen bewußt, daß ich eben nun, da ich das Tränentheater tadle, es in Wirklichkeit fortsetze; denn die Männer, die dies lesen, werden nur gottergeben mit den Schultern zucken und sich auf die Tränenflut einstellen. Die Frauen werden mich natürlich der Grausamkeit zeihen, aus Selbstbemitleidung zu heulen anfangen und dabei nach einer Schulter Ausschau halten, um sich darauf auszuschluchzen.

Der einzige Trost, den ich der Männerwelt anzubieten imstande bin, lautet: daß ich volles Verständnis für unsere Lage habe – und daß ich, wenn ich nur dürfte, allzu gerne über jeden einzelnen von uns eine Träne vergießen würde!

## WHAT ARE STYLISTIC AND RHETORICAL FIGURES?

Stylistic and rhetorical figures are intentional deviations from what is 'normal' or straightforward in the vocabulary, syntax, composition or argumentation of a text, with the purpose of reaching a certain effect.

It was the old masters of rhetoric who analysed and laid down almost all of the stylistic devices necessary in the process of communication, – which accounts for the Greek and Latin etymologies abounding in the following survey. They realized that the reader's intellect had to be addressed ('docere'), that his emotions had to be stirred ('movere'), and that his sensual perceptions had to be appealed to ('delectare').
Consequently they taught their students that they should have two aspects in mind:

1) the subject-matter ('res'), i.e. a clear understanding of it ('intellectio'), a suitable line of reasoning ('inventio') and a skilful presentation of the arguments ('dispositio');
2) the linguistic means of communication, i.e. the appropriate choice of words and rhetorical figures.

All the stylistic and rhetorical figures are the result of a deliberate change from what is normal in plain English, according to the categories of substitution, change in the word order, and the dropping and adding of elements in the fields of

1) semantics and syntax,
2) argumentation and
3) composition.

Apart from the rhetorical figures proper, the following survey includes such terms as may prove useful when dealing with questions of style.

## 5.1 STYLISTIC AND RHETHORICAL FIGURES IN SEMANTICS AND SYNTAX

### ► REGISTER [ˈredʒistə]

This term denotes the type of language appropriate to a particular situation. Thus, for example, the language used by a teacher in a class of infants will vary considerably from that in use at a political conference. The register depends on the subject, the situation and the addressee. So language has to be adapted to a wide variety of social situations ranging from a speech in Parliament to a chat at the fire-side. It may be factual, informative, formal, technical, as well as casual, intimate or emotional, and is, of course, closely linked with the author's → **style**.
Compare 1) the beginning of *Silas Marner* by George Eliot (published in 1861) with 2) that of *The Catcher in the Rye* by J. D. Salinger (published in 1951). Their wording is obviously based on different registers.

1) 'In the days when the spinning-wheels hummed busily in the farmhouses – and even great ladies, clothed in silk and thread-lace, had

their toy spinning-wheels of polished oak – there might be seen, in districts far away among the lanes, or deep in the bosom of the hills, certain pallid undersized men, who, by the side of the brawny country-folk, looked like the remnants of a disinherited race.'

2) 'If you really want to hear about it, the first thing you'll probably want to know is where I was born, and what my lousy childhood was like, and how my parents were occupied and all before they had me, and all that David Copperfield kind of crap, but I don't feel like going into it. In the first place, that stuff bores me, and in the second place, my parents would have about two haemorrhages apiece if I told anything pretty personal about them.'

Sometimes an author may deliberately use a word or a sentence which does not fit into the register of the context, for humorous purposes. George B. Shaw's comedy *Pygmalion* is based on the contrast between two different registers: the Queen's English and cockney. At Mrs Higgins's party, for instance, when Liza is asked: 'Are you walking across the park, Miss Doolittle?', she forgets the good diction she has just been learning and she answers: 'Walk! Not bloody likely. I am going in a taxi.'

**TA Register**

| | | | |
|---|---|---|---|
| The author | uses<br>employs<br>resorts to<br>makes use of | vulgar<br>slang<br>colloquial<br>familiar<br>dialect<br>current<br>common<br>formal<br>literary<br>poetic<br>learned<br>technical<br>scientific<br>legal<br>religious | words<br>terms<br>phrases<br>expressions<br>vocabulary<br>language |

| | | | | |
|---|---|---|---|---|
| A | word<br>phrase | belongs to<br>is characteristic of | familiar<br>ordinary<br>everyday | speech |
| | | | a certain | dialect<br>jargon |

## ▶ DENOTATION

(L de = 'from' + notare = 'to mark' = 'to mark out the exact meaning of'; G 'be-zeichnen')

Denotation is the direct explicit meaning of a word or expression as distinct from additional suggestions, i.e. → connotations, → implications, → overtones

## ▶ CONNOTATION [ˌkɔnəu ˈteiʃən]

(L cum- = 'along with' + notare = 'marking, signalling')

## ▶ IMPLICATION [ˌimpliˈkeiʃən]

(L im-plicare ≙ 'to enfold, to involve')

Both terms are used almost synonymously. They denote the conveying or suggesting of additional meanings by a word or phrase along with or apart from what it explicitly names or describes.

In literature, these additional implications or suggestions sometimes tend to overwhelm the explicit significance of a term. They could be compared to the overtones accompanying any note in music. For that very reason, the term **'overtone'** is also used in the sense of connotation or implication.

**Examples:** The word **'hearth'**, which literally means 'the floor of a fireplace', – this is the **de**notation! –, suggests in addition 'the fireside, warmth, safety, cosiness, a family and friends, the home itself' – these are the various **con**notations of the word – evoking associations of feelings, sensations and ideas.

'By his reference to the **need for strict economy,** the chairman implied that the financial position of the company was causing some concern'.

### TA Connotation, implication

| | | | |
|---|---|---|---|
| A | word<br>phrase | hints at<br>implies<br>suggests | something |
| | | hints<br>implies<br>suggests | that . . . |

| | | |
|---|---|---|
| We must be aware of the | implications<br>connotations | to be found in this . . . |

| | | | |
|---|---|---|---|
| A | word<br>phrase<br>metaphor | has | overtones of . . . |
| | | is loaded with implications | |

**▶ ASSOCIATION** [ə,sousi ˈeiʃən]
(L ad-sociare = 'to join, to unite')

This term is used to denote the feelings, thoughts, or recollections linked in the mind or associated in the memory with a thing or person. (→ connotation, → implication, → overtone)

**Example:** 'Words stir our feelings ... through their enveloping atmosphere of associations.' (J. L. Lowes)

**TA Association**

| | | | | |
|---|---|---|---|---|
| The author | links<br>connects | impressions<br>ideas | (rather) by association<br>(than by logic) | |
| Associations are | stirred<br>aroused<br>evoked | by certain stimuli | | |
| Impressions<br>Ideas | are | associated<br>connected | through | similarity<br>contrast |
| Connections between ideas are | established<br>influenced | by frequency | | |

**▶ STYLE** [stail]
(L stilus = 'stylus', ancient writing instrument)

Style – also referred to as 'diction' – is the manner of writing characteristic of a text, an author or a period. It refers to the **choice** (1) **and arrangement of words** (2), and the use of certain figures of speech (→ stylistic devices). Every writer has his particular way of expressing his ideas. His style may also vary according to his purpose.

**Examples:**

**Poetic:**

'It is not a story that falls easily into sequence... For the sea has claimed its own and spreads its rippled blanket over the site, and the great white bird that saw it all from the beginning to the end has returned to the dark frozen silences of the northland whence it came.'

(Paul Gallico, *The Snow Goose*)

**Vivid:**

'As soon as Dixon had joined the company within, the leisurely tempo of his day jerked abruptly into frenzy.' (Kingsley Amis, *Lucky Jim*)

## TA 1) The choice of words

<table>
<tr><td rowspan="4">The passage is full of<br>The text abounds in<br>The author uses</td><td>set<br>hackneyed<br>commonplace<br>trite</td><td>phrases</td></tr>
<tr><td>odd<br>specific<br>pedantic</td><td rowspan="3">words<br>terms<br>expressions</td></tr>
<tr><td>abstract<br>concrete</td></tr>
<tr><td>descriptive<br>suggestive</td></tr>
</table>

<table>
<tr><td colspan="2">The text contains</td><td rowspan="2">neologisms / contemporary words<br>archaisms / obsolete words<br>Americanisms<br>Germanisms<br>Gallicisms<br>latinized words<br>journalese<br>officialese</td></tr>
<tr><td>The author</td><td>uses<br>employs<br>has recourse to</td></tr>
</table>

<table>
<tr><td>He is a writer with a</td><td>poor / restricted<br>rich / large</td><td>vocabulary</td></tr>
</table>

<table>
<tr><td rowspan="3">A(n)</td><td rowspan="3">word<br>phrase<br>expression<br>figure of speech</td><td rowspan="3">is</td><td>effective<br>appropriate / apt<br>proper<br>to the point</td></tr>
<tr><td>misapplied<br>out of place<br>irrelevant<br>incongruous</td></tr>
<tr><td>vague<br>ambiguous<br>equivocal</td></tr>
</table>

p. t. o.

**TA 1) The choice of words** (continued)

| | | | | |
|---|---|---|---|---|
| The author | uses<br>employs<br>sustains | a | banal<br>conventional<br>standardized<br>dignified<br>exalted<br>elevated<br>poetic | diction |

## TA 2) The arrangement of words

Here are some qualities of style usually considered good or bad:

| GOOD | BAD |
|---|---|
| **plain**<br>simple<br>unaffected<br>neat<br>pure<br>matter-of-fact<br>sober<br>natural | **ornate**<br>artificial<br>affected<br>pompous<br>inflated<br>stilted<br>bombastic<br>high-flown<br>flashy |
| **concise**<br>terse<br>condensed<br>laconic<br>pithy<br>crisp | **wordy**<br>diffuse<br>lengthy<br>long-winded<br>round-about<br>desultory<br>loose |
| **clear**<br>intelligible<br>to the point<br>precise<br>vivid | **obscure**<br>confused<br>woolly<br>evasive |
| **vigorous**<br>powerful<br>forceful<br>impressive<br>passionate | **weak**<br>feeble<br>nerveless<br>colourless<br>bookish |

| | |
|---|---|
| **vigorous**<br>trenchant<br>lively<br>weighty<br>eloquent | **weak**<br>lax<br>dull<br>watery<br>slip-shod |
| **elegant**<br>polished<br>graceful<br>fluent<br>elevated<br>poetic<br>sublime<br>lofty | **clumsy**<br>awkward<br>laboured<br>crude<br>banal<br>cliché-ridden<br>trite<br>hackneyed |

## ► TONE

(L/Gk teinein = 'to stretch'; tonos = 'act of stretching a string; pitch, tone')

This term, originally denoting the accent or inflection of the voice as adapted to the emotion or passion expressed, is also used for the style or manner of approach in speaking or writing in general. It reflects the mood of the author and his attitude towards his subject.

**Humorous tone:**

> 'If you happen to have read another book about Christopher Robin, you may remember that he once had a swan – or the swan had Christopher Robin, I don't know which.'
>
> (A. A. Milne, *Winnie-the-Pooh*)

**Earnest tone:**

> 'The chapters that follow should be read against a background of thoughts about the Hungarian uprising and its repression, about H-bombs, . . . about those endless columns of uniformed boys, white, black, brown, yellow, marching obediently towards the common grave.'
>
> (Aldous Huxley, *Brave New World Revisited*)

**TA Tone**

| | | |
|---|---|---|
| The text is written<br>The description is given | in a tone of | contempt<br>irony<br>understatement |

p. t. o.

| | |
|---|---|
| The tone of the passage is | flippant<br>colloquial<br>humorous<br>playful<br>ironical |
| | solemn / grave<br>serious / earnest |
| | detached<br>provocative<br>conciliatory |
| The author seems to be | in high spirits<br>in a joking mood<br>in low spirits<br>downcast |

▶ **HUMOUR** [ˈhjuːmə]

(L humor = 'fluid of the body, considered to determine a person's temperament')

Humour is that quality in an expression of ideas which causes amusement by appealing to the reader's sense of the ludicrous or absurdly incongruous (i.e. his sense of humour.). There is no sting in it, no conscious superiority: it implies greater kindliness and sympathy than does **wit,** which is connected with intellectual brilliance.

> 'Humorists . . . are writers who, in deliberately adopting an absurd eccentric attitude in their thoughts, style and language, pretend not to notice these and imperturbably declaim the most logical **nonsense** in the world . . . with a twinkle in their eyes.' (R. Escarpit)
>
> Humour is such an essential part of the English style and character that 'the surest way to affront any Englishman is to suggest to him that he has no sense of humour'. (H. W. Garrod)

**Examples:**

> 'Of all the several ways of beginning a book which are now in practice throughout the known world, I am confident my own of doing it is the best – I'm sure it is the most religious – for I begin with writing the first sentence and trusting to Almighty God for the second.'
>
> (L. Sterne, *Tristram Shandy*)

'He stood before them with his body swayed, and bent forward just so far as to make an angle of 85 degrees and a half upon the plain of the horizon – which sound orators, to whom I address this, know very well to be the true persuasive angle of incidence; in any other angle you may talk and preach – 'tis certain –, and it is done every day, but with what effect, I leave the world to judge.' (L. Sterne, *Tristram Shandy*)

On open fire-places: '. . . At last you can lie down on the floor facing your homely, friendly fire and enjoy a really good book; it is true that your hair may catch fire if you are careless but you will always have the consolation that your feet get frozen at the same time.' (G. Mikes)

## TA Humour

<table>
<tr><td rowspan="2">This</td><td rowspan="2">text<br>story</td><td rowspan="2">is</td><td colspan="2">full of humour</td></tr>
<tr><td>written in a humorous</td><td>tone<br>vein</td></tr>
<tr><td colspan="3">The author aims at a comic effect when</td><td colspan="2">saying that . . .<br>comparing (A) with (B)</td></tr>
<tr><td>The humour in this text</td><td>springs from<br>originates in</td><td>the</td><td colspan="2">contrast between . . .<br>situation<br>witty retorts of . . .</td></tr>
<tr><td>Mark Twain is a</td><td colspan="4">humorous writer<br>humorist</td></tr>
</table>

▶ **IRONY** ['airəni]
(Gk/L = 'simulated ignorance')

Irony is a figure of speech by which the writer says the opposite of what he means, knowing that the waywardness of his expression will draw special attention to its actual meaning. As a means of the → sarcastic as well as the → humorous ways of writing, it is often used to blame.
This is, for **example,** what Dickens writes about the Old Bailey (London Central Criminal Court), as it was in 1780:

'It was famous for the pillory, a **wise old** institution, that inflicted a punishment of which no one could foresee the extent; also for the whipping-post, another **dear old** institution, **very humanizing** and **softening** to behold in action; also for extensive transactions in blood-money, another **fragment of ancestral wisdom,** systematically leading to the most frightful mercenary crimes that could be committed under heaven.'

Many ironical remarks, not to be taken literally, are made in everyday life. What they amount to becomes clear when the phrase 'I don't think (that) . . .' is added at the beginning of each of them:

– '(I don't think that) This is a pretty state of affairs!' (i.e. 'What a mess!')
– '(I don't think that) That's a fine thing to say!' (i.e. 'You ought to be ashamed of yourself for saying such a thing!')
– 'I'm having a tooth pulled out tomorrow – a pleasant prospect!' (i.e. 'I dread to think of it!')

**Note** that, in a wider sense, the word 'irony' is often used as a synonym of **'mockery'.**

### TA Irony

<table>
<tr><td rowspan="2">A text contains</td><td>sharp-edged<br>pungent</td><td>irony</td></tr>
<tr><td>ironical</td><td>statements<br>remarks<br>allusions</td></tr>
<tr><td>The author</td><td>speaks<br>writes<br>describes something</td><td>in a tone of irony<br>ironically<br>with irony</td></tr>
<tr><td colspan="3">He achieves an effect of irony by . . .</td></tr>
<tr><td>The reader is expected to</td><td>see<br>understand<br>grasp<br>become aware of<br>be sensitive to</td><td>the irony of . . .</td></tr>
<tr><td colspan="3">The author's irony is mainly directed against . . .</td></tr>
</table>

▶ **SARCASM** [ˈsaːkæzəm] → Satire
(Gk sarkazein = 'to tear flesh like dogs')

Unlike humour, which usually sympathizes with its object, sarcasm is always aggressive and intended to wound, as the etymology reveals.
In everyday life, it takes the form of such remarks as:

– 'Are you going to stop in bed all day?'
– 'That's right – smash every cup in the house!'
– 'I suppose you'll get this job finished by Christmas.'

Dylan Thomas gives a good example of sarcasm in *Quite Early One Morning*:

> 'When we returned to school the morning after the fight I had a glorious black eye. The teacher whose lesson we had missed looked at me with a sardonic expression on his face. "I see Mr Thomas has been straining his eyes, gentlemen. He must be careful not to do too much school work, mustn't he?"'

▶ **SATIRE** [ˈsætaiə]
(L satura = 'plate filled with various fruit')

Satire is a piece or form of writing based on the use of → humour, → irony, → sarcasm, for the purpose of exposing and discouraging vice and ridiculing foolish ideas or habits. Satirical writing is thus always didactic.
For **example,** in the following couplet, Alexander Pope satirizes the way justice is dispensed in the 18th century:

> 'The hungry judges soon the sentence sign,
> And wretches hang that jurymen may dine.'

Laurence Sterne holds up the scientists of his time to ridicule when writing:

> 'Now you must understand that not one of these was the true cause of the confusion in my Uncle Toby's discourse; and it is for that very reason I enlarge upon them so long, after the manner of **great physiologists** – to show the world what it did **not** arise from.'

**TA Satire, sarcasm**

<table>
<tr><td colspan="6">The writer is a satirist.</td></tr>
<tr><td colspan="6">This text is satirical.</td></tr>
<tr><td colspan="2" rowspan="2">The author</td><td>satirizes</td><td colspan="3">somebody<br>something</td></tr>
<tr><td>attacks</td><td>somebody<br>something</td><td>with</td><td>irony<br>satire<br>sarcasm</td></tr>
<tr><td>His</td><td>irony<br>satire<br>sarcasm</td><td>is directed against<br>attacks<br>exposes<br>ridicules<br>arouses contempt for</td><td colspan="3">human folly<br>a certain habit<br>a project vice<br>a certain idea<br>an institution</td></tr>
</table>

▶ **COMPARISON** [kəmˈpærisn]
(L cum = 'with' + parare = 'to couple'; par = 'equal')

Comparison is the act of judging to what extent two things or persons are similar.

▶ **ANALOGY** [əˈnælədʒi] = → Comparison
(Gk/L analogia = 'proportion')

Analogy means resemblance in some particulars between things otherwise unlike. Both → **simile** and → **metaphor** are based on analogy.

**Example:**

There is an analogy between the branches of a tree and those of a family.

Authors often base their conclusions on the use of analogy. If an author resorts to **false analogy,** he establishes unjustified conclusions.

**Example:**

We may draw an analogy between the branches of a family and those of a tree; but it would be wrong to argue that because the smaller branches of a tree have to be lopped from time to time and the larger ones sawn off, the same procedure should be adopted with the branches of a family.

Such an argument based on false analogy is a → **fallacy.**

**TA Analogy, comparison**

| | |
|---|---|
| A comparison consists of two | elements<br>parts<br>members |

| | | | |
|---|---|---|---|
| The author | draws<br>makes<br>forms<br>sets up<br>builds up<br>establishes | a comparison<br>an analogy | between (A) and (B) |

<table>
<tr><td rowspan="3">(A)</td><td colspan="3">has its analogy in</td><td rowspan="3">(B)</td></tr>
<tr><td>is<br>constitutes<br>develops into</td><td>an analogy</td><td rowspan="2">to</td></tr>
<tr><td>is</td><td>analogous</td></tr>
</table>

p. t. o.

**TA Analogy, comparison** (continued)

| | | |
|---|---|---|
| He compares | our political system **with** that of Sweden.<br>the heart **to** a pump. | |
| A comparison | holds<br>fails | |
| The author argues by analogy.<br>He pushes analogy too far. | | |
| This is a(n) | artificial<br>forced<br>false | analogy |

▶ **IMAGINATION** [ˌimædʒiˈneiʃn] → Image; → Simile; → Metaphor; → Symbol
(L imago = 'forming mental pictures')

Speaking of 'imagination', we refer to the creative faculty by means of which mental pictures of objects and acts not present are formed in the mind.
Many writers consider that literature is primarily and above all an effort of the imagination. Images are mental pictures.
As a stylistic device, an **image** is an expression which brings a vivid picture to the mind. It may be a → simile, → a metaphor, or a → symbol. The collective term for all images is **'imagery'.**

**TA Imagination, fancy**

| | | | | |
|---|---|---|---|---|
| The author seems to have a(n) | | strong<br>vivid<br>overflowing<br>morbid | | imagination |
| He | sees<br>pictures<br>conjures up | something in his mind's eye | | |
| The reader's imagination is | stirred<br>affected<br>caught<br>captured<br>held | by | the lively report<br>the vivid description<br>the article | |

p. t. o.

## TA **Imagination, fancy** (continued)

| | | | | |
|---|---|---|---|---|
| The | article<br>text<br>book | stirs<br>takes<br>holds<br>catches<br>grasps | the reader's | fancy<br>imagination<br>interest |

## TA Image, imagery

| | | | |
|---|---|---|---|
| The imagery used conveys a vivid picture to the mind. | | | |
| The author | speaks in<br>uses<br>employs<br>makes use of | optical<br>auditory<br>tactual | images |
| | | vivid<br>ready-made | |
| They | fit into the context<br>are suited<br>are appropriate | | |

▶ **SIMILE** [ˈsimili]
(L similis = 'like, similar')

A simile is a figure of speech in which two things or actions are compared because they have something in common though they are in all other respects unlike, in order to make the description more striking.
So 'Miss Amelia Jones is like her sister Dorothy' is **not** a simile, but merely a literal comparison. To make it a simile proper, the reader's imagination must be stirred, as in 'Miss Amelia Jones is like a fussy old hen'.
In a simile, the imaginative comparison is explicitly stated with the help of some such word as **'like'** or **'as'.**

There are scores of similes in current use:

... as dead as mutton ...
... as fit as a fiddle ...
... as happy as a sandboy
... as red as a beetroot ...
... like a bull in a china shop ...
... like a fish out of water ...

Literature, of course, abounds in them:

– 'As flies to wanton boys, are we to Gods,
They kill us for their sport.' (Shakespeare)

– 'For women are as roses whose fair flower
Being once displayed doth fall that very hour.' (Shakespeare)
– 'O'my love's like a red, red rose . . .' (Robert Burns)
– 'The holy time is quiet as a nun
Breathless with adoration . . .' (Wordsworth)
– 'I wandered lonely as a cloud . . .' (Wordsworth)
– '. . . blankets and mattresses hung like tongues from the windows.'
(Laurie Lee)

Many similes were good and convincing when first used, but they have been so often repeated that they no longer affect our imagination. This is true of all overworked figures that have become **clichés,** which should be avoided.

**TA Simile**

| | | |
|---|---|---|
| (A) is | like<br>as . . . as | (B) |
| The author | uses<br>employs | a simile to (purpose) |
| It is drawn from | nature<br>science | |
| This simile | indicates<br>suggests<br>implies<br>illustrates | (something)<br>that . . . |

▶ **METAPHOR** ['metəfə]
(Gk meta- + phero = 'to transfer')

A metaphor is a simile condensed: a simile says merely that one thing is **like** another, the metaphor that one thing **is** another.
For instance, the simile 'Miss Amelia Jones is **like** a fussy old hen' becomes a metaphor if **'like'** is dropped. Thus, in a metaphor, the imaginative comparison is implied by means of an identification of the two things compared.

Current language is full of metaphors:

. . . the sands of time . . .
. . . crocodile tears . . .
. . . the countess sailed across the room . . .

Some words are much more often used in their → metaphorical or figurative than in their → literal sense. For example, we more often hear of someone being petrified with fear than of something petrifying in the sense of 'turning into stone'.
And here are just a few examples taken from literature:

– 'All the world's a stage
  And all the men and women merely players . . .' (Shakespeare)
– 'Life's but a walking shadow . . .' (Shakespeare)
– 'O, full of scorpions is my mind, dear wife . . .' (Shakespeare)

'Swallowed half an hour before closing time, that second dose of soma had raised a quite impenetrable wall between the actual universe and their minds. **Bottled,** they crossed the street; **bottled,** they took the lift up to Henry's room on the twenty-eighth floor. And yet, **bottled** as she was, and in spite of that second gramme of soma, Lenina did not forget to take all the contraceptive precautions prescribed by the regulations.'

(From *Brave New World* by Aldous Huxley)

**TA Metaphor**

| | | | |
|---|---|---|---|
| The author | uses<br>employs<br>resorts to | extended<br>submerged<br>suggestive | metaphors<br>metaphorical language |
| Here, the metaphor 'darkness' | embodies<br>calls up a sense of<br>calls forth associations of | evil | |
| The power of the metaphorical use contributes to . . . | | | |
| The author describes something by | suggestive<br>strongly associative | metaphors | |
| He uses 'night' as a metaphorical equivalent of 'evil'.<br>'Night' is often (used as) a metaphor for 'evil'. | | | |

▶ **SYMBOL** [simbəl]

(Gk syn- = 'together' + ballein = 'to throw'; 'uniting the concrete and abstract meaning of a word')

A symbol is a sign, a concrete thing that stands for something abstract or invisible.

**Examples:**

- The Cross is the symbol of Christianity, the hammer and sickle that of Communism.
- The turtle dove is { a symbol / an emblem } of peace.
- The wedding ring is meant to symbolize eternal love.

**TA Symbol**

<table>
<tr><td>A symbol</td><td>represents<br>stands for</td><td>an idea<br>an abstraction<br>an organization</td></tr>
<tr><td>It</td><td>conveys<br>communicates</td><td>abstract conceptions</td></tr>
<tr><td>(A)</td><td>symbolizes<br>is a symbol of<br>is symbolic of<br>serves as a symbol of/for</td><td>(B)</td></tr>
<tr><td colspan="3">It evokes emotional responses.</td></tr>
</table>

## ▶ PERSONIFICATION [pəː,sɔnifi·keiʃən]

This term denotes a figure of speech in which inanimate or abstract things are referred to as if they were human beings. It is a kind of metaphor inasmuch as the inanimate thing is seen to have some similarity with human beings.

**Examples:**

- Justice is blind.
- Exploitation reared its ugly head.
- The moon stepped out of her mantle of cloud to smile momentarily upon us.
- Necessity is the mother of invention.
- England is the mother of Parliament.
- Philosophy is the mother of all arts.
- 'Come, sealing Night,
  Scarf up the tender eye of pitiful Day . . .' (Shakespeare)
- 'I am the daughter of Earth and Water' (Shelley)

### TA Personification

| | | |
|---|---|---|
| Eros<br>Cupid | represents<br>is a personification of<br>personifies | love |

| | | | | |
|---|---|---|---|---|
| Justice | is | represented<br>personified<br>embodied | as | a blindfolded woman |
| Love | | | | Cupid |

| | | |
|---|---|---|
| The author | represents<br>personifies<br>embodies | justice as a blindfolded woman |

► **ALLITERATION** [ə,litə'reiʃən]
(L ad- = 'to' + litera = 'letter')

It is the repetition of a consonantal sound, usually at the beginning, of two or more neighbouring words for the purpose of special emphasis. This stylistic device is mostly used to convey auditory images.

**Examples:**

– '**S**ister **S**usie's **s**ewing **s**ocks for **s**oldiers.'
– 'After life's **f**it**f**ul **f**ever, he sleeps well . . .' (Shakespeare)

### TA Alliteration

| | |
|---|---|
| In this sentence, four of the six words | alliterate (with each other)<br>form an alliteration<br>begin with alliterating letters |

► **REPETITION** [,repi'tiʃən]
(L re- = 'again' + petitionem = 'seeking')

Repetition of words or phrases is sometimes made use of for the purpose of emphasis.

**Example:**

'Scrooge was his **sole** executor, his **sole** administrator, his **sole** assign, his **sole** residuary legatee, **sole** friend, and **sole** mourner.' – (Dickens)

Repetition can easily be overdone. Besides, students should beware of it in their own essays, as its use is more likely to be penalized as bad style than regarded as an effective figure of speech!

**TA Repetition**

| | | | |
|---|---|---|---|
| This text abounds in | unnecessary<br>monotonous<br>emphatic | repetitions | |
| The author's use of repetition is | | monotonous<br>emphatic | |
| He is repetitive in what he says. | | | |
| He | uses<br>employs<br>resorts to | repetition for the purpose of | emphasis<br>persuasion |
| He uses repetition | to drive his argument home<br>to make his point more forcefully<br>to draw the reader's attention to . . . | | |

▶ **ACCUMULATION** [ə,kjuːmju'leiʃən]
(L ad- = 'to' + cumulus = 'heap'; 'heaping up')

Accumulation denotes the heaping up of similar words and phrases within a few lines.

**Example:**

'What a jovial and merry world this would be, may it please your worship, but for that inextricable labyrinth of debts, cares, woes, grief, discontent, melancholy, large jointures, impositions, and lies!'

(L. Sterne, *Tristram Shandy*)

**TA Accumulation**

| | | | |
|---|---|---|---|
| The author | uses<br>employs<br>resorts to | accumulation of | adjectives<br>clichés<br>examples<br>images |
| | accumulates | | |

▶ **PARALLELISM** ['pærəlelizm]
(Gk para- = 'beside' + allelon = 'one another')

Writers often make use of the device of parallelism: that is, they give two or more parts of the sentences a similar form so as to give the whole a definite pattern. This symmetry tends to produce an agreeable rhythm. It also helps to bring out the point of a paragraph – to emphasize a contrast, for example, by balancing some words or parts of speech against each other.

**Example:**

'**We charge him with** having broken his coronation-oath – *and we are told that he* kept his marriage-vow!
**We accuse him of** having given up his people to the merciless inflictions of the most hard-hearted of prelates – *and the defence is that he* took his little son on his knee and kissed him.
**We censure him for** having violated the articles of the Petition of Right – *and we are informed that he* was accustomed to hear prayers at six o'clock in the morning.' (Macauly)

**TA Parallelism**

<table>
<tr><td colspan="2">The author</td><td>uses<br>employs<br>forms</td><td colspan="2">parallelisms</td></tr>
<tr><td colspan="5">Parallelism occurs in . . .</td></tr>
<tr><td colspan="3">There are parallelisms of</td><td>words<br>structure</td><td>in the first paragraph</td></tr>
<tr><td>A</td><td>word<br>sentence</td><td colspan="3">is parallel to another</td></tr>
<tr><td colspan="5">Words are balanced against each other.</td></tr>
</table>

▶ **HYPERBOLE** [haiˈpəːbəli]
(Gk hyper = 'over, above, exceeding' + ballein = 'to throw'; exceeding a limit)

A hyperbole is a figure of speech using **exaggeration** – i.e. going beyond the limits of truth –, not to persuade or to deceive, but to emphasize a feeling or to produce a humorous effect. It is not intended to be taken literally.

**Examples:**

– 'I loved Ophelia: forty thousand brothers
Could not, with all their quantity of love,
Make up my sum.' (Shakespeare)

– 'I have been watching two gentlemen building a block of flats here in St John's Wood ... They have been on the job since 1940 and they can be perfectly sure that their children and grandchildren will have secure and permanent employment.' (George Mikes)

**TA Hyperbole, exaggeration**

| | | |
|---|---|---|
| The author | uses<br>employs<br>speaks in<br>writes in | hyperbole |
| The politician<br>The narrator | gives a hyperbolical | speech<br>description of ... |
| The statement ... is | an exaggeration<br>a hyperbole | |
| It is an exaggeration to | state<br>say<br>write | that ... |
| This text | abounds in<br>is full of<br>contains many | hyperboles<br>exaggerations |
| The author | makes exaggerative statements<br>falls into gross exaggerations | |

▶ **UNDERSTATEMENT** → Litotes

'Understatement' is the reverse of 'exaggeration': it is a statement below the truth. The author deliberately expresses an idea too weakly, either for the sake of moderation or for the purpose of irony. It should be noted, by the way, that the habit of understating things is a typical feature of the English language and of the English character on the whole.

**Example:**

– 'That's rather nice' may be an understatement for 'How delightful'.

– 'The Englishman understates his case. Had there been any Englishmen present at the original, biblical deluge, they could have looked round and remarked quietly: "Bit wet today, isn't it?"' (G. Mikes)

### ▶ LITOTES ['laitəuti:z, 'laitəti:z]
(Gk litos = 'plain, meagre')

A litotes, as a figure of speech, is a type of understatement which expresses an affirmative idea by the negation of its opposite, to give special emphasis to it.

**Examples:**

- 'Our success is due **in no small measure** (i.e. mainly due . . .) to the hard work done by Mr Thompson.'
- 'It was **not a bad party at all** (i.e. an excellent party).
- 'He's **no fool** (i.e. a very intelligent person).'

### TA Understatement, litotes

| | | | |
|---|---|---|---|
| The author | uses<br>employs | a litotes<br>an understatement | in line . . . |
| He rather understates the . . . | | | |
| It is an understatement to | state<br>say<br>write | that . . . | |
| What he really means is . . . | | | |

### ▶ EUPHEMISM ['ju:fimizm]
(Gk eu- = 'well' + pheme = 'speech')

Euphemism is a figure of speech intended to hide the real nature of something unpleasant or taboo by using a mild or indirect term for it. Sometimes, euphemism may be necessary to spare a person's feelings. But it often originates in prudery or a false sense of refinement.

**Examples:**

| | |
|---|---|
| – 'stomach' or 'tummy' | for 'belly' |
| – 'He expectorated.' | for 'He spat.' |
| – '. . . the underprivileged' | for '. . . the poor' |
| – 'He has passed away.' | for 'He has died.' |
| – 'Would you like to wash your hands?' | for 'Would you like to go to the toilet?' |

– 'How sleep the brave who sink to rest
By all their country's wishes blest!' (Collins)

**TA Euphemism**

| | | | | | |
|---|---|---|---|---|---|
| The author uses | pleasant<br>mild<br>vague<br>polite | expressions<br>terms | for | harsh<br>blunt<br>unpleasant<br>blasphemous<br>cruel | ones |

| | | | | |
|---|---|---|---|---|
| Instead of | telling the whole truth,<br>openly criticizing, | he | uses<br>employs<br>resorts to | euphemisms |

| |
|---|
| He avoids naming things directly |

▶ **PERIPHRASIS** [pəˈrifrəsis] or **circumlocution** [ˌsəːkəmləˈkjuʃn]
(Gk peri- = 'round, about' + phrazo = 'declare')
(L circum = 'round, about' + locutio = 'way of writing or speaking')

A periphrasis is a round-about way of saying a simple thing. It is used to avoid repetition or to lend dignity to a sentence, – sometimes even for humorous effect. It can, of course, lead to verbosity.

**Examples:**

'I am driven to the conclusion that the possibility of a lapse of memory on your part cannot be altogether dismissed as an utter impossibility.' (George Mikes gives this sentence as the equivalent of 'You are a damn liar', humorously adding that a foreigner has to spend some time in England before he understands such a periphrasis!)

'It cannot be denied that Lamb's most serious frailty was his habit of partaking too freely of alcoholic stimulants.' (= ... that he drank too much ...)

**TA Periphrasis, circumlocution**

| | |
|---|---|
| The author uses | periphrases<br>circumlocutions<br>round-about phrases |

| | | |
|---|---|---|
| He | expresses<br>says | something by periphrasis |

| | | |
|---|---|---|
| This sentence | is<br>contains<br>presents | a long periphrasis for ... |

| | |
|---|---|
| This is a round-about way of | putting things<br>saying that ... |

▶ **ELLIPSIS** [iˈlipsis], pl. ellipses [iˈlipsiːz]
(Gk en- = 'in' + leipo = 'leave'; something left out)

It is the shortening of a sentence by the omission of one or more words that may be easily understood from the context. It is in common use to avoid repetition but may also be used for artistic effect.

**Examples:**

**Normal usage:**

– 'All turned out as (had been) expected.

**As a stylistic figure:**

– I went to Oxford as one goes into exile; she to London.' (Wells)
– 'Coming in languidly, on the far side of the little Bay, nosing his sinuous way along – the eel.' (Strong)

**TA Ellipsis**

| | | | |
|---|---|---|---|
| The sentence '. . .' is elliptical | | | |
| The author uses | ellipsis for | poetic<br>comic | effect |
| | a crisp style abounding in ellipsis | | |

▶ **ALLUSION** [əˈluːʒən]
(L ad- = 'to' + ludo, lus = 'play'; G 'An-spielung')

An allusion is an implied indication. It denotes an indirect reference to people or things outside the text in which it occurs, without mentioning them in a straightforward way.

**Example:**

In an end-of-term speech, a headmaster might quote Goldsmith's famous lines, thus alluding to the best 'Abiturient' of the year:
'And still they gazed, and still the wonder grew
That one small head could carry all he knew.'

**TA Allusion**

| | | | | | |
|---|---|---|---|---|---|
| The author | repeatedly alludes<br>makes frequent allusions | to the Bible | | | |
| This | phrase<br>sentence<br>paragraph | is<br>contains | a(n) | obvious<br>obscure<br>ironic | allusion to |

▶ **PUN** = play on words

A pun is a – usually humorous – play on words having a similar sound but different meanings. The English language seems to lend itself to puns more than most languages because of its many homophones[1]) and homonyms[2]).

**Examples:**

'Is life worth **living**?' – 'It depends on the **liver**!'
Here the pun is based on the homonyms 1) 'liver' = 'one who lives' and 2) 'liver' = 'the glandular organ'.

'At the drunkard's funeral, four of his friends carried the **bier**.'
This time, the pun is based on the homophones 1) 'bier' = 'a movable stand on which a coffin is taken to grave' and 2) 'beer' = 'alcoholic drink'.
Homophones, being spelt differently, lose their ambiguity as soon as they are written or printed – and the joke falls flat. It is better to listen to such puns than to read them.

And this is the famous pun used by Lady Macbeth after her husband has murdered King Duncan:
'If he do bleed, I'll **gild** (1) the faces of the grooms withal, for it must seem their **guilt** (2).'
It is based on the homophones 1) 'to gild' = 'to smear with blood' (gold being thought of in Elizabethan times as red) and 2) 'guilt' = 'responsibility for wrong-doing'.

**TA Pun**

| | |
|---|---|
| There is a pun in a | phrase<br>sentence |

| | | | | | | |
|---|---|---|---|---|---|---|
| The author | uses<br>employs<br>makes | a(n) | funny<br>ingenious<br>subtle | pun | on<br>upon | the word in order to ... |

| | | |
|---|---|---|
| He puns on a | word<br>phrase | for ironical purposes<br>to attract the reader's attention |

---

1) A word with the same sound as another (Gk homo = 'like' + phon- = 'sound').
2) A word with the same form as another but with a different sense (Gk homo = 'like' + onyma = 'name').

▶ **PARADOX** [ˈpærədɔks, -iz] (pl paradoxes)
(Gk para = 'beside, beyond' + doxa = 'opinion')

A paradox is a statement that is seemingly contradictory or opposed to common sense, and may yet be found to contain some truth on closer examination.

**Examples:**

– Hasten slowly. (L Festina lente!)
– Mobilizing for peace.
– Paradoxically enough, the more terrible the prospect of thermonuclear war becomes, the less likely it is to happen.
– 'The child is father of the man.' (Wordsworth)
– 'He who goes against the fashion is himself its slave.' (L. P. Smith)
– 'The sober British worker does not waste his job by doing it.' (G. Mikes)
– 'We want none of your Lisson Grove prudery here, young woman. You've got to learn to behave like a duchess.' (G. B. Shaw, *Pygmalion*)
– 'So fair and foul a day I have not seen.' (Shakespeare, *Macbeth*)

**TA Paradox**

| | | | |
|---|---|---|---|
| The author | says<br>states<br>expresses | something | paradoxically<br>as a paradox<br>with apparent paradox |

| | | | |
|---|---|---|---|
| A | phrase<br>sentence | is<br>constitutes | a paradox |

| |
|---|
| Paradoxically enough, something is . . . |

▶ **CLIMAX** [ˈklaimæks, -iz] (pl. climaxes)
(Gk klimax = 'ladder')

A climax is a figure of speech in which a series of expressions rises step by step, beginning with the least important idea and ending with the most important. The term may also be used to refer only to the last expression in the series.
In the same way, climactic text structuring means arranging material in order of importance, with the most important arguments coming last.

**Examples:**

– 'Some books are to be tasted, others to be swallowed, and some few to be chewed and digested.' – (Bacon)

– 'For some men gambling leads to penury, penury to petty theft, petty theft to robbery, robbery to armed violence, and armed violence to murder.'

The climax of a story or play is a major turning point in its action or the point of greatest dramatic interest.

**TA Climax**

<table>
<tr><td colspan="2">The author brings</td><td colspan="2">a sentence<br>a paragraph<br>a development</td><td>to a climax</td></tr>
<tr><td colspan="5">He works the argument up to a climax</td></tr>
<tr><td colspan="2">A sentence<br>A paragraph</td><td colspan="2">leads to<br>rises to<br>develops to<br>comes to<br>reaches</td><td>a climax</td></tr>
<tr><td>The</td><td>ideas<br>sentences<br>arguments</td><td colspan="3">follow a climactic arrangement</td></tr>
<tr><td colspan="2">The author climaxes a</td><td colspan="2">paragraph<br>story</td><td>by . . .</td></tr>
<tr><td colspan="5">The paragraph climaxes in . . .</td></tr>
<tr><td>This</td><td>scene<br>dialogue<br>passage</td><td>is</td><td>the climax of<br>at the climax of</td><td>the story<br>the play</td></tr>
</table>

▶ **ANTICLIMAX** [ˌæntiˈklaimæks]
(Gk anti- = 'opposite, against' + klimax = 'ladder')

▶ **BATHOS** [beiθɔs]
(Gk = 'depth')

Both terms denote the sudden fall in writing or speaking from an idea of importance or dignity to something trifling or ridiculous in comparison, especially at the end of a series. This figure is sometimes deliberately used for humorous effect. Made unintentionally, the joke may be even greater – at the author's expense, of course! 'From the sublime to the ridiculous, there is only one step.' (Napoleon)

**Examples:**

– 'The love of God, justice and sports cars . . .'
– 'The bomb completely destroyed the new cinema, several dozen houses, the cathedral and my dustbin.'

**TA Anticlimax**

| | | | | |
|---|---|---|---|---|
| The | sentence<br>paragraph | introduces<br>leads up to | an anticlimax | |
| (A) | forms<br>is | a | sudden<br>humorous<br>ludicrous | anticlimax |

▶ **ANTITHESIS** [æn'tiθəsis; pl. -iːz] → Parallelism, balance
(Gk anti = 'against' + tithenai = 'to set'; = 'to set against one another'; cf. 'opposed' L opponere = 'gegenüberstellen')

As a rhetorical figure, antithesis denotes the opposing of ideas by means of grammatically parallel arrangements of words, clauses or sentences so as to produce an effective **contrast.**

**Examples:**

– People who never look **backward** to their *ancestors* will not look **forward** to *posterity.*
– '**God** made the *country* and **man** made the *town.*' (Cowper)
– 'True wit is Nature to advantage drest
  What **oft** was *thought,* but **ne'er** so well *exprest.*' (Pope)

**TA Antithesis**

| | | | |
|---|---|---|---|
| A) and B) | form<br>constitute | an antithesis<br>a contrast | |
| A word<br>A sentence<br>A paragraph | forms<br>constitutes | the antithesis<br>an antithesis<br>a contrast | to another one |
| The author effectively balances | | words<br>sentences<br>paragraphs<br>ideas | against each other |

## 5.2 RHETORICAL FIGURES IN COMPOSITION

Any deviation from what is considered to be the natural organization of a text – e.g. time order, space order, topical order, cause-effect order, problem-solution order – may have the purpose of arousing the particular interest of the listener or reader.

▶ **FLASHBACK** → Anticipation
(= 'Rückblende')

The flashback is a literary or theatrical technique – often used in narrations, in films or television – that involves the interruption of the chronological sequence of events. At this point, earlier scenes or events are interjected, giving a vivid picture of the (hero's) past.

**Example:**

> '"My son!" groaned the boss. But no tears came yet. In the past, in the first months and even years after the boy's death, he had only to say those words to be overcome by such grief that nothing short of a violent fit of weeping could relieve him. Time, he had declared then, he had told everybody, could make no difference.'
>
> (K. Mansfield, *The Fly*)

▶ **ANTICIPATION** [æn,tisiˈpeiʃən] → Flashback
(L ante = 'before' + capere = 'to take'; = 'Vorwegnahme')

The anticipation as a stylistic technique is the reverse of the flashback. The author interrupts the chronological sequence of events to present or allude to events which will happen in the relative future. His aim is to make developments transparent, quite often with emotional overtones.

**Example:**

> 'As for the child, he would see that it was cared for: he would never forsake it; he would do everything but own it.'
>
> (George Eliot, *Silas Marner*)

**TA Flashback, anticipation**

<table>
<tr><td rowspan="2">The author</td><td>employs<br>makes (frequent) use of</td><td>flashbacks<br>anticipation</td><td rowspan="2">(in order to . . .)</td></tr>
<tr><td colspan="2">flashbacks (in a masterly way)<br>backflashes<br>anticipates</td></tr>
<tr><td colspan="4">The (hero's) past recurs in a series of flashbacks</td></tr>
</table>

▶ **DIGRESSION** [dai'greʃən] → diversion
(L dis = 'not' + gressus from gradior = 'step'; = 'not in step')
(cf. G 'Exkurs' = 'out of step')

Digression denotes the act of departing from the main compositional plan in a discourse or any other organized literary work. It is meant mainly to entertain the audience or to distract from the real problem. Occasionally, it may help to support the arguments inasmuch as the main topic is exposed under a new aspect.

**Example:**

In his novel *Tristram Shandy,* Laurence Sterne, being aware of spending more time on digressions than on the actual story of his hero, thus comments upon his own technique: 'Digressions, incontestably, are the sunshine; they are the life, the soul of reading; take them out of this book, for instance, you might as well take the book along with them; one cold eternal winter would reign in every page of it.'

**TA Digression**

| | | | |
|---|---|---|---|
| The author provides<br>The text is interrupted by | a lengthy digression about . . . | | |
| The author | digresses<br>wanders away | from the main | subject<br>theme<br>topic |
| The text is amusingly digressive. | | | |

See also: → **Parallelism**
→ **Antithesis**
→ **Climax**

## 5.3 RHETORICAL FIGURES IN ARGUMENTATION: FALLACIES

A text which contains some of the following tricks of rhetorical argumentation, i.e. fallacies ['fæləsiz] (L fallax = 'deceiving') reveals that the author is not being honest: he may either try to hide something or he may even be a fanatical one-sided ideologist who tries to fool and deceive the public in a demagogical way.

▶ **SPECIOSITY** [spiːʃiˈɔsiti] → Sophistry
(L speciosus = 'beautiful; pretending to be fair')

Speciosity denotes arguments which are deceptively pleasing in form or look, i.e. superficially fair and correct, but are not so in reality. A specious argument, or sophism, is one that sounds plausible and reasonable enough but does not bear close inspection.

**Example:**

A student once did not feel like going to school and decided to make a day-trip to the mountains instead. The following day he said to his teacher: 'I am very sorry it was literally impossible for me to do my homework in the afternoon, since I couldn't even attend school in the morning.'
This is a specious excuse because it is meant to give the teacher the impression that the student was seriously ill.

▶ **SOPHISTRY** [ˈsɔfistri] → Speciosity
(Gk sophos = 'wise'; sophistes = 'teacher of rhetoric')

Sophistry denotes specious argumentation, i.e. clever reasoning intended to deceive. Such arguments are called sophisms. The term goes back to a class of teachers of philosophy and rhetoric in ancient Greece who developed an elaborate system of argumentation. They taught their pupils how to support **any** thesis by means of subtle, often false reasoning which seems correct at first sight but is actually fallacious.

**TA Speciosity, sophistry**

| | | |
|---|---|---|
| The author | employs<br>makes use of | specious arguments<br>sophisms |
| His reasoning is<br>His arguments are | rather specious<br>fallacious | |

▶ **BEGGING THE QUESTION** / petitio principii (= assumption of the beginning)

'Begging the question' is a fallacy assuming the truth of the very thing being argued about or to be proved.

**Example:**

If somebody argues that laws are unnecessary because a country could be better run without them, his (false) argument is in fact that laws are unnecessary because they are unnecessary. He does not prove anything, he is only begging the question.

The same trick is used in **assumptive phrases** (L ad-sumere = 'annehmen' = 'to take for granted') which verbally imply what is to be proved by sound argument, such as:

– 'It is beyond doubt that . . .'
– 'It is only too clear that . . .'
– 'No thoughtful person will deny the fact that . . .'
– 'Any honest person will concede that . . .'
– 'Ladies and Gentlemen, I sincerely feel that . . .'

► **ARGUING IN A CIRCLE** / petitio principii (= 'assumption of the beginning')

This is the same fallacy as → 'begging the question', since the author who argues in a circle simply takes for granted in the premise what is to be proved or demonstrated: he uses a premise (an assumption made for the purpose of the argument) to prove a conclusion, and then uses the conclusion to prove the premise. This fallacy is quite obvious in short texts, but it may be less transparent or somewhat concealed in longer ones.

**Example:**

'To allow every man an **unbounded freedom of speech** must be *advantageous to the state,* for it is highly *conducive to the interests of the community* that each individual should enjoy **complete liberty in expressing his sentiments'.**
(Here the author conceals his circular argument by using different words, or highflown periphrases, for the same thing in the decisive places:
unbounded freedom = complete liberty . . .
advantageous to the state = conducive to the interests of the community)

**TA Begging the question, arguing in a circle**

| | | | |
|---|---|---|---|
| The author | is begging the question<br>obviously argues in a circle | when stating | that . . . |
| It is a mere assumption to state | | | |
| The author obviously | assumes<br>takes for granted<br>goes on the assumption | | |

▶ **NON SEQUITUR**
(L = 'it does not follow')

In argumentation, the 'non sequitur' is an illogical inference, also called 'the fallacy of false cause': the speaker/writer draws a wrong conclusion from the premises.

**Example:**

'Driving on the motorway gives Mr Smith a headache.
At the moment he has a headache.
Therefore he has been driving on the motorway.'

This inference is unjustified: the cause of the headache may be driving on the motorway, but it can also be indigestion, lying in the sun, influenza, etc.'

**TA Non sequitur**

| | |
|---|---|
| The author draws a wrong conclusion from the fact that . . . | |
| His inference is unjustified | |
| He wrongly infers<br>He is wrong in inferring | that . . . |

▶ **FALSE ANALOGY** → Analogy

▶ **AMBIGUITY** [ˌæmbigˈjuiti] = Equivocation
(L ambo = 'both' + agere = 'to drive' = 'moving in two directions')

An ambiguity is sometimes unintentional. In deceptive rhetoric, however, it is the deliberate wording of a phrase or passage in such a way that it can be taken in two ways.

▶ **EQUIVOCATION** [iˌkwivəˈkeiʃən] → = Ambiguity → Innuendo
(L aequus = 'equal' + vox = 'voice' = 'with two meanings equally possible')

Equivocation denotes a form of speaking or writing that is intentionally vague, ambiguous or evasive. 'A lie may be told by silence, by equivocation, by a glance of the eye' (John Ruskin). And sure enough, equivocation is a way of expressing things which helps to hide the truth, or, as William Penn puts it, it is 'half way to lying, as lying is the whole way to hell.'

**Example:**

Being asked his opinion of Italians, Mr Benson replied: 'It takes all sorts to make a world.'
This answer is equivocal, leaving the questioner in doubt as to his real views.

**TA Ambiguity, equivocation**

<table>
<tr><td>Mr A's</td><td>statement<br>answer</td><td>is</td><td rowspan="2">ambiguous<br>equivocal</td></tr>
<tr><td colspan="3">The wording of this passage is deliberately</td></tr>
<tr><td>There is an</td><td>ambiguity<br>equivocation</td><td colspan="2">in the first paragraph</td></tr>
<tr><td colspan="4">The fallacy in this text arises from the ambiguous use of . . .</td></tr>
</table>

## ▶ RHETORICAL QUESTION

(Gk rhetor = 'orator'; 'rhetorical' = characteristic of an efficient 'orator')

A rhetorical question is a statement turned, for the sake of effect, into a question to which no answer is expected. This very common rhetorical figure somehow shifts the speech into a dialogue so as to give the listener the false impression that he is actively taking part in a debate, and persuade him to accept the argument more readily.

**Examples:**

'Who does not love his country?'
(= Of course, everybody loves his country)
'Who wishes a despotic government?'
(= Of course, no one wishes a despotic government)
'Who doesn't want to go on holiday?'
(= Of course, everybody wants to go on holiday)

**Note** that rhetorical questions are not necessarily fallacies: they are often used by orators to bring liveliness into their speeches.

## ▶ EMOTIVE LANGUAGE → Argumentum ad hominem, ad populum

Emotive language is intended to play on the irrational feelings of the hearer/reader. It is often used instead of logical argument in order to influence the hearer's judgement. Such words as 'true', 'honest', 'sound', 'proper', 'good', 'bad', for example, are sometimes misused and need wary watching on the part of the listener.

▶ **IRRELEVANCY** [iˈrelivənsi]
(L in = 'not' + relatus = 'connected', = 'not to the point')

Irrelevancy, a common form of fallacy, is the deliberate diversion of attention from the matter in dispute. Lacking sound arguments, a dishonest or demagogical writer or speaker will often resort to the following tricks of rhetoric: in order to sway the hearer, he will try to blur his intellectual understanding by

1) flattering him (→ argumentum ad hominem)
2) diverting his attention (→ evasion, → diversion)

▶ **ARGUMENTUM AD HOMINEM** [ˈaːgjumentəm æd ˈhɔminəm]

He may first appeal to the particular self-interests, sympathies and prejudices of the person concerned, and, for that purpose, resort to → emotive language.

**Examples:**

- 'Of course, **you** are not in favour of raising the taxes as planned by the Government'
- 'Only a bright young man like **you** can do such a job. But Mr. X, your colleague, is just the sort of moron to doubt it.'

▶ **ARGUMENTUM AD POPULUM** [ˈaːgjumentəm æd ˈpɔpjuləm]

In case of a larger audience, the speaker may play on the emotions of a whole group, crowd, social class or nation.

**Examples:**

- 'This policy is directed against the innermost interests of the working-classes.'
- 'Such a law would be unfair to women.'
- 'It is un-English to do anything like that.'
- 'In these days of hardships, let us all be guided not by the head, but by the heart – the great heart of humankind.'

**TA Argumentum ad hominem, ad populum; emotive language**

<table>
<tr><td rowspan="2">The speaker</td><td>appeals to<br>plays on</td><td>the audience's<br>the hearer's</td><td>interests<br>sympathies<br>prejudices</td></tr>
<tr><td>exploits<br>knows how to manipulate</td><td>the instincts<br>the emotions<br>the hopes<br>the fears</td><td>of the audience</td></tr>
</table>

▶ **EVASION** [iˈveiʒən]
(ex = 'out' + vadere = 'to go' = 'to escape')

The speaker may 'evade the point' altogether, i.e. deliberately avoid answering a question or stating his position directly and candidly.

**Example:**

> 'In spite of all his wrigglings, evasions and sophistries, he was forced to come back to the point by his opponent in the debate.'

▶ **DIVERSION** [daiˈvəːʃn]
(L dis = 'asunder, away' + vertere, versum = 'to turn', = 'to turn aside, to go a different way')

A demagogue will often, instead of tackling the problem openly, try to draw away the attention of the opponent or that of the audience from the main point of discussion. The contention is not refuted; instead, the speaker simply goes on to quite a different issue.

**Example:**

> "'What is going to happen to all that milk?' said someone. 'Never mind the milk, comrades!' cried Napoleon . . . 'The harvest is more important . . .'
> So the animals trooped down to the hayfield to begin the harvest, and when they came back in the evening it was noticed that the milk had disappeared."

(Orwell, *Animal Farm*)

**TA Evasion, diversion**

<table>
<tr><td rowspan="2">The speaker</td><td colspan="2">evades</td><td colspan="2">the question<br>the point</td></tr>
<tr><td colspan="2">fails to answer<br>avoids answering</td><td colspan="2">the question</td></tr>
<tr><td rowspan="2">He</td><td colspan="2">makes a diversion</td><td></td><td rowspan="2">by saying that . . .</td></tr>
<tr><td colspan="2">turns the attention from<br>diverts the audience from<br>distracts the audience from</td><td>the main issue</td></tr>
<tr><td>His</td><td>answer<br>remark</td><td>is</td><td colspan="2">irrelevant<br>not to the point</td></tr>
</table>

▶ **DISTORTION** [disˈtɔːʃn]
(L distorquere = 'to twist')

A more artful trick than those listed so far is the distortion of the opponent's assertion, or the extension of a statement beyond what he means. It is easy, then, to discredit him for something he did not really say.

**Example:**

Mr A: 'I am strongly in favour of abolishing nuclear **bombs**!'
Mr B: 'Mr A fails to see and concede that to abolish nuclear **fission** means to prevent progress.'

**TA Distortion**

<table>
<tr><td rowspan="2">He</td><td colspan="2">extends the opponent's assertion</td><td rowspan="2">when stating that . . .</td></tr>
<tr><td>distorts the opponent's</td><td>thoughts<br>motives</td></tr>
</table>

▶ **INSINUATION** [in,sinjuˈeiʃən]

▶ **INNUENDO** [ˌinjuːˈendəu, -z]
(L in + nuere = 'to nod' = G 'ein-nickend' = 'implying by nodding')

The insinuation, or innuendo, is a sly and backbiting fallacy which consists in a veiled or equivocal allusion reflecting on the reputation, ability, character of the person referred to. It is an indirect suggestion of something unpleasant, but unverified and unproved.

**Examples:**

– 'I do not know him very well, so perhaps I had better not say too much about him.'
– 'It is curious that Mrs Smith is now wearing a watch similar to the one lost by my wife.'
– 'The bank was robbed some time ago. Haven't you noticed that the Joneses have got heaps of money all of a sudden?'

▶ **SUGGESTIO FALSI** [səˈdʒestiəu fɔːlsai]
(L = 'the suggestion of an untruth')

A suggestio falsi is the → insinuation of something untrue. It may be a statement that is not necessarily untrue in itself but implies something that is.

**Example:**

Mrs Smith: 'The Joneses are living as husband and wife, but are they really married?'
Mrs Black: 'Thank goodness we're more tolerant these days than we used to be.'

Mrs Black thus leaves Mrs Smith under the false impression that she knows the Joneses not to be married.

It is obvious that insinuations of that sort (just as, to some degree, distortions of statements) only aim at damaging the reputation of the person or group concerned. They overstep the limits of permissible rhetoric, and a speaker who makes use of them runs the risk of being charged with **slander** by his opponent.

**TA Insinuation, suggestio falsi**

<table>
<tr><td rowspan="2">The author</td><td colspan="3">insinuates that . . .</td></tr>
<tr><td>tries to undermine X by</td><td colspan="2">sly insinuations<br>innuendos</td></tr>
<tr><td colspan="2">The electoral campaign was punctuated by</td><td>innuendos<br>insinuations</td><td>on both sides</td></tr>
</table>

▶ **SUPPRESSIO VERI** [sə'presiəu 'viːrai]
(L = 'the suppression of a truth')

This means deliberately concealing facts which might be to the disadvantage of the speaker or to the benefit of his adversary.

▶ **PERSUASIVE DEFINITION**
(L persuadere = 'to persuade')

As the etymology reveals, a persuasive definition, often used in persuasive argumentation, is not aimed at fixing the exact, objective meaning of a word. Instead, the speaker deliberately shifts that meaning in order to get his opponent round to his opinion.

**Example:**

A beatle fan who is out to persuade his grandfather that pop music is better than classical music employs the following persuasive definition: 'Pop music is really classical music free of artificial constraint.'

# 6. TEXT PRODUCTION

The study of rhetoric has been described as the study of the best ways to define, develop, arrange and support one's ideas in order to achieve one's purpose. A closer study of rhetoric is therefore not only apt to develop a sense of awareness in the reader as necessary for text comprehension, text analysis and appreciation; it will also provide the writer with the most effective options or choices in terms of rhetoric when producing a text of his own. It will show him how to present his ideas in a clear and simple, yet effective way – in oral and in written communication.

Although this section will concentrate on text production proper, you can, of course, make use of the subsequent material and tables for purposes of text analysis and appreciation as well, provided you adapt them to your specific needs.

## 6.1 WHAT YOU AS A WRITER OR SPEAKER MUST KEEP IN MIND

Whenever you wish to produce a rhetorically efficient text of your own, you must keep the following aspects of the process of communication in mind:

1) the sender (i.e. the writer or speaker);
2) the addressee (i.e. the reader or hearer);
3) the purpose of your text;
4) its topic and topical coherence;
5) the structuring of your text, i.e. its outline and functional coherence.

### 6.1.1 The sender

- What are **your qualifications** to deal with the subject as a speaker or writer?
- Is the information you give comprehensive, up to date, realiable and convincing? – **Gather information!**
- How can you express and present your ideas in the most intelligible, consistent and convincing form? – **Define key-terms! Present your ideas in a consistent and convincing order!**

### 6.1.2 The addressee

- Is the reader or hearer likely to be interested in the topic(s) or will you have to **arouse his interest** – particularly in the introduction, but, in fact, throughout the text?
- Are the readers' or hearers' qualifications above, equal to or below your standard? – **Use an adequate register**, taking the addressee, the situation and your purpose into account!

### 6.1.3 Your purpose

- What is your **main purpose**? – Do you mainly intend:
  - to **inform or instruct** the reader or hearer;
  - to **entertain** him;
  - to **explain** how you see and interpret a certain situation (expository writing);
  - to **persuade or convince** him to adopt your views (argumentative writing)?
- **Choose the adequate text type and text form!**

### 6.1.4 Topic and topical coherence

- What is your **topic** exactly? – **State and define it in clear terms!**
- Bearing the restricted time and space available in mind, do you have to narrow or **limit your topic**:
  - by deliberately considering only one aspect;
  - by limiting it in point of time or space;
  - by simplifying or generalizing?
- What is the **central idea**, the gist, **of your message**?
  - State it in **one topic sentence** in the introduction or some other prominent place of your text.
  - Guarantee **topical coherence** throughout the main body by repeating topical terms.
  - **Reinforce the central idea in your conclusion** by restating – in epigrammatic form! – the gist of your message.

### 6.1.5 Text structuring and functional coherence

- How can you – in your introduction, particularly in longer texts – **inform the reader about your intended procedure**, i.e. the outline of your text and your text structuring?
- How can you guarantee **functional coherence**, i.e.

  - **develop your ideas step by step,**
  - provide appropriate **transitions** and
  - effective **long-distance and short-distance connectives** between individual ideas and supporting material?
- How can you **draw clear conclusions** from preceding material or arguments?

The above survey of the process of communication shows that some of the aspects have been dealt with in the preceding sections of this book; others – and this is shown by experience! – do not cause any real trouble. So the subsequent chapters of this section can concentrate on those three aspects which are fundamental to most texts – irrespective of text type or text form:

1) **How to make ideas clear**
2) **How to develop ideas or support arguments**
3) **How to organize or structure ideas** and how to achieve functional coherence

Special emphasis will thereby be laid on the specific difficulties for foreign students at an advanced stage, particularly on **how to achieve topical and functional coherence.**

## 6.2 HOW TO MAKE IDEAS CLEAR

Each writer or speaker must be aware that the reader or hearer will – at one point or other – ask the inquisitive question:

'What do you mean exactly?'

No matter whether you try to determine the meaning of a certain word or phrase in a text or whether you want to define a key-term for your own expository or argumentative writing, you must always use a language which is likely to be understood by an average reader or hearer.

Before presenting the various techniques of determining the range of meaning of individual words, terms or notions, it is necessary to show you how to incorporate these 'explanations' into the context. This may be achieved by their statement or restatement.

### 6.2.1 Statement of 'explanations'

The following linking phrases may help you to incorporate 'explanations' into your writing:

**TP Statement of explanations**

<table>
<tr><td rowspan="2">Here<br>In this sense<br>In this context<br>As used by<br>Mr X</td><td rowspan="2">the</td><td rowspan="2">word<br>term<br>phrase</td><td rowspan="2">'....'</td><td colspan="3">means '......'<br>means that ......<br>denotes .....</td></tr>
<tr><td>is best</td><td>defined<br>described<br>determined</td><td>as ...</td></tr>
<tr><td colspan="4">The term '.....', often read or heard,</td><td colspan="3">means '......'<br>denotes '....'</td></tr>
<tr><td colspan="3">Speaking of '....', we</td><td colspan="4">mean '......'<br>refer to '........'</td></tr>
</table>

### 6.2.2 Reformulation and restatement of explanations

In fact, it takes time for some statement to sink in, to be fully grasped or even to be accepted. Any sort of restatement will at this stage give the reader or hearer a fair chance of better understanding – irrespective of the type of reformulation. Some may just give the reader time to breathe in an otherwise concise text, as in the following instance: 'I think so; **in fact,** I am quite sure.'; others contain the classical techniques of determining the range of meaning of words, such as synonyms, antonyms or definitions. No matter which you want to incorporate into your writing, the following linking phrases may be of some help to you.

**6.2.2 Reformulation and restatement of 'explanations'**

- I think so; **in fact**, I am quite sure.
- Only one boy was absent, **namely** Henry.
- This is a fine place for a vacation; **indeed,** it is the best I have found so far.
- Britain had many colonies; **as a matter of fact**, they covered 40 per cent of the globe.
- It wasn't a very good dinner, **to say the least of it** (= without saying more!).
- He was not to be trusted; **in other words**, he was a liar.
- **Another way of putting it** would be to state in straighforward terms that he was a criminal.
- From then on, he did not make an effort, **that is (to say)** he let himself drift.
- The four text types are manifested in actual text forms, **i.e.** in short-stories, novels, etc.

p. t. o.

– He came home very late last night, { **or better** / **or rather** / **or** } early in the morning.

– A narration is a composition in chronological order, or, { **to put it (more) simply,** / **in simple words/terms,** / **in simpler words/terms,** } the telling of a story.

– A narration is the telling of a story, or, { **technically speaking,** / **to put it more exactly,** / **to give a definition,** / **according to (authority),** } a composition in chronological order.

– He is mad; **scientifically speaking** he suffers from a neurosis.

**▶ How to determine the meaning of individual terms and notions**

Various procedures are available to achieve this aim. A term may be defined by means of synonyms, antonyms, definitions, etymologies, or enumerations. In addition, a notion may be 'unfolded' thus giving rise to a longer explanation – or explication (→ expository texts) – in which the author will often resort to comparisons.

### 6.2.3 Synonym ['sinənim]

(Gk syn = 'together' + onyma = 'name')

A synonym is a word or term that is similar in meaning to another so that it can be substituted for it in a statement without essentially changing its sense. Most of the time, synonymous terms are not exactly equivalent. For this reason, it is sometimes necessary to modify them by means of adverbs. The word 'delighted', for instance, is synonymous with 'greatly pleased'. Moreover, beware that the term substituted may belong to a different register.

Synonym: [x] ≈ [a]

**TP Synonym**

– 'Wary' **means roughly the same as** 'cautious'.

– 'Wary' **is** { **synonymous with** / **a synonym of** } 'cautious'.

– **A synonym of** 'wary' **is** 'cautious'.

It depends on the context which of these terms best renders the meaning of 'wary': 'cautious', 'wide-awake', 'alert', 'heedful', 'prudent', 'careful', 'watchful' or 'considerate'.

### 6.2.4 Antonym [ˈæntənim]

(Gk anti = 'the opposite of' + onyma = 'name, word')

An antonym is a word or term which has roughly the opposite meaning of the word that is to be explained.

antonym: $\boxed{x} \not\approx \boxed{a}$

**TP Antonym**

- **An antonym of** 'wary' **is** 'careless'.
- 'Careless' is { **an antonym of** / **the opposite of** } 'wary'.
- 'Wary' **is opposite in meaning to** 'careless'.

Again, it depends on the context which of the following terms is the most exact antonym: 'careless', 'incautious', 'rash', 'impulsive' or 'inconsiderate'.

### 6.2.5 The Aristotelian or genus-differentia definition

[ði: ˌæristɔˈtiːliən ɔː ˈdʒiːnəs ˌdifəˈrenʃiə ˌdefiˈniʃən]
(L de = 'from' + finis = 'end, limits' = 'to establish the boundaries or range of something')

Employing the genus-differentia definition, the writer establishes the range of meaning by

1) indicating the genus or class that includes it in the **inclusive term** (L genus proximum, G 'Oberbegriff') and
2) adding the **specific differences** or distinguishing marks (L differentia specifica, G 'Einengung').

Aristotelian definition: $\boxed{x} \approx \boxed{A} \pm \boxed{a_1}\boxed{a_2}\boxed{a_3}$

**Examples:**

- An hour (x) is the 24th ($a_1$) part ($a_2$) of the day (A).
- A chair (x) is a movable ($a_1$) seat (A) that is designed to accommodate one person ($a_2$ : purpose) and usually has four legs ($a_3$) and a back ($a_4$).

The following questions may help you to arrive at the distinguishing marks:

1) What does x consist of?
2) What does x look like?
3) What is its purpose?

With some words, the **etymology** may contribute to make the meaning much more transparent. Very often, an additional **example or illustration** will also help to make the notion more vivid and concrete.

**Example:**

Speaking of 'metaphysics' (Gk meta = 'after' + physika = 'the things of nature, physics'), we refer to the branch of philosophy that is concerned with the things beyond external nature: so it deals with the very nature of existence, truth, knowledge and the question of God.

### 6.2.6 Enumeration [iˌnjuːməˈreiʃən]

(L ex + numerare = G 'Auf-zählung')

An enumeration is best used when an inclusive class term is to be explained. The number and characteristics of its constituent elements is then given in detail.

Enumeration: $\boxed{X} \approx \boxed{a_1}\,\boxed{a_2}\,\boxed{a_3} \cdots \boxed{a_n}$

**Example:**

**Speaking of furniture (X), we refer to (we mean)** convenient or decorative **articles, such as** tables ($a_1$), chairs ($a_2$), wardrobes ($a_3$), desks ($a_4$), etc, needed in living quarters or offices.

### 6.2.7 The long definition or explication

(L ex-plicare = 'to unfold, to explain'; G 'entfalten')

The types of explanation treated so far serve two purposes:

1) in text production, to give some preliminary idea of the key-terms of the subject in the introduction;

2) in text analysis and appreciation, to determine the author's or a person's concept of certain facts, ideas or events.

If the gap of information between the author and the reader is too wide, the expert author must try to give the somewhat uninformed reader a clear idea of his subject in an expository text.
This is how Kenneth J. Heller tries explain, or 'explicate', to students who have not before realized the complexity of language studies some of the most important aspects of linguistics:

**Example** **What is Language?**

'First, language is a set of sounds. This is also true of animal communications, but the system of communication which is most strikingly like language, that of bees, is a set of body movements, not sounds.
Second, the connection of sounds and objects is arbitrary. Not even words which imitate the sounds of objects are the same in different languages: a cock goes cock-a-doodle-doo in English, cocorico in French and kikeriki in German. This means that the sounds of speech are passed on to all members of any community by older members of that community. Language is a social activity. On the other hand, a cat mews and purrs even if cut off from all other cats. Animal communication is instinctive not social.
Third, language is systematic. Language elements are systematically arranged in recurrent patterns. Any sentence is a set of elements in which the individual elements can be substituted. A parrot may be able to say 'Birds can talk' but he can never go on from here and form sentences like 'People can talk' or 'Birds can fly'. His utterance is a unit, human language is a substitution frame.
Fourth, language is a set of symbols. We can talk about things which are not present, e.g. apples which are not in the room. Language which occurs without an immediately present stimulus is called 'displaced speech'. It is what enables us to know something of the past and of the world beyond our range of vision and hearing at a given moment. Animals are incapable of displaced speech.
Fifth, language is complete. All human language has been found to be so elaborate that its speakers can make a language response to any experience they may undergo. On the other hand bees cannot make an utterance equivalent to 'The beekeeper is coming'. Even in a language like ancient Greek that has no word for car a speaker would have been perfectly capable of describing an automobile or of coining a new word for it had he seen one. The vocabulary of a language is always expansible, always 'open' – except in languages that have gone out of use'.

(*Modern Life*, p. 73: Special contribution by Kenneth J. Heller)

### 6.2.8 Making ideas clear by means of → comparison

(L cum = 'with' + par = 'equal' = 'to show the similarities between A and B')

If a writer or speaker wants to explain complex facts, ideas, events, institutions or problems to somebody who has not yet much insight, he can compare them to something similar the reader or hearer can be expected to be familiar with. In a narrower sense, the term comparison denotes the listing of similarities; in a wider sense, it may also include some differences. When comparing two things, keep in mind that there is no absolutely correct comparison between two phenomena; demagogues, for that very reason, often use false → analogies to manipulate the audience.

**Examples:**

See how Janet Ross and Gladys Doty, in their essay on rhetoric, succeed in giving the reader a clear idea of the process of writing by extensively comparing it to the work done by an architect. (→ exposition, pp. 97 f.).
See also 'The Royal Referee' (*Modern Life*, p. 180), where the task of an English monarch is compared to that of a football referee.

### 6.2.9 How to ensure topical coherence,

or how to make your train of thought consistent and conspicuous throughout your writing.

1) State your topic clearly in the introduction: starting from background information, 'zoom in' and focus the reader's attention on the central idea. State it in one topical sentence in affirmative form.
2) Remind the reader of your topic repeatedly throughout your composition. Convenient points to do so will be when you move from one main item to another or when you go on from one type of developing or supporting material to another, e.g. from examples to quotations.
3) Restate your topic in epigrammatic and memorable form in the conclusion.

**Example:**

Note how topical coherence has been guaranteed in the following text: (The relevant words and phrases are set out in bold type)

**'Of all the subjects I have studied in high school, Latin has proven most valuable to me. It** has increased my knowledge in many fields. Through the intensive study of **Latin words and forms**, I have been able to expand my English vocabulary, for many of our English words are **derived from Latin**. I have also learned **grammar and sentence construction** since **the study of Latin** involves concentrated work on both of these subjects. **Latin** has given me **an understanding of ancient Rome,** which has had a great influence on our own civilization. **Through Latin** I have become familiar with the lives and accomplishments of **great Roman orators, poets and generals** such as Cicero, Virgil and Caesar. I have also gained **a knowledge of mythology**, a subject which is all around us in the form of paintings, statues, operas, and even current Broadway plays. Although many consider **the study of Latin** a waste of time, **I believe that I could not possibly have put my time to better use than I did in learning Latin.**

(From Warriner's *English Grammar and Composition,* p. 355)

In this text, it was quite easy to ensure topical coherence since the passage is short and concentrates on **one clear topic: 'The benefit you get from studying Latin at school.'** It goes without saying that the process of subordinating ideas and incorporating supporting material into a longer text is much more difficult and needs special attention and practice.

## 6.3 HOW TO DEVELOP IDEAS OR SUPPORT ARGUMENTS BY MEANS OF FACTS, DETAILS, EXAMPLES, ILLUSTRATIONS, STATISTICS, AND QUOTATIONS FROM AUTHORITIES

to answer the reader's or hearer's ever-present questions:

1) How do you know?
2) Why do you think so?

Since the reader is not likely to have the same range of experience as you, he will always tend to question even those conclusions which seem to be safe and sound to you, because you based them on the experience **you** have made in life, in other words, on what you have read, seen or heard.

To persuade or to convince the reader of the conclusiveness of your reasoning, you must consequently place him in a position to retrace and verify your steps of experience.

### 6.3.1 Give indisputable facts and details to develop your ideas or to support your arguments

Facts are statements of things that exist or have been done. They can be verified and thus help you to illustrate your ideas or to support your arguments in concrete terms so as to make them more plausible to the reader or hearer.

In an essay on Thomas Carlyle you might mention the following facts taken from *The Oxford Companion to English Literature,* for example, thus showing that you have conscientiously gathered information on the subject and that your essay deserves to be trusted.

**Example:**

'Thomas Carlyle (1795–1881) was born at Ecclefechan, in Dumfriesshire, of peasant stock. He was educated at the parish school, then at Annan Academy, and at the age of 15 entered Edinburgh University. He was subsequently a schoolmaster at Annan and Kirkcaldy, but soon took to literary work, contributing to Brewster's 'Edinburgh Encyclopaedia', studying German literature, and writing his 'Life of Schiller', which appeared in the 'London Magazine' in 1823–4 and was separately published in 1825.'

### 6.3.2 Give examples and illustrations so that the reader can imagine what you are talking about

When presenting, or, arguing on, complex problems, do not merely speak in abstract terms, but make use of examples and illustrations. They will help you to make things clear and make the point in your line of argumentation, since

1) they make your presentation more vivid by stimulating the reader's imagination,
2) often contain human interest aspects and
3) help the reader or hearer to grasp problems much more clearly after understanding one concrete instance.

**Example:**

'A work of art must communicate a kind of philosophy, make me laugh or cry. I've been dubbed a 'social' painter. I feel that anyone who puts brush to paper is a social painter. Every fear and hope and desire of mankind is my particular interest. In 'The Red Stairway', **for example,** the crippled man is climbing upward. I wanted to say something about the indestructibility of mankind.'

(American painter Ben Shahn on his art; slightly adapted)

### 6.3.3 Quote figures or statistics to make your point

Statistics – i.e. figures inferred from scientifically chosen instances of a matter – provide sensible information, if they are relevant, reliable and representative.

**Note:** To carry conviction, figures must be presented correctly and effectively, in other words:

1) they must be up to date,
2) they must be accurate,
3) they must come from a reliable and verifiable source (which must be given) and
4) they must be presented in a rememberable form, e.g. 'half a million, exactly 496,786'.

Study how R. R. Pedley in the following article *Comprehensive Disaster* has made use of statistics to prove the inefficiency of comprehensive schools. Note especially how he makes his point in the last few lines.

**Example:**

> '. . . Certainly, judged by such 'productivity' criteria as public examination results, university scholarships, university acceptances, the prospects of the bright children in comprehensive schools are by no means bright. One of the more fashionable comprehensive schools is Wandsworth in London – its 'successes' were bandied about the 'House of Commons' in 1965 – Wandsworth, in fact, claims an 'academic' intake of 120. This school 'succeeded' in 1964 in gaining 40 boys 2 or more A-level passes. In the same year Chislehurst and Sidcup, also with an academic intake of 120, produced 105 boys with 2 A-level passes. 24 boys left Wandsworth for universities, 68 left Chislehurst and Sidcup similarly destined. . . . Three good maintained grammar schools (say, Harrow County, Chislehurst and Sidcup and Tiffins) gain between them more university scholarships in a year than any 50 comprehensive schools . . .'
> (R. R. Pedley, Comprehensive Disaster, in: *Fight for Education,* The Critical Quarterly Society, London 1968, p. 46)

### 6.3.4 Quote authorities

**a) whose judgement the reader will accept**
**b) who have phrased the idea in a classical form**

Sometimes you may have the feeling that the reader or hearer might not be willing to accept your arguments because you do not happen to be an expert in that particular field. You may also have the bitter feeling that your linguistic and rhetorical competence fails to carry conviction. In this situation, you may quote an authority – i.e. a person or a source of information generally accepted.
In 1968, C. B. Cox and A. E. Dyson wrote a 'Letter to Members of Parliament' in Great Britain to warn them against the imminent dangers orig-

inating in progressive education. Under the heading 'Progressive Collapse', they quoted the views of many personalities on education, and particularly those of John Osborne – a famous writer who was known to hold rather leftist views.

**Example:**

'... Meanwhile, discontent with progressive collapse ... extends even to well-known rebels of yesteryear. Here is an extract from the *Observer* of 7th July 1968, where Kenneth Tynan discusses students with John Osborne:

TYNAN: You weren't exhilarated by the recent events at the Sorbonne?
OSBORNE: No, not at all. And to that extent, I suppose people could say that one has become right wing. What happened at the Sorbonne seemed more animal than human to me ...
TYNAN: The students would call it a protest against exploitation.
OSBORNE: Were they being exploited? I don't know. I thought they were expecting a great deal. In any case, disappointment is the salt of life ...
TYNAN: Do you believe in government by an élite?
OSBORNE: No, but – I know this sounds very blimpish – the prospect of rule by instant rabble doesn't appeal to me either.'

(From: *Fight for Education,* The Critical Quarterly Society, London 1968, p. 5)

### 6.3.5 How to incorporate developing and supporting material into your train of thought or line of argumentation

The following linking phrases will help you to integrate details, facts, figures and statistics, quotations from authorities, etc., into your writing.

**TP Exemplification, particularization, restriction**

– Many great men have risen from poverty, Lincoln and Edison, **for example.**
– Many great men have risen from poverty, **for instance (e.g.)** E. and L.
– Beauty exists in many shapes, **such as** the sun, the moon.

| | | | | |
|---|---|---|---|---|
| – One | **example**<br>**illustration**<br>**instance** | out of many | would be useful<br>should be added | to explain the ... |

p. t. o.

**TP Exemplification, particularization, restriction** (continued)

| | | | |
|---|---|---|---|
| – This idea can best be | demonstrated<br>illuminated<br>clarified<br>specified | by an | **example**<br>**illustration**<br>**anecdote** |

| | | |
|---|---|---|
| – May I make the point by<br>– May I prove my point by | quoting (an authority)<br>drawing upon a source | |
| | drawing upon<br>citing<br>referring to | an example |

– Here is perhaps an appropriate point to give an **example.**
– At this point, perhaps, an **example** should be given.
– To round off the picture, we must give a concrete **example.**
– Other **instances** of '......' are to be seen in the fact that ...
– There is no need to enumerate all the relevant **examples** and **instances,** but a word or two must be added about ...

| | |
|---|---|
| – **As to**<br>– **As for**<br>– **With regard to**<br>– **Talking of** | children, it must be stated that .... |

– Here are some more **examples** of ...

| | | | | |
|---|---|---|---|---|
| – Many more | **instances**<br>**examples**<br>**illustrations** | could be added, | **notably**<br>**primarily**<br>**particularly**<br>**especially**<br>**mainly** | in the field of ... |
| | | | **in particular** | those ...<br>the one |
| | | | **at least one ...** | |

– In this field, however, the { **chief** / **main** } **emphasis** shall be laid upon ...
– Among the most important **instances** of ......... are ...
– Nowhere is this clearer than { **in the field of ...** / **with** (minority groups) }

## 6.4 HOW TO ORGANIZE IDEAS AND STRUCTURE TEXTS

A sentence, paragraph, passage or section of a text is made coherent by relating ideas to one another. Apart from **topical coherence** – which is achieved by coming back to the topical terms at certain intervals – coherence (L con = 'together' + haerere = 'to stick'; G 'Zusammenhang') is ensured by arranging relevant ideas in a definite order and using transitions to move smoothly from one idea to the other. The linguistic elements by means of which this **functional coherence** of a text is achieved are called **'linking phrases'** or **'connectives'.** Since experience shows that students have some difficulties in this field, we have tried to present the most common connectives in this chapter of the book, no matter whether they connect ideas inside sentences (i.e. short-distance connectives), from sentence to sentence or from paragraph to paragraph (i.e. long-distance connectives).

### 6.4.1 How to present a topic in the introduction

(L intro = 'to the inside' + ducere, duct- = 'to lead'; G 'Einleitung')

You cannot start a text without

1) arousing the reader's or hearer's attention,
2) informing him on the topic you intend to deal with in the topical sentence, and
3) telling him something about your planned order of procedure.

The first purpose of an introduction has rightly been compared to a 'lure', i.e. something brightly coloured and attractive used as a sort of bait to arouse the reader's or hearer's interest. In any introduction, you should therefore try to establish a relationship to the reader's core of interest, for instance by means of references to current affairs, newspaper articles, statistics, recent events, etc, and then 'zoom in' on the subject like a camera focusing on one object.
At this stage, you should state your topic in a clear topical sentence and finally tell the reader something about the order in which you intend to present your ideas to enable him to follow your train of thought or line of reasoning from the very beginning to the very end.

### 6.4.2 How to structure the main body of a text*)

To give the reader or hearer a fair chance of following the presentation of your ideas step by step, you should always make sure you follow a

*) It goes without saying that introduction and conclusion are omitted in texts of merely paragraph length. In that case, the main body is the whole text.

definite order. The most frequent patterns of organization will be presented on the following pages. Special care will thereby be accorded to providing students with suitable connectives.

#### 6.4.2.1 Topical order

The most common arrangement of ideas is **topical order** which is achieved by structuring the subject according to some logical division or some principle of classification intrinsically originating in the key-terms of the topical sentence. This pattern of organization can, of course, not be systematicized; only an example of an outline of such a text-structuring can be given. As for the linguistic form of outlining, two are available: the **word outline** and the **sentence outline.**

**Example of outlining:**

**Topic:** 'Volleyball is an ideal game for students'

**a) Word outline:**

1. **Pleasure**
   1.1 Recreation after study
   1.2 Joy of competition
2. **Health**
   2.1 Stimulation of bodily functions
   2.2 Increase in mental alertness
3. **Citizenship**
   3.1 Development of team-work
   3.2 Development of fair play

**b) Sentence outline:**

1. It is **fun** to play volleyball, since
   1.1 it allows for recreation after study and
   1.2 gives the joy of competition.
2. It is **healthy** to play volleyball, since
   2.1 it stimulates bodily functions and
   2.2 helps to increase mental alertness.
3. It is a good **training in citizenship,** since
   3.1 it develops a spirit of cooperation and
   3.2 is a good exercise in fair play.

**Note:**

– Word outlines or sentence outlines must always precede a long text, e.g. a 'Facharbeit'!

– Besides, in a text analysis, you may be asked to 'outline a text' in one of the two ways described above.
– Most important: this outline of your topic must by all means remain prominent in the main body of your text as the so-called train of thought or line of reasoning.

#### 6.4.2.2 Order of enumeration

A listing arrangement of items must of course always be preceded by an introductory clause of the following type:

**TP Enumeration: introductory clause**

| | | |
|---|---|---|
| – There are three **main reasons** for my decision.<br>– **Various factors** may account for (terrorism).<br>– When discussing (**the issue of** racial segregation in South Africa), we must bear **several points** in mind.<br>– This policy could only work **under certain** ideal **circumstances:** | | |
| – Living in a big town has certain | | **advantages**<br>**disadvantages** |
| – Such a decision | has had<br>might have | a threefold **consequence**<br>**various consequences** |

The stages of the enumeration itself can be varied. The following linguistic choices are available for this purpose.

**TP Enumeration: main body**

| | | |
|---|---|---|
| One | Two | Three |
| First | Second | Third |
| Firstly | Secondly | Thirdly |
| In the first place | In the second place<br>In the next place | In the third place |
| For one thing . . . | . . . for another . . . | Another thing is . . . |

p. t. o.

**TP Enumeration: main body** (continued)

| | | |
|---|---|---|
| First of all<br>To begin with<br>To start with | Then<br>Besides<br>Moreover<br>Furthermore<br>In addition to that | Then again<br>Last of all<br>Lastly<br>Finally |
| The first thing I want to say is that ...<br>Let me begin by saying that ... | The next thing is ...<br>The next point I want to make is ...<br>What comes next is ... | The final point is ... |

**Examples**

(a) This is a way of expressing disagreement in several steps:

| | |
|---|---|
| **To begin with,** | I am not quite sure whether ... |
| **Besides,** | I have some doubts about ... |
| **Then again,** | I seriously question his contention that ... |

(b) A girl gives her reasons for preferring coeducational schools:

| | |
|---|---|
| 'In spite of the many arguments offered by those who favour women's colleges, I have decided to go to a coeducational school. There are three **main reasons** for my decision. | |
| **First (of all)**<br>**To start with**<br>**In the first place**<br>**Firstly** | I think I will have more fun at a coeducational school. |
| **Secondly**<br>**Then**<br>**In the second place**<br>**Moreover**<br>**Another thing is** | I think that we ought to have the male viewpoint in our classes ... Mixed classes are more interesting and enlightening. |
| **And thirdly**<br>**Finally**<br>**Lastly** | education is supposed to be a preparation for life. How can you prepare for life in a world where both sexes are not constantly together! |

### 6.4.2.3 Order of importance (climactic order)

The various items listed in your text may have the same degree of importance. Sometimes, however, they will have more or less weight; in that case, you should always proceed from the least important to the most important in order to retain the interest of the reader, particularly when presenting evidence in support of, or against, an argument or opinion.
Here are various ways of emphasizing the degree of importance of a particular item in relation to the preceding one or to the rest of your text.

**TP Same degree of importance**

<table>
<tr><td colspan="2">It is also important to mention that . . . .<br>It also deserves mentioning that . . . . . .</td></tr>
<tr><td>In the same way<br>Likewise</td><td>it is important to mention that . . .<br>it deserves mentioning that . . .</td></tr>
<tr><td>Similarly<br>Equally</td><td>important is the fact that . . .</td></tr>
</table>

**TP A higher degree of importance**

<table>
<tr><td colspan="3">More important still is (the fact) that . . .</td></tr>
<tr><td>A more important</td><td>reason<br>advantage<br>consequence</td><td>is the fact that . . .</td></tr>
<tr><td>He understands English and,</td><td>better still,<br>what is better,<br>what is more,<br>what is more important,</td><td>can speak it very well.</td></tr>
<tr><td>He understands English and can speak it very well,</td><td colspan="2">which is even better.<br>which is better still.<br>which is still more important.</td></tr>
<tr><td>He doesn't tell the truth</td><td colspan="2">– worse still, he keeps telling lies.<br>and, what is worse, he keeps telling lies.</td></tr>
</table>

**TP The highest degree of importance**

<table>
<tr><td colspan="4">Most important of all is the fact that . . .</td></tr>
<tr><td>The most important</td><td>factor<br>advantage<br>reason<br>consequence</td><td>of all is<br>the fact that</td><td rowspan="2">(in the country the air is less polluted than in towns.)</td></tr>
<tr><td colspan="3">And, what is most important,<br>Last but not least<br>And } above all<br>But }</td></tr>
<tr><td colspan="4">And finally, the air in the country is less polluted than in towns –<br>which is perhaps the { most important point. / greatest advantage of all.</td></tr>
</table>

**Example of climactic order:**

The general introduction of comprehensive schools would have **a threefold consequence**:
**To begin with,** it would make the construction of huge buildings necessary. **Then, what is more,** it would entail a serious problem of reorganization. **But above all,** our brighter pupils would no longer be motivated, which means that the level of education would be considerably lowered.

### 6.4.2.4 Time order / Chronological order

Time order is used in narrations or in expository writing in which a process is described from beginning to end. Some patterns of time order run parallel to those of enumeration, e.g. when retracing the main stages in
- a period of history
- somebody's life
- a novel.

**First example**

The author mentions three main stages in Mr X's life:

| | |
|---|---|
| **At first**<br>**At the beginning** | things ran smoothly. |
| **Then**<br>**Afterwards**<br>**After that**<br>**Later (on)** | he got into financial troubles. |

p. t. o.

| | |
|---|---|
| **Finally**<br>**Eventually (= finally!)**<br>**In the end**<br>**At the end of (his career)** | he had to sell his house. |

**Second example**

The history of industrialization can be divided into **several stages**:

| | | |
|---|---|---|
| **Originally**<br>**Formerly**<br>**Once**<br>**In the old days**<br>**Long ago** | workers were all farmhands and the common land belonged to everybody. | |
| (So the first industrial workers had | **previously**<br>**formerly**<br>**once** | been farmhands.) |
| **Later(on)**<br>**Subsequently**<br>**Around** 1850 | they moved into towns to find jobs in the new-born industry. | |
| **In the course of** the 20th century | their lot has been considerably improved and their housing conditions greatly improved. | |
| **Not so long ago** | they were even granted the right to participate in management decisions. | |
| **Ever since** Bismarck | German workers have enjoyed a comparatively high degree of social security. | |
| **Recently**<br>**Lately** | it has been found out that they earn more than clerks. | |
| **Now** | automation is causing new troubles. | |

**6.4.2.5 Order of comparison and contrast**

You may sometimes want to express the idea that something happens or happened in spite of certain factors (events or circumstances). In the following phrases, you will find various short-distance connectives to render this idea.

## TP Concessive contrast

<table>
<tr><td rowspan="2">There was no news;</td><td colspan="2">Jane, however, did not give up hope.</td></tr>
<tr><td>yet (still)<br>nevertheless<br>in spite of that<br>despite that<br>even so</td><td>Jane did not give up hope.</td></tr>
<tr><td rowspan="2">He had treated her badly;</td><td colspan="2">but she loved him all the same.</td></tr>
<tr><td>yet<br>still</td><td>she loved him.</td></tr>
<tr><td>Despite<br>In spite of<br>For all<br>Notwithstanding</td><td colspan="2">his wealth, he did not find a girl to marry him.</td></tr>
<tr><td colspan="3">He will never succeed, however hard he may try.<br>Cheeky as he was, she dared not answer him.<br>Strange though it may appear, I think that . . .</td></tr>
<tr><td>Although<br>Though</td><td colspan="2">they were poor, they were always neatly dressed.</td></tr>
<tr><td>It is strange,</td><td>but<br>yet</td><td>true.</td></tr>
<tr><td>He looked honest;</td><td>actually<br>(but) in fact</td><td>he was a rogue.</td></tr>
<tr><td colspan="3">Contrary to popular notions it has been found out that . . .</td></tr>
</table>

**Example:**

The truth is that our Christian civilization is riddled through and through with dilemma. We believe in the brotherhood of man, **but ([and] yet/[and] still)** we do not want it in South Africa. We believe that God endows men with diverse gifts, and that human life depends for its fullness on their employment and enjoyment; we are afraid, **however**, to explore this belief too deeply. We believe in help for the underdog, **but in spite of that (but at the same time; nevertheless)** we want him to stay under.

Another sort of contrast will be expressed when you have

1) to weigh the pros and cons of **one thing,** or
2) to weigh the pros and cons of **two or more things** by comparing and contrasting them as in the following tables:

**TP Weighing the pros and cons of one thing**

| | | |
|---|---|---|
| The rent is high, | **but (then)**<br>**but otherwise**<br>**on the other hand** | the house is satisfactory. |
| London is a noisy place, | | it is a place where you get entertainment. |
| **On the one hand**, a new car is expensive, **on the other hand,** a breakdown is unlikely. | | |

**TP Weighing the pros and cons of two or more things**

| | |
|---|---|
| London is a noisy place, | **whereas** Iona is extremely quiet.<br>Iona, **on the contrary,** is extremely quiet. |
| The Isle of Mull lies far from the mainland;<br>{ Iona, **however**, is more remote still.<br>{ **but** Iona is **even** more remote. | |
| **Unlike** most villages in Scotland, Aviemore is terribly commercialized. You will find more entertainment at Aviemore. **But on the other hand,** the setting cannot compare with that of Ullapool. | |

To introduce an **elaborate comparison** of similarities alone (i.e. a comparison proper) or of similarities **and** differences (i.e. a comparison in a wider sense, including a contrast) you may use the following phrases:

**TP Introductory clause to an elaborate comparison**

| | | | | |
|---|---|---|---|---|
| At this point it is | useful to **make a comparison between A and B**<br>important to see **how A compares with B** | | | |
| A **comparison** | **between A and B** | | | **will show that . . .** |
| | **of A** | **and with** | **B** | |

To elaborate a comparison, you may then proceed in two different ways:

1) items of similarity or difference may be compared or contrasted one by one (as in the first of the following two examples), or
2) all the items of A may be presented first – followed by all the items of B.

**First example:**

| | |
|---|---|
| **Text structuring:** | $A = / \neq B$<br>$a_1 = / \neq b_1$<br>$a_2 = / \neq b_2$<br>$a_3 = / \neq b_3$ |

**The difference between democracy (A) and communism (B) in practice is clearly shown by a comparison between the USA and Russia.**

**In the USA,** the people are supreme, and the government is their servant.

**In Russia,** the government is supreme, and the people are its servants.

**The United States Constitution** guarantees to American citizens the right to choose their leaders. The two-party system insures them a choice.

Control of the government **in Russia** rests in the hands of a small group of leaders. Voting is a farce because there is only one party – the Communist party, and any citizen who dares to oppose the ruling group receives harsh treatment.

**In America** the government guaranteees the people complete freedom to worship as they please,

but **in Russia** the leaders discourage religion and religious worship.

Freedom of speech **in America** gives everyone the privilege of saying exactly what he thinks, even to the point of criticizing his government.

Freedom of speech does not exist **in Russia**. The people, living in constant fear of their government, are afraid to express any views contrary to those of the party.

(From: Warriner, *English Grammar and Composition,* p. 372)

**Second example:**

| | |
|---|---|
| **Text structuring:** | $A : a_1 \quad a_2 \quad a_3$<br>$= / \neq$<br>$B : b_1 \quad b_2 \quad b_3$ |

**The difference between communism (A) and democracy (B) in practice is clearly shown by a comparison between Russia and the USA.**

To begin with, in the political system of **Soviet Russia,** people are not allowed to express any views incompatible with the so-called interests of the workers and farmers, or rather, those of the party clique in power. In fact, control of the government rests exclusively in the hands of this small group of party functionaries forming the Central Committee. Voting is thus a farce, and any citizen who dares to criticize or oppose this ruling group is either repressed, sent to a forced labour camp or expelled. To put it in a nutshell, the government in Soviet Russia is supreme, and the people are its servants.

In the **United States of America**, on the other hand, matters are very different – though by no means perfect, of course. There, the freedom of speech gives everyone the right of saying what he thinks, even to the point of criticizing his government. Moreover, the United States Constitution guarantees to all American citizens the right to choose their government. An actual choice is guaranteed by the two-party system. So we may rightly say that in the United States of America the people are supreme and the government is meant to be their servant.

(Adapted from preceding text)

**6.4.2.6 Dialectical order** [ˌdaiəˈlektikəl]

(Gk dialektike = 'the art of discussing'; from dia = 'across' + legein = 'to speak'; same etymology as the word 'dialogue'!)

It is exclusively used in **argumentative essays**, discussions or debates, where conflicting views are weighed up with the purpose of persuading the reader/hearer to adopt a certain attitude, or even of prompting him to some action.

As far as the structure is concerned, an argumentative essay can be divided into four parts:

1) the introduction to the topic/problem
2) the presentation and critical appreciation of the views you oppose
3) the presentation of the views you defend
4) the conclusion, summing up your argument and stating your final decision

**TP Dialectical order: the introduction of the topic**

| | | |
|---|---|---|
| It has often been | said<br>claimed<br>assumed | that . . . |

p. t. o.

## TP Dialectical order: the introduction of the topic (continued)

| |
|---|
| A was once thought to . . ./Gone are the days when . . . |
| There has been a heated controversy on the question whether . . .<br>The proposal to (do something) has raised a storm of angry protests. |
| Basically, A and B are the same thing. But no matter how . . . A is, it can never equal B. |
| Since the term '. . . . . . .' is often used loosely, it is frequently misunderstood. It is often wrongly associated with . . . But, in fact, it . . . |

## TP Dialectical order: the main body – opposing other views

| | | | | |
|---|---|---|---|---|
| Those who advocate A attack B for various reasons.<br>Those out to support A often argue that such a procedure will . . .<br>They are among the first to point out that . . . . | | | | |
| Firstly<br>Secondly<br>Finally | they | argue that . . . . . ., which is bad enough<br>claim that . . . . . . ., which is even worse.<br>insist that . . . . . ., which is the worst of all. | | |
| In | their view<br>his opinion | A | is<br>constitutes | a real problem<br>a serious danger |
| Although there is no denying the fact that . . . | they fail to see . . .<br>they fail to acknowledge . . . | | | |
| They are completely wrong when | assuming<br>claiming | that . . . | | |
| It is simply not true that . . . | | | | |
| This is simply wrong, since A is | only<br>exclusively<br>solely | concerned with . . . | | |
| They argue that . . ., but, | what is worse,<br>even worse,<br>still worse, | they claim that . . . | | |
| As I see it, these critics unduly generalize and exaggerate. | | | | |

p. t. o.

**TP Dialectical order: the main body — opposing other views** (continued)

| | |
|---|---|
| They fail to | take all the relevant facts into consideration<br>acknowledge certain facts<br>appreciate definite trends<br>weigh all the arguments in a fair way<br>draw the proper inferences and conclusions |

So, all their arguments are true to a certain extent, but somehow they are all unconvincing

Unfortunately, some people are easily persuaded by such fine-sounding arguments for the simple reason that . . .

**TP Dialectical order: the main body — defending your own views**

So much for the 'cons'; let us now turn to the 'pros'.
In spite of all the conflicting views, there seems to be some common ground between A and B in the field of . . .
In fact, what seems more important to me than the arguments propounded above is the fact that . . .

| | | |
|---|---|---|
| I | think/feel<br>assume/fear | that . . . |

'. . . . . . . .' is generally accepted as having obvious advantages.

| | | |
|---|---|---|
| In my view<br>In my opinion<br>As far as I can see<br>If we consider it from the point of view of . . . | A | seems to . . .<br>is likely to . . .<br>is bound to . . . |

| | | | |
|---|---|---|---|
| As for<br>As to<br>As regards<br>With regard to<br>With respect to<br>With reference to<br>Talking of | the question of economy | I would like to point out that . . . | |
| | | it should be | mentioned that . . .<br>pointed out that . . .<br>noted that . . . |
| As far as the question of . . . is concerned, | | it might be stated that . . .<br>it is obvious that . . . | |

p. t. o.

**TP Dialectical order: the main body – defending your own views** (continued)

| | | |
|---|---|---|
| By the by<br>By the way<br>Incidentally<br>In passing | it should be stated/mentioned<br>it should not remain unmentioned | that . . . |
| So I think there is a very good reason for me to assume that . . .<br>The more so, since there is increasing evidence as to . . .<br>It is much more likely that . . .<br>No one would seriously deny that . . .<br>Although it must be admitted that . . ., there is no denying the fact that . . .<br>I would like here to raise the question whether there might not even be . . . | | |

**TP Dialectical order: the conclusion – an appeal to the reader**

| | | |
|---|---|---|
| Owing to all these considerations it becomes plausible that . . . | | |
| So, | to sum up and to make the point,<br>in short,<br>in brief, | I am opposed to A, but very much in favour of B |
| I am completely unsympathetic to A, since I feel committed to B. | | |

**Note:** Two examples of argumentative writing based on dialectical structure – one on political activities at school, and one on the death penalty – can be found on pp. 88–90, with the relevant structural material.

### 6.4.3 How to draw inferences or conclusions from developing and supporting material

Inferences are often drawn in the course of a text – whether

1) you establish some logical connection between ideas or facts ('therefore/this is the reason why . . .'), or
2) you integrate supporting material into your train of thought ('. . . which tends to prove that . . .')

But most important of all is the final conclusion where you must reinforce your topic and make your point in a straightforward and convincing way.

**TP Consequences resulting from reasons given before**

| | | |
|---|---|---|
| He has committed a crime. | **Accordingly**<br>**Therefore**<br>**For that reason** | he must be imprisoned |
| The crops were a failure. | **So**<br>**Therefore**<br>**Consequently**<br>**In consequence**<br>**As a consequence**<br>**As a result**<br>**For that reason**<br>**That is (the reason) why** | prices rose |
| He saved the life of an Indian chief, **thus** gain**ing** the Indians' confidence. | | |

**TP Drawing conclusions from supporting material** (facts, statistics)

| | | | |
|---|---|---|---|
| In 1848 they found a skull that was more evolved than that of an ape but less so than that of a man | **which** | **shows**<br>**proves**<br>**goes to prove**<br>**tends to prove** | **that** man has not always existed in his present form. |
| **This implies that** human beings have evolved from some lower form of life. | | | |
| **In other words we may** | **say**<br>**state**<br>**infer**<br>**conclude** | **that** (human beings . . .) | |
| **Thus**<br>**And so**<br>**In that case** | it is only too obvious that . . .<br>I am probably right in inferring that . . .<br>we are certainly justified in saying that . . . | | |

**TP Final conclusion**

| | |
|---|---|
| **To conclude**<br>**In conclusion** | we may say that . . .<br>we are certainly justified in saying that . . . |

p. t. o.

**TP Final conclusion** (continued)

| | | |
|---|---|---|
| **All in all** | | we may say that . . .<br>we can only come to the conclusion that . . . |
| **Taking everything into** | **account**<br>**consideration** | |
| **Summing up**<br>**To sum up**<br>**To put it in a nutshell**<br>**In short**<br>**Briefly**<br>**In a word**<br>**In one word** | we may say that . . .<br>I should say that . . . | |

# 7. LETTER-WRITING

Letters may be divided into three types: **personal letters, formal letters** and **business** or **professional letters.** For the purpose of preparing yourself for an examination, however, business letters can be ignored. You will have to write such letters only when actually employed in a particular firm, and your employer will then tell you the sort of letter he wants you to write. In examinations you may have to write either of these letters:

1) a letter to a friend;
2) a letter to the editor of a newspaper;
3) a letter of application.

The first one is a personal letter; the other two are formal letters. Their subject-matter will of course be determined entirely by the test questions, but there are several points that you should know about these letters in general.

## 7.1 THE 'LETTER TO A FRIEND'

What is meant by 'friend' here is a close personal friend you are on intimate terms with and you'd therefore address by his or her first name.

In an examination you won't have to bother about such things as what to write on the envelope and how to write your address and the date. For examination purposes you can start your letter off with the salutation, e.g. 'Dear John'. Here one usually writes 'Dear' plus the name one would use when speaking to the person one is writing to. There must always be a comma after the salutation and when 'Dear' is placed first in this way it is written with a capital letter. The text of the letter likewise begins with a capital letter and the first word is placed about two or three centimetres from the margin, like this:

Dear Margaret,
      What a long time . . .

Common alternatives to 'Dear Margaret', are 'My dear Margaret', and 'Dearest Margaret', (only to very close friends). There are a number of other alternatives, but they do not concern us here.

The body of the letter – what you write between the salutation and the valediction ('Yours sincerely',) – is obviously the most important part of any letter. It is, however, impossible to lay down any absolute rules about how this section of the letter should be written. Letter writing, like any other form of composition, is an individual matter, dependent on personal tastes and peculiarities. To some people facility of expression and good style are natural gifts; the general rule, however, seems to be that they have to be acquired by hard practice.

The style of a personal letter will, of course, be much more familiar than that of other types of composition. In real life it is even full of slang and colloquialisms. A personal letter written for examination purposes, however, should not contain slang and the many slipshod expressions current in everyday speech, for it is intended to test the candidate's ability to write correct English of good style. The ideal to be aimed at is a style that is easy and natural without being slovenly and vulgar. Contracted forms are of course permitted.

When writing a letter, you should keep the following general principles in mind:

- A letter, like any other piece of continuous writing, ought to be divided into paragraphs, and the ideas it puts forward should be arranged in a suitable order.
- A letter usually divides clearly into three parts. In the first part, reference is made to the reason for writing the letter. In the second part, the subject can be developed at whatever length is necessary. The third part of the letter is a polite conclusion. This last part is usually made into a distinct paragraph however short the letter.
- In an examination you should invent some 'background' to your letter to make it more realistic and more interesting, and not rest content merely to put down just the bare information stated in the question.

Frequently the letter is finished with some wish, e.g.

I hope you will have a very nice holiday.

Yours sincerely,

Sometimes this final sentence is used to send messages to someone else, e.g. 'Please remember me to your parents.' A warmer, more cordial note is introduced by such phrases as:

**TP**

With best wishes,
All the best,
With kind regards,
With kindest regards,
Kind regards,
With all good wishes,
All good wishes,
Best regards,

After that a conventional phrase is used to close the letter. The most common endings are:

**TP**

| |
|---|
| Yours,<br>Yours ever,<br>Ever yours,<br>Yours as ever,<br>Yours sincerely,<br>Sincerely yours,<br>Yours very sincerely, |

Remember that all these expressions start with a capital letter and are followed by a comma. Here is an example:

... With all good wishes,
Yours sincerely,
John.

At the very end of the letter you sign your name. It is essential that the signature should match the salutation. So if you have addressed the person you are writing to by his/her first name, then you also sign only your first name here.

## SOME USEFUL PHRASES

### TP Thanking your friend for a letter

| | | | | |
|---|---|---|---|---|
| Thank you for your | interesting<br>informative<br>absorbing | letter, which | has just arrived. | |
| | | | arrived<br>I received | this morning.<br>last week.<br>on Thursday.<br>two days ago. |
| I was very | glad<br>happy | to get your letter, which | arrived<br>I received | today, etc. |

### TP Apologizing for not having written for a long time

<table>
<tr><td rowspan="2">I'm sorry</td><td>I haven't written<br>for not writing</td><td>for so long,</td><td rowspan="3">but</td><td rowspan="3">I've been very busy.<br>I simply didn't get round to it.<br>I've been more than busy with . . . for the last two months, etc.</td></tr>
<tr><td colspan="2">it has taken me so long to reply,</td></tr>
<tr><td colspan="3">Many apologies for not having written earlier,</td></tr>
</table>

### TP Introducing the subject

| |
|---|
| I have just this moment received your letter and am writing back at once because . . .<br>Many thanks for your last letter in which you suggest that I should tell you about . . .<br>I must write at once and tell you about . . .<br>In my last letter I promised I'd tell you about . . .<br>I hate to bother you, but I have a (small) problem and you are perhaps the only one who will understand.<br>My problem is that . . . |

### TP Letter endings

<table>
<tr><td>I (do) hope you are</td><td colspan="2">(still) keeping well.<br>well.<br>quite well again.</td></tr>
<tr><td>I am looking forward to</td><td>seeing<br>hearing from</td><td>you soon.</td></tr>
<tr><td colspan="3">Please write soon.<br>Please write when you can.<br>I wish you could have been with us.<br>Do let us know how you are getting on.<br>This letter is rather short, I'm afraid, as I'm hard pressed for time at the moment. I'll write a longer letter as soon as there is more time.<br>(Instead of these phrases you can use any of the conventional phrases listed above, such as 'With best wishes,'. Or you can combine the two and write something like:<br>I hope you are keeping well. With best wishes,<br>Yours sincerely,</td></tr>
</table>

## 7.2 THE 'LETTER TO THE EDITOR OF A NEWSPAPER'

Letters published in newspapers usually take a peculiar form, e.g. 'Sir – In answer to your reader . . .', with 'Yours etc.' as the valediction, and either without the writer's address or with that address appended below the writer's name. Or, a reader's letter may be printed without a salutation and a valediction altogether, giving only the writer's name and the town he is writing from. This is now the most commonly used form.
As a student, you should not imitate these forms, but set out your letter in the usual way. Most of what has been said about the layout of personal letters applies here, too, but there are a few minor differences: The salutation is always 'Dear Sir,', the valediction 'Yours faithfully,' and the writer signs his name in full; contracted forms should be avoided and the general tone of the letter ought to be more formal.
When writing a letter for publication in a newspaper or magazine, or when writing such a letter for examination purposes, you should bear in mind that letters to the press should always be short, to the point, and well-reasoned. You ought to make it clear as early as possible in your letter what it is you are writing about, and if the letter has arisen from something that appeared in the newspaper you are writing to, you should refer to it as exactly as possible, giving, for example, the title of the article, and the date of the edition of the paper in which it appeared. This may be important for creating some 'background' to your letter in an exam situation.
The tone of the letter should be both restrained and trenchant, and you must make every effort to express your point of view with precision, logic and politeness. It is important that you should make the last sentence as telling as possible.
The subject matter of the letter may be almost anything, and on any one day in *The Times*, for instance, there may be letters dealing with such different matters as the rights and wrongs of fox-hunting, world poverty, the weather, justice for nurses, animals in space, the design of new stamps, the functions of the monarchy, and the powers of the police. In an examination, the following types of letter are possible:

- **letters making suggestions or stating opinions and beliefs:** These may cover local, national, or international affairs; or they may be on more general topics, such as cruelty to animals, the degeneracy of modern youth, and so on.

- **letters of complaint:** These complaints could be about something that has appeared in the newspaper; on the other hand, the complaints could be about some aspect of politics, local government, other people's behaviour, etc.

- ▶ **letters of appreciation:** These are the reverse of the letters of complaint – they express the writer's pleasure at something he has seen in the paper or his feeling that some praiseworthy aspect of public life or conduct should be made known through the newspaper.

**Note:** This last type of letter is regarded as particularly difficult by students. They feel it ties them down too much to only the positive side of a problem and may then not give them enough to say.

Letters are usually of more than one type. For instance, a letter of complaint will often contain suggestions for a remedy, and many letters stating beliefs will also contain criticism of people holding contrary ideas. The main thing is to plan the letter really well. In a letter of complaint, for instance, you must first of all show that you are specially qualified to deal with the subject in question; then the various points should be set out as briefly as possible and some evidence put forward in an orderly fashion to support your complaint; finally you may urge others to join in your protest or express the hope that a change in the situation you are complaining about will be effected soon.

## SOME USEFUL PHRASES

### TP Asking for publication of the letter

| | | |
|---|---|---|
| I beg<br>I should like to be permitted<br>... prompts me to ask for | a few lines of your space<br>space in your columns<br>some space in your paper | to urge a plea which ...<br>to point out that ...<br>to make a suggestion which ...<br>to draw the attention of your readers to ... |

### TP Openings showing approval

I quite agree with Mr Hudson's letter (14th October) in which he pleads ...
I would like to endorse Mr Anderson's views about ...
Your recent article on ... was very timely. The dangers of ... cannot be overlooked any more.
I would like to draw the attention of your readers to ...
The concern you have shown about ... is highly commendable and I would like to congratulate F. Freeman on his splendid article on ... (7th June).

**TP Openings showing disapproval**

> I wonder whether the press is adequately aware that ...
> I am writing to you, following Mrs Grimsby's letter of 24th April.
> It is simply not true ...
> I was disturbed to read your article about ...
> I am writing to complain about the article last week about ...
> What nonsense Frank Drummond writes in your issue of last Saturday.

**TP Neutral openings**

> I wish to draw the attention of your readers to ...
> By way of comment on Mary Holland's interesting article (19 March) I would like to point out that ...
> I was interested to read Mr Wells' letter of 2nd June about ...
> With reference to the letter of 13 February about ..., I feel I must inform you that ...
> I would like to point out that ...
> I am writing to you in the hope that ...

It is, of course, not at all necessary to use any of these or similar openings – it is sometimes a good idea to come straight to the point:

> Have we all gone mad? Having followed the discussions about nuclear reactors, fast breeders, and what not, I seriously wonder what will become of this nation ...

People writing to the press often feel the need to state their qualifications for writing on a given topic, or the special reasons which have prompted them to do so.

**TP Stating one's qualifications**

> As a schoolteacher of many years' experience, I think that ...
> As a ratepayer, I consider that ...
> As a concerned parent, I would like to know why ...
> I have lived in this city or near it all my working life. I believe that ...

## 7.3 THE 'LETTER OF APPLICATION'

This is one of the most important types of formal letter – for obvious reasons. However, letters of application are not too difficult to write, if you keep in mind the main requirements, and write in simple direct English using the sentence patterns given below. Although the exact wording must vary from individual to individual and from job to job, certain standard sentence patterns can be followed. In general the letter should contain the following four sections:

1) an introduction stating how the post came to your notice;
2) a statement of all relevant information about yourself – your age, education, qualifications, etc.
3) reasons for your wanting the job and reasons why your employer-to-be should find you particularly suitable for the particular job;
4) your availability for interview plus mention of the fact that a stamped, addressed envelope (s.a.e.) has been enclosed.

In real life, a letter of application would probably also contain photostat copies of your school leaving certificate and various testimonials, a curriculum vitae, and a statement of referees to whom your prospective employer could write to ask their opinion about your suitability for the job. All this is not necessary, of course, when writing a letter of application as part of an examination. You should, however, mention these things, **as if** you had really enclosed copies of all the necessary documents in your application.

As in all other formal letters you should start your letter with 'Dear Sir,' and end it with 'Yours faithfully,'. In tone, the letter of application should be restrained, though not so conventional that no personality at all shows through and it must sound keen and competent without appearing to boast. On the other hand, there are a number of things to avoid when writing a letter of application. So do not say that you will be suitable because you are a clever person – this your employer-to-be can judge for himself. Nor should you try to flatter him and say he is such a famous man that you feel you must work for him. Another thing to be avoided is giving a personal reason for needing the job, e.g. 'I am very anxious to get the job because my wife is expecting her fourth child.'; appointments are usually made on grounds of ability, suitability, personality, etc., not out of charity. Nor must you jump from one point to another just as ideas come into your head. This gives the impression of being disorderly and casual. Again, the letter must be written from the reader's point of view, not from the writer's; information essential to the prospective employer must be set out clearly and anything irrelevant omitted. On the other hand it is tactless to make demands and stipulate conditions when asking to be considered for a post. Above all you must not criticise your present or former employer; employers inevitably tend to sympathise with other employers. The safest way is to follow certain standard patterns.

## SOME USEFUL PHRASES

### TP For the introduction

| | | | | |
|---|---|---|---|---|
| I wish to apply for<br>I am interested in<br>I should like to apply for<br>I should like to make application for | the post of | head engineer<br>manager<br>translator<br>guide, etc. | in your | office,<br>company,<br>firm etc., |

| | | |
|---|---|---|
| (which I saw) advertised in | today's<br>yesterday's | 'Daily Telegraph'.<br>'Daily Mail', etc. |

| | | |
|---|---|---|
| The Headmaster of my school<br>The Principal of my college<br>Mr Smith, etc. | told me<br>has informed me | of the vacancy. |

| | | | |
|---|---|---|---|
| I have | read<br>seen | your advertisement for the post of . . . in | today's . . .<br>yesterday's . . . |

| |
|---|
| I wish to apply for this post.<br>I am interested in this post, etc. |

| | | |
|---|---|---|
| In | reply<br>answer | to your advertisement in this morning's 'Daily Post', I wish to submit this application for the post you mention as being vacant. |

### TP Stating your qualifications

| |
|---|
| I enclose details of my career and qualifications, and photostat copies of my School Leaving Certificate and testimonials.<br>You will find a full account of my career and qualifications on the attached personal record sheet, and I have also added the names of two referees and copies of two recent testimonials. |

Stating qualifications and giving reasons for wanting and feeling suited for a job are closely related. It is, therefore, not always possible to make a sharp distinction between the two and some overlapping may occur.

## TP Giving reasons for wanting the job

<table>
<tr><td rowspan="3">You will notice that</td><td colspan="2">I have worked in England for three years.<br>I have qualifications in French and Spanish.<br>my present work is very similar.<br>my career so far has given me experience in office routine and in dealing with people.<br>I obtained particularly good results in languages.<br>my science subjects are particularly good, etc.</td></tr>
<tr><td>I am used to</td><td>travelling.<br>meeting tourists.<br>giving talks.<br>demonstrating articles.<br>working on my own, etc.</td></tr>
<tr><td colspan="2">I have had considerable experience as a(n) . . .<br>I therefore feel competent to carry out the duties involved in the post advertised.<br>I am anxious to get on and believe I should prove thoroughly satisfactory.</td></tr>
<tr><td rowspan="2">I think the post will give me more</td><td colspan="2">responsibility.</td></tr>
<tr><td>scope for my</td><td>English.<br>linguistic abilities.<br>interest in . . .</td></tr>
<tr><td rowspan="2">My present post</td><td colspan="2">requires too much travelling.</td></tr>
<tr><td>does not</td><td>give me much responsibility.<br>use my qualifications (fully), etc.</td></tr>
<tr><td colspan="3">Although I am very happy in my present job, I am now looking for a position which will give me more responsibility and the chance of promotion.</td></tr>
<tr><td colspan="3">I have had considerable experience as a(n) . . . and have . . ., but it has always been my ambition to find (a permanent position in a firm of international standing).<br>My ambition is not so much to obtain a good salary now as to secure a post which would give scope for my energies, and enable me to gain advancement later on.</td></tr>
</table>

## TP Your availability for interview

<table>
<tr><td colspan="2">I am available for interview</td><td colspan="2">at any time.<br>at any time suitable to you.</td></tr>
<tr><td colspan="4">I am sorry that I shall be away for the next two weeks on a business trip for my present firm, but I shall be available for interview, if required, after 9th September.</td></tr>
<tr><td rowspan="3">I should be {pleased<br>glad</td><td rowspan="2">to call on you</td><td colspan="2">if desired.</td></tr>
<tr><td>at any time</td><td>by appointment.<br>which is convenient to you.</td></tr>
<tr><td>to come for</td><td colspan="2">a personal interview at your convenience.<br>an interview if you find that my qualifications and experience are adequate for the post in question.</td></tr>
<tr><td colspan="4">If you could grant me an interview, I should be pleased to call whenever convenient to you.<br>If you feel that my qualifications meet with your requirements, I shall be pleased to come for an interview.</td></tr>
<tr><td colspan="4">I hope to hear from you soon.<br>I enclose a stamped, addressed envelope (= an s.a.e.) for your reply.</td></tr>
</table>

Imagine yourself in an examination now. The text you have to deal with is in some way or other concerned with language – the problems of an international language, billingual education, English as a second language, etc. Since the questions on the worksheet always arise from the text or take further one of the problems it mentions, the worksheet might in this case include questions such as:

- Explain why you are learning English as a second (or third) language.
- What are the arguments for and against an international language?
- 'Being bilingual creates more problems than it solves.' Comment on this statement.
- Why are some languages liable to die out?

This hypothetical worksheet might also have a section on letter-writing with the following tasks:

(a) Write **a letter to a friend** telling him about the problems you have with learning a foreign language.
or
(b) Write **a letter to the editor of a newspaper** complaining about the choice of foreign languages offered in the local school.
or
(c) Write **a letter of application** offering your services as an interpreter and translator.

These are the letters you might write in each case; the words in bold type are the ones that have been taken over from the collection of useful phrases above.

**Note:** Here, as so often, you will have to use your imagination to make your answers more lively and realistic by creating some 'background' to your letters.

(a) **Model of a 'personal letter'**

Dear Mike,

**I hate to bother you, but I have a small problem and you are perhaps the only one who will understand.**

**My problem is that** I hate Latin and yet have to study it. My dad, who is a doctor as you know, practically forced me to take it as he is still hopeful that I'll take over his practice one day, but I'm not at all sure that I want to be a doctor; I'd rather be an electronics engineer. So, as far as I'm concerned, Latin is no use to me at all.

To make matters worse, our teacher is as antique as the language. He bores me stiff, but I can't go to sleep during his lessons – I'm sitting right in front of him and he would notice.

I honestly don't know what to do about the whole thing. I've thought over a number of possible ways of getting rid of Latin, but none of them has a chance to succeed. Do you perhaps know of something that might work?

Sorry for talking about myself all the time, but this Latin business does get on my nerves.

**Please write when you can. All good wishes,**

**Yours as always,**
John.

(b) **Model of a 'letter to the editor'**

Dear Sir,

**I would like to be permitted some space in your paper to urge** other parents to join me in my fight to have Russian removed from our language programmes.

**As a citizen of the United Kingdom,** I would like to know why my son is being required to take Russian as his first foreign language at the local Comprehensive School. I feel that a more appropriate language would be German or French. After all, we expect our children to fight Communism and not to learn its language; nor do we want them to be infected with Communist ideas under the pretence of learning what is termed 'one of the most important languages in the world.'

However, the school authorities have brushed off my protests, and so **I am writing to you in the hope that** other people will complain, too. Perhaps a change can be brought about through our joint efforts.

**Yours faithfully,**
William B. Hamilton.

(c) **Model of a 'letter of application'**

Dear Sir,

**I should like to apply for the post of** interpreter and translator at your London headquarters **advertised in today's 'Daily Telegraph'.**

**You will find a full account of my career and qualifications on the attached personal record sheet, and I have also added the names of two referees and copies of two recent testimonials.**

**You will notice that** my mother is English and my father German, so I am bilingual in those languages, and I also speak French and Italian fairly fluently. **I have had considerable experience as an** interpreter, **and have** translated a great deal of technical material, **but it has always been my ambition to find a permanent position in a firm of international standing.**

**If you feel that my qualifications meet with your requirements, I shall be pleased to come for an interview. I enclose an s.a.e. for your reply.**

**Yours faithfully,**
Gerhard Krieger.

**Note:** You will have noticed that it pays to know some standard openings and endings because letter-writing is so highly conventionalized, and letters of application can practically be written entirely with the help of certain set phrases.

## 8. TRANSLATING FROM ENGLISH INTO GERMAN

Translation – both from and into the foreign language – is regarded with deep suspicion by many, particularly by the adherents of an entirely monolingual approach to foreign language teaching and learning; any intrusion of the learner's mother tongue is anathema to them. There are others who are all in favour of teaching translation as a valuable skill, and some speak even of 'the art of translation.' There is some doubt, on the other hand, as to whether translation as a skill can be taught at all systematically, and there are yet other groups who would allow translation only during the elementary stage of foreign language learning, but not later, or only when the advanced stage has been reached, but not before. There are probably a few more groups, and they all put the stress in some other place. Translation is, therefore, a highly controversial subject. A look at the syllabuses for the teaching of English (and French) of the various 'Bundesländer' and the place they accord translation within the concept of the individual syllabus as a whole makes this abundantly clear – each emphasizes some other aspect of translation.

In this situation it is difficult to give general advice. All that can be done here is to draw your attention to a number of points that seem essential to success in translating from English into German. Translation from German into English seems to be used mainly for teaching points of grammar during the elementary and intermediate stages of language learning and can therefore be excluded here. It is only during the very advanced stage of a university course in 'Anglistik' that this form of translation is taught as a special skill.

Before we can say anything else we have to make one thing clear. Students often assume that translating into one's own language is 'easy' once they know the meaning of all the words in the foreign text. This is to say they seem to think that anybody who has reached a certain command of another language is automatically qualified to translate from this language into his own. This is, however, a grave misunderstanding of the nature of translation. At the bottom of it seems to be the idea that it is mainly the transference of words and sentences from one language into another what translation is all about. If translation could in actual fact be reduced to the substitution of one set of words for another, whilst concepts remained unchanged, then it would indeed be easy to translate. The trouble is, however, that, strictly speaking, it is not words, sentences or a text which are translated, but concepts and statements, i.e. that which constitutes the semantic content of speech. It is thoughts which are translated, not linguistic devices.

What follows from all this is that the most important thing for you to do whenever you are confronted with a text you have to translate is to try to understand this text as well as you possibly can. Unless you have really understood what the author wants to say and not only what the words 'mean', you cannot hope to give a good translation of this text. If you cannot get at the deeper meaning behind the words, if you miss stylistic devices, and if you cannot read between the lines, you won't be able to arrive at a good translation, but will simply substitute words from your own language for the foreign words. To what extent you can in fact understand a text in this way largely depends on your command of the foreign language in general, but also on what you know about text types and text forms and about stylistic devices.

The first step, therefore, in increasing your competence as a translator should be to study chapter 3 ('Text Types, Text Forms, Text Groups') and chapter 5 ('Survey of Stylistic Devices') really well. This will put you in a position to determine more easily the text type a text mainly belongs to; it may also enable you to say something about register, tone and style of the texts in question and about the stylistic devices the author made use of. This in turn will make it easier for you to choose the right words and expressions for your translation. If the passage you have to translate is written in a humorous tone, for instance, then you should try to re-echo that humorous tone in your translation. Whether you will in fact succeed will of course depend on your command of your own language. (For a demonstration of how the humorous tone of an English text can actually be reproduced in a German translation cf. 'A Woman's Tears' and the corresponding translation in ch. 5.)

After all that has been said about the importance of understanding a text in all its points – even those the author only implied – it should now go without saying that the least you must do is to read the text two or three times very slowly, paying great attention to detail, before you can start translating it. You ought to read a translation text a good deal more slowly than one for comprehension – almost as if you were reading a poem. Many things can become clear in this way you might otherwise have overlooked, e.g. the stylistic figures the author employed. Be sure to ask yourself what their function is in the particular context they appear in and in the text as a whole. And always remember – the better you understand a text, the better your translation of it will be. It may even become possible to guess correctly one or two words you're not quite sure of.

The next step in increasing your competence as a translator should be to make sure you know the syntactic and stylistic peculiarities of English that most often cause difficulty when they have to be translated into

German and that you also know how to deal with them. A good deal will depend on practice then, but it is always a good idea to find out first what you should be on the look-out for. The main problem areas can be classed under six heads:

1) participle and gerund constructions;
2) different stylistic features;
3) translation through a negation of the opposite;
4) foreign words;
5) literal or free translation;
6) lack of concentration.

### 8.1 Participle and gerund constructions

a) **the participle remains untranslated:**

| | |
|---|---|
| – The complaints **made** about the ringing of the church bells ... | Die Klagen über ... |
| – It was General de Gaulle's conviction that he, **acting** as an independent agent, could reconcile East and West. | ... daß er als unabhängiger Vermittler ... |

b) **a different construction is used in the translation:**

| | |
|---|---|
| – Uncle Henry, **leaning** against the door-post, described the great flood of 1929. | ... lehnte sich an ... **und** beschrieb ... (co-ordination) |
| – The poor man was ruined, his children **flung** on the streets. | Der arme Mann war ruiniert; seine Kinder wurden auf die Straße geworfen. (new main clause) |
| – **Considering** our lack of experience, we did quite well. | **In Anbetracht** ... (nominal expression) |
| – He is like a savage **concealing** primitive rites and taboos from an inquisitive explorer. | Er ist wie ein Wilder, **der** ... (relative clause) |
| – The people couldn't help **thinking** him guilty. | Mußten die Leute ihn nicht für schuldig halten? (rhetorical question) |
| – **On learning** about the ememy's plans, General H. ... | **Als** General H. von den Plänen des Gegners erfuhr, ... (temporal clause) |
| – He took no notice of this, **being** deeply interested in what was happening at the other side. | ... **weil** er ... (clause of reason) |

| | |
|---|---|
| – He sat with them, **listening** mainly, until near midnight. | ... **wobei** er ... (modal clause) |
| – She had read of such things **being** possible. | ... **daß** solche Dinge möglich seien. (that-clause) |
| – We'll leave, weather **permitting.** | ... **falls** das Wetter es zuläßt. (conditional clause) |

## 8.2 Different stylistic features

Generally speaking, a nominal style is preferred in English whereas in German verbal and adverbial constructions are more common. Similarly, the passive voice is used less frequently in German than in English. You ought to take these different stylistic features of the two languages into account in your translations – as in the following examples:

a) **nominal constructions in English – verbal constructions in German**

| | |
|---|---|
| – the **question** is | es **fragt** sich |
| – It is my personal **belief** | Ich persönlich **glaube** |
| – It might have been expected that the public would take more **interest** in local than in national questions. | ... sich aufgeschlossener **zeigen** würde ... |

b) **nominal style in English – adjectival or adverbial style in German**

| | |
|---|---|
| – at the **top** of their **voices** | so **laut** sie konnten |
| – They walked back **in silence.** | ... **schweigend** ... |
| – He was in the **depths** of despair. | Er war in **tiefster** Verzweiflung. |

c) **verbal constructions in English – adverbial constructions in German**

| | |
|---|---|
| – as **is well-known** | **bekanntlich** |
| – **I'm sorry to say** he died last night. | ... **leider** ... |
| – **I am sure** that he will be here by eight o'clock | ... **sicherlich** ... |

d) **passive voice in English – active voice in German**

| | |
|---|---|
| – What more **is wanted?** | Was will **man** mehr? |
| – The war would **be won** by those who would gain and keep superiority in machine technics. | Die, die ..., **würden** auch den Krieg **gewinnen**. |
| – In our time, the acquisitive, rather than the creative and spiritual instincts **are encouraged.** | Unsere Zeit **fördert** mehr die auf Erwerb ausgerichteten als die schöpferischen und geistigen Instinkte. |

### 8.3 Translation through a negation of the opposite

This is often a useful trick when you can't get round a difficult word or phrase in your translation. Here are a few examples of how this can be done:

| | |
|---|---|
| – a sensible, but **dull** precaution. | eine vernünftige, aber **wenig phantasievolle** Vorsichtsmaßnahme |
| – We too can **prosper**. | Auch uns braucht es **nicht schlecht zu gehen**. |
| – She gives the impression of **outdoorness.** | Sie macht **nicht** den Eindruck eines **Stubenhockers.** |

### 8.4 Foreign words

This is an old problem and one that can't be solved once and for all. The German language is full of English words like 'star,' 'comeback,' 'establishment' or 'make-up'. When words such as these have become fully assimilated you can use them for your own translation if any of them turn up in an English text. You needn't hesitate about technical terms either; words like 'character' and 'aristocracy' (politics); 'epic' and 'parody' (literature); or 'inflation' and 'product' (economics) need of course not be 'translated' into German – it would be extremely difficult anyhow. But there are a number of foreign words for which genuinely German words exist: 'majority' (Majorität – Mehrheit), 'complexity' (Komplexität – Vielschichtigkeit), 'co-ordinate' (koordinieren – aufeinander abstimmen), and so on. In all these and in similar cases it is not the foreign but the German word you ought to use.

### 8.5 Literal or free translation?

Here it is even more difficult to lay down any hard and fast rules. One thing seems clear – whenever there is any danger of the original 'coming through' in your translation or whenever your version of the text is very clumsy you will have to find some other way of expressing what is meant. This may become possible by means of a change in the word order, a verbal construction in the place of a nominal one, of translating two words as only one (a sober and temperate figure = eine nüchterne Gestalt), and so forth. You should be wary, however, of making any big changes. What you have to do is to translate the text, not to rewrite it in your own words in the sense of a paraphrase.

## 8.6 Lack of concentration

Many mistakes are made through a lack of proper concentration. The little word 'of' is a case in point; study the following examples:

| | |
|---|---|
| – Criticism **of** the government was not allowed. | Kritik **an** (nicht: der) Regierung ... |
| – suspicion **of** foreigners | Mißtrauen **gegenüber** (nicht: der) Ausländern |
| – He followed her about with his eyes, in which there was a strange expression **of** watchfulness and longing. | ... Ausdruck **von** (nicht: der) |

**Tenses** are another constant source of mistakes. In particular, make sure that you translate sentences in the present perfect tense and in the future tense correctly; very often the present tense is needed in German:

| | |
|---|---|
| – I've been in London for two weeks. | Ich **bin** seit zwei Wochen in London. |
| – If I'm late, I'll take a taxi. | ... **nehme** ich ... |

In your translations, try to take into account the fact that the German language tends to use so-called **'fill-words'** a great deal:

| | |
|---|---|
| – but didn't you hear anything? | aber hast du **denn** nichts gehört? |
| – I haven't heard anything, but I believe you. | Ich habe **zwar** nichts gehört ... |

Remember also that you need the subjunctive in German for an English indicative occasionally, especially in reported speech.

**When writing down your translation of the text, you should keep the following points in mind:**

1) Don't write anything down unless you are fairly sure that you won't have to change it again. Experience has shown that people are very reluctant to make any necessary changes once they've formulated a sentence and written it down.
2) Try to write 'good' German. Don't look either at the original text nor at your translation of it for a minute or two – to clear your mind – and then read the finished version of your translation again concentrating only on the impression the German text now gives; you might notice clumsy passages then you'd overlooked before. If you do come

across clumsy sentences or phrases try to rephrase them in a more elegant fashion.

3) You should follow the rules of punctuation and orthography in your translation; monosyllabic and bisyllabic numbers, for instance, must be written as words and not as figures: 'fünfzehn', not '15'. Mistakes in this area will hardly have any influence on the mark you get for your translation, but spelling mistakes, left-out commas, etc. create a very bad impression. You should do everything in your power not to annoy the corrector.
4) It is not a good idea to have a fully worked-out rough copy first and then to make a fair copy at the end. Time and again words, clauses, even whole paragraphs, are left out in the process of producing a fair copy and, unless you also hand in your notes, this is the only one that counts. So whenever you feel sure about a sentence write it straight down on the sheet of paper you're going to hand in.
5) Don't give alternative solutions in brackets. It is your job as a translator to make up your mind for **one** solution only. Giving a free translation of a sentence in your text and supplying a literal translation in brackets (to show that you have understood the original) is not permissible. For some strange reason there are always one or two students who don't accept this and insist on giving alternative solutions. In these cases the corrector either crosses out the solution in brackets, if it is correct, or counts it as an error if it isn't.

**Example:**

Here now is a practice text. Read it slowly several times and try to understand it as well as you can; then translate it and compare your translation with the annotated one given below.

**On Cleopatra and her Visit to Rome**

Last year the Queen of Egypt began requesting permission to pay a visit to Rome. I finally granted it and have offered her for residence my villa across the river. She will stay at least a year in Italy. The whole matter is still a secret and will not be announced to the City until the very eve of her arrival. She is now approaching Carthage and should be here in about a month.

I confess that I look forward to this visit with much pleasure, and not only for the reason which first leaps to the mind. She was a remarkable girl. Even at twenty she knew the loading capacity of the major wharves of the Nile; she could receive a deputation from Ethiopia and refuse all its requests, and make the refusals appear to be benefits. I have heard her scream at her ministers' stupidity during a discussion, and she was not only right, but right with a wealth of detailed information.

Indeed, she is one of the few persons I have known who have a genius for administration. Conversation will be a pleasure again. There are few pleasures equal to that of imparting to a voracious learner the knowledge that one has grown old and weary in acquiring.

And yet she is lying, intriguing, intemperate, indifferent to the essential well-being of her people, and a light-hearted murderess. I have been receiving a series of anonymous letters warning me of her propensity to murder. I have no doubt that she is not long separated from a beautifully wrought cabinet of poisons, but I know also that at her table I need no taster. The prime object of her every thought is Egypt, and I am its first security. Egypt will never recover its greatness; but Egypt, for what it is, lives by me.

When I first met her, she was proud to state that there was not one drop of Egyptian blood in her veins. I advised her to forget that she was a descendant of Macedonian mountain brigands. She followed my advice. She is now the true Pharaoh and the living incorporation of the Goddess Isis. This is as it should be. The adherence of a people is not acquired merely by governing them to their best interests. We rulers must spend a large part of our time capturing their imaginations. In the minds of the people, Fate is an ever-watching force, operating by magic and always malevolent. To counter its action we rulers must be not only wise but supernatural, for in their eyes human wisdom is helpless before magic.

From: Th. Wilder, *The Ides of March: Caesar's Journal*

Apart from asking yourself the obvious questions about the contents of this text (What is it all about? How does Caesar see Cleopatra? What is his relationship to her?, etc.) you should also ask yourself the following questions before you start translating:

What kind of text is it?

It belongs mainly to the narrative text type and is obviously an extract from a diary – Caesar's diary.

Is there anything remarkable about the language of the text?

It is written in fairly formal English, which does not, however, give the impression of being stilted, but clearly shows the polished style of a well-educated man for whom writing is easy.

Consequently, you ought to try to reproduce in your translation this fairly formal language attempting at the same time to recapture the easy flow of Caesar's polished style. Don't overdo it, though; your translation should still read like an extract from Caesar's diary and not like a speech before the Senate with Caesar trying to defend his invitation of Cleopatra.

**On Cleopatra and her Visit to Rome**

Last year the Queen of Egypt began requesting permission to pay a visit to Rome. I finally granted it and have offered her for residence my villa across the river. She will stay at least a year in Italy. The whole matter is still a secret and will not be announced to the City until the very eve of her arrival. She is now approaching Carthage and should be here in about a month.

**Über Cleopatra und ihren Besuch in Rom**

Letztes Jahr ersuchte die Königin von Ägypten erstmals[1]) um die Erlaubnis, Rom einen Besuch abstatten zu dürfen. Ich habe sie schließlich erteilt und habe ihr meine Villa jenseits des Flusses als Wohnsitz angeboten. Sie bleibt[2]) mindestens ein Jahr in Italien. Die ganze Angelegenheit ist noch geheim[3]) und wird der Stadt erst[4]) im letzten Augenblick[5]), am Vorabend ihrer Ankunft, bekanntgegeben. Sie nähert sich eben[6]) Karthago und sollte in etwa einem Monat hier sein.

I confess that I look forward to this visit with much pleasure, and not only for the reason which first leaps to the mind. She was a remarkable girl. Even at twenty she knew the loading capacity of the major wharves of the Nile; she could receive a deputation from Ethiopia and refuse all its requests, and make the refusals appear to be benefits. I have heard her scream at her ministers' stupidity during a discussion, and she was not only right, but right with a

Ich gestehe, daß ich diesem Besuch mit großer Freude entgegensehe, und nicht nur aus dem Grund, der sich einem zuerst aufdrängt[7]). Sie war ein erstaunliches[8]) Mädchen. Bereits im Alter von zwanzig[9]) Jahren kannte sie das Fassungsvermögen aller[10]) größeren Nilhäfen[11]); sie konnte eine Abordnung aus Äthiopien empfangen und alle ihre Bitten ablehnen und die Ablehnung als Entgegenkommen[12]) erscheinen lassen. Ich habe sie während einer Beratung angesichts

---

[1]) Gerundkonstruktion adverbial aufgelöst.

[2]) Englisches Futur im Deutschen mit Präsens wiedergegeben.

[3]) Nominalkonstruktion adjektivisch aufgelöst.

[4]) 'not . . . until' positiv ausgedrückt (vgl. oben 'negation of the opposite').

[5]) 'im letzten Augenblick': ein Versuch, 'very' wiederzugeben.

[6]) 'eben': ein Versuch, die Verlaufsform mitzuübersetzen.

[7]) Nominalkonstruktion verbal aufgelöst.

[8]) Trifft das Gemeinte wohl besser als das wörtliche 'bemerkenswertes'.

[9]) 'zwanzig' ausschreiben.

[10]) Ein Versuch, den genauen Wortsinn von 'major' wiederzugeben.

[11]) 'wharf': eigentlich 'Anlegeplatz'; 'Nilhäfen' verdeutlicht das Gemeinte sicher besser.

[12]) 'refusals' und 'benefits' im Deutschen besser mit Singular übersetzt, wenn man das Wortpaar 'refuse – refusals' bzw. 'ablehnen – Ablehnung' beibehalten will.

wealth of detailed information. Indeed, she is one of the few persons I have known who have a genius for administration. Conversation will be a pleasure again. There are few pleasures equal to that of imparting to a voracious learner the knowledge that one has grown old and weary in acquiring.

der Dummheit ihrer Minister toben hören; und sie war nicht nur im Recht, sondern konnte sich dabei auf eine Fülle von genauen Angaben stützen[13]). Sie ist in der Tat eine der wenigen Personen, die ich kenne[14]), die eine geniale Begabung[15]) für die Verwaltung[16]) haben. Es wird wieder eine Freude[17]) sein, mich mit ihr zu unterhalten[18]). Es gibt wenige Freuden, die der gleichen, einem lernbegierigen Schüler das Wissen zu vermitteln, bei dessen Erwerb[19]) man alt und grau[20]) geworden ist.

And yet she is lying, intriguing, intemperate, indifferent to the essential well-being of her people, and a light-hearted murderess. I have been receiving a series of anonymous letters warning me of her propensity to murder. I have no doubt that she is not long separated from a beautifully wrought cabinet of poisons, but I know also that at her table I need no taster. The prime object of her every thought is Egypt, and I am its first

Und doch ist sie verlogen, ränkesüchtig, unbeherrscht, gleichgültig gegenüber dem wahren Wohl ihres Volkes und eine Frau, die sich aus einem Mord kein Gewissen macht[21]). Ich habe eine Reihe von anonymen Briefen bekommen[22]), die[23]) mich vor ihrem Hang zum Mord warnen. Ich hege[24]) keinen Zweifel, daß sie sich nicht lange von einem kunstvoll gearbeiteten Giftschränkchen trennt, aber ich weiß auch, daß ich an ihrer Tafel keinen Vorkoster

---

13) Eine wörtliche Übersetzung scheint nicht möglich.
14) Present perfect mit Präsens wiederzugeben.
15) Einen Anklang an 'genius' wenigstens im Attribut beibehalten.
16) Im Deutschen mit Artikel.
17) 'Freude' statt 'Vergnügen' (das in diesem Satz besser wäre) wegen des nachfolgenden 'pleasures', das nicht mit 'Vergnügungen' wiedergegeben werden kann.
18) Die wörtliche Übersetzung: 'Die Unterhaltung wird wieder eine Freude sein' wirkt etwas steif.
19) Gerundkonstruktion in einen Nominalausdruck aufgelöst.
20) 'grau' ist hier wohl dem wörtlichen 'müde' vorzuziehen.
21) Es bestünde noch die Möglichkeit, 'light-hearted' mit 'kaltblütig' wiederzugeben und so die Konstruktion des Originals zu wahren, aber dadurch würde der Sinn leicht verfälscht; 'eine Frau, die sich bei einem Mord nichts denkt' wäre der Sprachebene des Originals nicht angemessen.
22) Präsens hier nicht möglich.
23) Partizipkonstruktion in einen Relativsatz aufgelöst.
24) 'hege' statt 'habe' an dieser Stelle trägt zur Wahrung des Sprachstils des gesamten Textes auch in der Übersetzung bei.

security. Egypt will never recover its greatness; but Egypt, for what it is, lives by me.

When I first met her, she was proud to state that there was not one drop of Egyptian blood in her veins. I advised her to forget that she was a descendant of Macedonian mountain brigands. She followed my advice. She is now the true Pharao and the living incorporation of the Goddess Isis. This is as it should be. The adherence of a people is not acquired merely by governing them to their best interests. We rulers must spend a large part of our time capturing their imaginations. In the minds of the people, Fate is an ever-watching force, operating by magic and always malevolent. To counter its action we rulers must be not only wise but supernatural, for in their eyes human wisdom is helpless before magic.

brauche. Ihr ganzes Sinnen und Trachten[25]) gilt Ägypten, und ich bin seine erste Sicherheit. Ägypten wird seine Größe niemals wiedererlangen, aber Ägypten, so wie es ist, lebt durch mich.

Als ich sie zum ersten Mal traf, wies sie stolz[26]) darauf hin, daß in ihren Adern nicht ein Tropfen ägyptischen Blutes fließe[27]). Ich riet ihr zu vergessen, daß sie von makedonischen Bergräubern abstammt[28]). Sie folgte meinem Rat. Sie ist jetzt der wahre Pharaoh und die lebende Verkörperung der Göttin Isis. So sollte es auch sein[29]). Man gewinnt[30]) die Zuneigung eines Volkes nicht einfach dadurch, daß man es zu seinem Besten regiert. Wir Herrscher müssen einen großen Teil unserer Zeit darauf verwenden, seine Fantasie zu fesseln[31]). In der Vorstellung[32]) des Volkes ist das Schicksal eine ständig wache Macht, die durch Zauber wirkt und immer bösartig ist.[33]) Um ihrem Wirken zu begegnen, müssen wir Herrscher nicht nur weise, sondern mit übernatürlichen Kräften ausgestattet sein[34]); denn in den Augen des Volkes[35]) ist menschliche Weisheit dem Zauber gegenüber hilflos.

---

[25]) Eine wörtliche Übersetzen scheint nicht möglich.
[26]) Verbale Konstruktion adverbial aufgelöst.
[27]) Konjunktiv im Deutschen bei indirekter Rede.
[28]) Nominalkonstruktion verbal aufgelöst.
[29]) 'auch' ist an dieser Stelle ein notwendiges Füllwort.
[30]) Aktivische Übersetzung.
[31]) Plural mit Singular wiedergegeben.
[32]) Siehe 31.
[33]) Partizipkonstruktion durch einen Relativsatz aufgelöst.
[34]) Eine wörtliche Übertragung scheint nicht möglich.
[35]) 'in den Augen des Volkes' statt 'in seinen Augen', um keine Mißverständnisse hinsichtlich des Bezugs des Possessivpronomens aufkommen zu lassen.

# 9. WRITING A RESEARCH PAPER ('FACHARBEIT' – 'SEMINARARBEIT')

A research paper is an extensive, formal composition giving the information you have gathered from reading in a number of sources. The preparation of such a research paper generally requires several weeks and involves several skills, such as using the library facilities and works of reference, note taking, organizing material, footnoting, etc.
In view of the importance of this paper, you should arrange to have enough time to devote to it to ensure that your work will be thorough and unhurried. Research work is careful work. Don't be satisfied with a paper that will merely 'get by'. Take pride in the amount of information you can give in approximately 10 to 15 pages, in the accuracy of your work, and in the neatness of its appearance.
The basic stages in writing this paper are as follows:

1) Choosing the topic;
2) Preparing a working bibliography;
3) Composing a preliminary outline;
4) Carrying out the research;
5) Assembling notes and writing the final outline;
6) Writing the first draft;
7) Revising the first draft and typing out the final version.

## 9.1 Choosing the topic

Four considerations are involved in the selection of a topic:
- you must really find it interesting;
- the topic must lend itself to research in several sources;
- these sources must be available in the libraries you use;
- you must narrow down your topic to manageable proportions.

The best kind of subject is one you really want to know more about and on which information can be found in many different sources. No matter how interesting to you a topic may be or how suitable for research, you won't be able to take it if you can't get the source material. Some compositions, it is true, can be written 'out of your head' without recourse to the library or to the opinions of others. Most compositions, however, will send you on a hunt for information. Consequently, if you find that your library does not have enough information on your chosen topic, you will have to select another.

Most topics are too large to receive adequate treatment within the set limits and so they must be narrowed down to manageable proportions. The best way to do this is to go to the library and do some reading in general reference works. This should enable you to get a better idea of the scope and structure of your topic. At this stage you should select some aspect of your original choice and draw up a provisional plan. Then you will be ready to begin the research proper.

## 9.2 Preparing a working bibliography

The first problem in preparing a research paper is locating books and periodicals that contain material pertinent to what you are writing about.
Start by consulting encyclopedias for a short overview of the entire area of your research topic. Then go and see what you can find out from the card catalogue in the library. The card catalogue indexes books by author, title, and subject. Usually the best way is to begin by looking under the general subject you are writing on. The next step is to try the Reader's Guide or other periodical indexes, or indexes in special subject matter fields. The Reader's Guide indexes articles from periodicals covering a wide variety of fields; it is continually brought up to date and, like the card catalogue, lists articles by author, title, and subject. You should consult the subject entries first. Naturally, you can expect to find a great number of periodicals in English only in the biggest libraries in Germany; so do not hesitate to ask the library staff for any help you may need – it is sometimes possible to get an article you need through inter-library loan. A last, often overlooked, source of further material on your topic is the bibliography that often appears at the end of an article or at the end of a chapter of a book.
When using these sources to find material, compile a list of all the books and articles which promise to be useful to you. Be sure to notice the copyright date – some material may be out of date. Record each book or article on a card – one source to a card – and record

- the author's name;
- the title;
- the facts of publication (place, date).

You will need this information later in making a bibliography and giving credit for material that you used in your paper. Unfortunately, there is no generally recognized way of writing bibliographical data. The following method, however, is very widely used.

**Note:** Any other method which gives all the necessary information will do just as well, of course. The main point is that once you have decided to use a particular method you stick to it throughout.

**Books:**

– author's name: last name first, then initials of first names, or the editor's name followed by the abbreviation ed., e.g.
  Haggard, E. W.,
  Robinson, J. A. T., ed.,
– title (volume, if necessary): make sure you give the full title and not only the one that appears on the outside cover – it may be a shortened title; you should underline the title, e.g.
  Levin, B., The Pendulum Years. Britain and the Sixties,
– facts of publication: place and year of publication; don't forget to mention the number of the impression if there are more than one, e.g.
  Levin, B., The Pendulum Years. Britain and the Sixties, London 1970$^{3}$.

The publisher is also mentioned sometimes, but this is not strictly necessary.

**Articles:**

– author's name (cf. above)
– title of article: put quotation marks round it, e.g.
  Leonard, G. B., 'Language and Reality,'
– name of magazine: begin with in: ... and underline the name of the magazine, e.g.
  Leonard, G. B., 'Language and Reality,' in: Harper's Magazine
– volume number and number of magazine (with date), e.g.
  Leonard, G. B., 'Language and Reality,' in: Harper's Magazine, vol. 249, no. 1494 (November 1974)
– page numbers, e.g. ... no. 1494 (November 1974), 46–52.

This, then, is the way you should note bibliographical details down on your cards; the most convenient size is A7 (half-postcard size). There are two more things, however, that you should bear in mind. It is a good idea to include in the upper left-hand corner of the card the call or order number of the book in question; you will find it on the respective card in the card catalogue. And you ought to number the cards clearly in the upper right-hand corner. These card numbers will be used later, when you are taking notes, to save you the task of copying details about the source with each note you jot down from that source. Instead of the complete source, you will merely write the number of the source.

By the time you have looked through all available sources of information, you will have a stack of cards – the working bibliography – representing the sources you plan to read.

### 9.3 Composing a preliminary outline

Before you can take notes in an organized way, you must have some idea of the topics on which you will need information. To formulate a list of such topics, read one or two brief treatments of your subject in encyclopedias or other reference works. Another approach is to anticipate the important questions your paper will have to answer. Write down what seem to be the major divisions of the subject. A list of these constitutes your preliminary outline.

This outline, of course, will not be complete. No doubt you will need to change it in many ways as you learn more of your subject. But you must have some plan for your paper before you can profitably undertake the next step. As you gather material, you may want to omit topics about which you find little source material and add others that appear to be interesting or significant. In other words, this tentative outline will prove extremely useful to guide you in your reading and note-taking.

Here is a specimen of such a preliminary outline for a research paper on **'Needed Changes in the Role of the U.S. Vice-President'**

1. The problem
   - 1.1 Succession to the Presidency
   - 1.2 Factors which govern selection of candidates
   - 1.3 The lowered prestige of the office
2. The original concept of the office
   - 2.1 Opinions of early statesmen
   - 2.2 Powers granted by the Constitution
3. Causes of the decline in prestige of the office
   - 3.1 Two-party system
   - 3.2 Twelfth Amendment
   - 3.3 Calibre of Vice-Presidents
4. Methods of raising the prestige of the office
   - 4.1 Improvement in method of nomination
   - 4.2 Improvement in method of election
   - 4.3 Changes in the powers of the Vice-President

## 9.4 Carrying out the research

Your task now is to determine what you need to read carefully and possibly take notes on and what you can reject. You will find that it doesn't often happen that a whole book, or even a whole chapter or article, will be of use to you as subject matter for any given topic. To find what you need for your paper, you will have to turn to many books and articles, rejecting most of them altogether and using from others a section here and there. Since you cannot take the time to read each book carefully you must **use the table of contents and the index,** and you must learn to scan the pages rapidly until you spot the passages you need. It is a good idea to **read the opening and summary paragraphs** first; they will usually tell you if it's worthwhile to read the rest, too.

Even more important, perhaps, than locating pertinent material in your sources is **note-taking.** Whenever you have to take a very large number of notes from quite a wide variety of sources, the efficiency of the method you use is very important indeed. You need a system which involves a disciplined approach to note-taking and which is extremely flexible. A card system satisfies both these requirements and is, for this reason, used by most people doing research. The card system involves keeping two sets of cards, one set for the sources of information (cf. no. 2 above), the other for notes. It is advisable to use a bigger card size for note-taking (A6 = postcard size or bigger).

The notes you take should fall under one or another of the topics in your outline. At the top of each note card write the outline topic with which the note deals. In the upper right-hand corner write the number of the source as you indicated it on the card in the working bibliography. Always write the page number after every idea you jot down. You will need this page number for the footnotes in your paper. It is essential that you should **use a separate card for each source.** This permits you to file your cards under the proper topic. Often more than one card will be necessary for a topic.

When it comes to **note-taking** itself, three things need to be remembered:

- **do not take too many notes;**
- **sort out separate pieces of information** that may go into different parts of your paper;
- **take notes in your own words.**

This last problem is the greatest. If you take notes in the words of the author, these words tend to be transferred to the finished paper. This may lead to a 'derived' style that is easy to detect for an experienced corrector. Worse still, the use of the words of others as if they were your own is plagiarism, which is a serious offence. If you are copying a passage that you expect to quote, write down the material exactly as the author wrote it, and put quotation marks round it. In general you should do very little copying. A research paper should not consist of a mere list of quotations. You are expected to gather facts and ideas from your sources, digest them thoroughly, and then put them forward in your own words. Quote verbatim only when the words of the source are especially important and especially well chosen. Too many quotations will make a very weak paper. Express your own ideas in your own words.

### 9.5 Assembling notes and writing the final outline

As soon as you have enough notes to ensure adequate treatment of your topic, you should start arranging your notes in the order in which you will use them. At this point you will find the topic-headings on the cards very useful. Reject those cards which no longer seem relevant and assemble the rest in chapter groups. You will then have before you a number of piles of information, each pile representing one division of your topic. Arrange this material in ascending order of importance.
You will find it necessary at this stage to prepare your final outline, because some of the topic-headings on the cards must obviously become subdivisions, whereas others now become major topics.

### 9.6 Writing the first draft

With your outline to guide you and your notes on each topic conveniently arranged, you are ready to write the first draft. This first draft is an important step in the whole process of creating a research paper and should on no account be left out in an attempt to save time. The temptation to do this may be very great – but you must resist it. Experience has shown again and again that students who try to leave out this step and to produce a final version of their papers without first writing a rough draft often run into trouble and instead of saving time actually have to spend more time: They start on chapter one, taking a long time over various details and rewriting passages again and again till they are at long last satisfied with what they have written. They do the same thing with chapter two and then suddenly find that they are running out of time at this rate, which usually means that chapters three, four and five get written very hurriedly. In the end there may not even be time to check the paper as a whole, and so instead of handing in a well-balanced paper they must be satisfied with what they have managed to put together at the last possible moment. It is a lot easier to make corrections and various improvements once you have finished all the chapters of your paper; it can also be done a lot more quickly. Remember that you can then make any necessary changes in the light of the whole paper and not only of an isolated chapter.

So don't worry unduly over details of style and don't delay your work trying to think of a clever introduction. The introduction ought in fact to be written **after** you've finished everything else and not at the very beginning of your work. You may start anywhere you like; the important thing is to make a start, to put your ideas on paper, and to write rapidly. Do things in the right order – first put the entire paper together and then worry about questions of style, etc.

As you incorporate in your paper the ideas on your note cards, be very careful to indicate their source on your manuscript, **whether you are giving the ideas in your own words or quoting the wording of the source.** In writing this rough draft it will be sufficient to indicate the source of material by simply writing down after each idea the source number from the working-bibliography card, and the page number. You need not bother to copy long quotations into this rough draft; merely jot down enough information to help you find the quotation later when writing your final draft.

Use long quotations only sparingly. A research paper is meant to show that you can collect material from a number of sources and use it for your own purposes. There is no need to demonstrate that you have read a certain source by quoting large chunks from it; it is far better to summarize in your own words what the source says and refer to the exact page in a footnote. **By quoting several lenghty passages you cannot hope to show your wide reading but only an inability on your part to present the ideas these passages put forward in your own words.**

### 9.7 Revising the first draft and typing out the final version

The writing of the final draft should be relatively easy. Troublesome problems of organisation have already been solved in writing the first draft, and so you are now concerned primarily with form.

#### a) Transitions

Supply the necessary transitions (cf. the various linking phrases in ch. 6 'Text Production') and try to make your sentences sound smooth and connected, not like a miscellaneous assortment of sentences hastily thrown together. A first draft may be written rapidly, but be very careful with your revised final copy.

### b) Footnotes

Sources of quoted material or of ideas taken from sources, even though they are written in your own words, are normally acknowledged in footnotes. At the end of the material to be credited, put a number slightly above the line to correspond to the number you will use for your footnote at the bottom of the page. Numbers should usually run consecutively throughout your entire paper. You can take all the data necessary for your footnotes from your source cards. Since you will have a full bibliography, you may omit the facts of publication in your footnotes and also use a shortened title. So, instead of writing

[8]) cf. Levin, B., *The Pendulum Years. Britain and the Sixties,* London 1970[3], 88

you can simply write

[8]) cf. Levin, *The Pendulum Years,* 88

In longer papers it is not uncommon to write all your footnotes on a separate sheet heading it 'Notes'.

The abbreviations most commonly used in footnotes are as follows:

| | |
|---|---|
| **c., ca.** | about (L circa) |
| **cf.** | compare (L confer) |
| **ch., chs.** | chapter, chapters |
| **ed.** | editor, edited, edition |
| **et. al.** | and others (L et alii) |
| **f., ff.** | and the following page, pages |
| **ibid.** | in the same place (L ibidem) |
| **id.** | the same (L idem) |
| **impr.** | impression |
| **l., ll.** | line, lines |
| **loc. cit.** | in the place cited (L loco citato) |
| **n.d.** | no date given |
| **n.p.** | no place given |
| **op. cit.** | in the work cited (L opere citato) |
| **p., pp.** | page, pages |
| **passim** | frequently found in a work (= L) |
| **q.v.** | which see (L quod vide) |
| **tr.** | translated, translator |
| **vide** | see (= L) |
| **vol., vols.** | volume, volumes |

**c) Bibliography**

At the end of your research paper give a bibliography of all the printed material you have used in preparing your paper. Usually your bibliography will include the same works that you credited in your footnotes, but you may list additional helpful works that you consulted but did not have to quote from. The form of your bibliographical entries is the same as that in your source cards. List these biographical items in alphabetical order by the author's last name, or by the first important word of the title if no author is given (A and The are not counted).

**d) Presentation**

- Type the final version on A4-size paper, but use one side of the paper only.
- Do not overcrowd the page. Leave at least 4cm on the left-hand side and about 2cm on the right-hand side and also sufficient space at the top and bottom of the page.
- Indented quotations and footnotes should be single-spaced.
- Paginate the manuscript in Arabic numerals. The title page counts as page 1, the table of contents as page 2, but they do not receive a page number. The first page of the text gets a 3, and so on. Write this number in the middle at the top of the page.
- Enclose the paper in a file with a metal clip.

The complete paper will consist of the title page, the table of contents (= your final outline), the paper itself, the bibliography and perhaps a list of notes, if you prefer this to writing footnotes at the bottom of each page. There may also be a last page on which you state, and then sign this statement, that you wrote the paper yourself and have acknowledged all your sources.

# INDEX

## ACKNOWLEDGEMENTS

List of quoted copyright material and copyright holders:

Arthur C. Clarke: a passage from 'The Reluctant Orchid' and from 'All the Time in the World'; Joint Matriculation Board: 'Class Distinctions' from the the G. C. E. O-Level Paper, November 1970; Max Hueber Verlag: extract from 'Britain. A Short Introduction for Students of English' by John Bourke; Oxford University Press: 'Not Quite Straight' from 'Advanced Comprehension Pieces for Overseas Students' by L. A. Hill and D. J. May; Longman Group Ltd.: nonsense text 'Pugglemess term lately over' from 'Teaching English as a Second Language' by J. A. Bright and G. P. McGregor; Janet Ross and Gladys Doty: 'Rhetoric: What is it and why study it?' from 'Writing English. A Composition Text in English as a Foreign Language'; Cambridge University Press: 'The bohemian marihuana smoker' from 'Inside Meaning. Proficiency reading comprehension' by Michael Swan; Holt, Rinehart & Winston: William Faulkner's Nobel Prize Accepting Speech, from 'Interpreting Literature' ed. by K. L. Knickerbocker & H. W. Reninger; Ernst Klett Verlag: 'What is Language?' by K. J. Heller, and 'Please Do Not Spit' by Alan Warner, both from 'Modern Life. Lese- und Arbeitsbuch für die Ober- und Studienstufe' ed. by H. J. Lechler et al.; Helen Monfries: model interpretation of an extract from E. M. Forster's 'Abinger Harvest' from 'An Introduction to Critical Appreciation for Foreign Learners'; Manz Verlag: 'On Cleopatra and her Visit to Rome' from 'Die Übersetzung aus dem Englischen ins Deutsche' by Josef Raith; Harcourt, Brace and Company, Inc.: 'The difference between democracy and communism', 'Studying Latin at School', and specimen of a preliminary outline for a research paper on 'Needed Changes in the Role of the U. S. Vice-President' from 'English Grammar and Composition. Complete Course' by John E. Warriner.

In a book of this type it is inevitable that the ideas of many other writers will be reflected and developed. In place of a selected bibliography, here are the publications we are particularly indebted to, and without which this book could not have been written:

Bright, J. A. & McGregor, G. P., *Teaching English as a Second Language. Theory and techniques for the secondary stage,* London (Longman) 1976[2]
for the sections on vocabulary and reading;

Deakin, B., *Letter Writing in English,* London (BBC English by Radio and Television) 1976[3]
for letter-writing;

Fischer, W., *Die englische Herübersetzung in der Schule. Hilfen zur Übersetzung Englisch–Deutsch. Ein Arbeits- und Lesebuch für die Oberstufe zur Vermeidung von Fehlern,* Frankfurt a. M. (Diesterweg) 1974
for translating into German;

Fowler, H. W. & Fowler, F. G. (eds.), *The Concise Oxford Dictionary of Current English,* Oxford (Oxford University Press) 5th ed. 1964
for many definitions and examples;

Friederich, W., "Übersetzen systematisch lehren", in: *Der fremdsprachliche Unterricht,* no. 4 (November 1976), 48–57
for translating into German;

Gläser, R. (tr.), *Stilistik der englischen Sprache,* Leipzig (VEB Verlag) 1966; author-

ized transl. of Kuznek, M. D. & Skrebnev, J. M., *Stilistika anglijskogo jazyka,* Leningrad 1960
for problems of style;
Gordon, I., *Practical Letter-Writing with Exercises and Worked Examples,* London (Heinemann) 1974[5]
for letter-writing;
Hornby, A. S., et al. (eds)., *Oxford Advanced Learner's Dictionary of Current English,* London (Oxford University Press) 3rd ed. 1974
for the section on working with the dictionary and many definitions and examples;
Mayr, E., "Englisch", in: Dickopf, K., (ed.), *Fremdsprachen. Englisch – Französisch – Latein,* Fischer Kolleg 7. Das Abiturwissen, Frankfurt a. M. (Fischer Taschenbuch Verlag) 1973
for developing students' competence in text production and working with texts;
Pink, A. & Thomas, S. E., *English Grammar, Composition and Correspondence,* London (Donnington Press) 12th ed. 1974
for problems of style and language appreciation;
Raith, J., *Die Übersetzung aus dem Englischen ins Deutsche,* München (Manz) 1975[2]
for translating into German;
Ridout, R. & Clarke, D. W., *A Reference Book of English. A General Guide for Foreign Students of English,* London (Macmillan) 1970
for intelligible basic information on linguistic and literary facts of English;
Ross, J. & Doty, G., *Writing English. A Composition Text in English as a Foreign Language,* New York (Harper & Row) 2nd ed. 1975
for a comprehensive system of text production;
Schlüter, K., *Grundkurs der Rhetorik,* München (DTV, Wiss. Reihe) 1974
for an analysis of the process of argumentation;
Sedlak, W., *Concepts for the Teaching of English Literature,* München (ISP Handreichungen) 1978
Swan, M., *Inside Meaning. Proficiency Reading Comprehension,* Cambridge (Cambridge University Press) 1975
id., *Understanding Ideas. Advanced Reading Skills,* Cambridge (Cambridge University Press) 1976
for problems of text comprehension and language appreciation and for questions set in papers (both books);
Warriner, J. E., *English Grammar and Composition. Complete Course,* New York (Harcourt, Brace & Company) 1957
for material on summary and paragraph writing and for the section on writing a research paper;
*Webster's Third International Dictionary of the English Language, Unabridged,* Springfield, Massachusetts (G. & C. Merriam Company) 1971
for definitions and examples;
Werlich, E., *The Field System Dictionary for Text Analysis,* Dortmund (Lensing) 1976[6]
for the most comprehensive collection of relevant word fields, phrases and fields of collocation;
id., *A Text Grammar of English,* Heidelberg (UTB Quelle & Meyer) 1976
for a comprehensive survey of working with texts;
Zandvoort, R. W., *A Handbook of English Grammar,* London (Longman) 1972[6]
for problems of word formation, esp. with prefixes.